This personal story of transition in a part of southern Nigeria is told by Okogun Omovuon whose supernormal enterprise became legendary. Okogun authorized the account by entrusting its production to his son, Joseph, a distinguished scientist still steeped in traditional culture. Joseph's commentary encapsulates Okogun's story. The literary compound produced by the synthesis of these two supplementary points of view is this (auto)biography.

Thus, while focussing on the modern reader, it fulfils its ideological responsibility of projecting its culture's point of view.

The book's subject should interest anthropologists, sociologists and historians, especially given its privileged insider viewpoint. The general reader too would be fascinated by the epic dimension added to the story by Okogun's heroic response to the challenge of the limited opportunities of his time and place.

Dan S. Izevbaye, Ph.D. FNAL

Emeritus Professor of English, University of Ibadan, Ibadan, and Professor of English Literature, Bowen University, Iwo, Nigeria, West Africa

The Life and Times of John Okogun Omovuon, 1905-1993, provides an excellent overview of Esan ethnography in a perspective that is thoughtful and scholarly; in a style that is lucid and readable.

The transposition of John Okogun Omovuon from the time he lived as an enigma makes the work an invaluable companion to contemporary research in History and Social Sciences of Ewohimi-Esan and Edo generally.

Since indigenous knowledge depreciated from early 20th century to recent times, this book provides a general material that makes the cosmology of Esan people come alive. I therefore have no reservation but to recommend the biography of John Okogun Omovuon for general reading.

Anthony Irenosen Okoduwa, Ph.D.

Professor of History and International Studies
Ambrose Alli University, Ekpoma, Nigeria

This text is not just about the biography of an enigmatic and indomitable John Okogun, but a true history of the rich cultural values and heritage of the homogeneous people of Esan, the Central Senatorial District of Edo State, Nigeria.

The intellectually endowed John Okogun was raised in a humble family background in Ewohimi, where Gerontocracy, like in other parts of Esan, is practised. This had a tremendous impact on his early life, which to a great extent influenced his religious beliefs, occupation and his zeal for excellence in all of his human endeavours.

Truly, a man for all seasons, his life proved him to be a man of sound moral character with a clear vision and mission for the good of his family, community and humanity.

This biographical text is a " Must Read " for everyone who is interested in cultural diversity, the essence of family life, love of human relationships and growth and development of mankind with the fear of God at heart.

Sir. Prof. Matthew O. Omo-Ojugo, Ph.D., JP

Ambrose Alli University, Ekpoma, Nigeria

This is a treasure of cultural and social-historical facts which is a welcome addition to Esan history. I am particularly happy that Prof Joseph Okogun took the pains to document the life and times of John Okogun Omovuon, an entrepreneur, innovator, thinker, and community activist. Perhaps it is his multi-talented and integrated personality that earns him the title of an 'enigma'. Posterity will remain grateful to the author for this important contribution to Ewohimi history at a time when our young people are fast losing knowledge of their ancestral history.

Rev. Fr. Anselm Adodo, Ph.D., OSB

Pax Herbal Clinics & Research Laboratories,Benedictine Monastery, Ewu-Esan, Nigeria

Pope Francis has vigorously challenged and awakened the consciences of this generation against the evils of a throwaway culture, that makes people easily want to throw things, history, information and people away, rather than fixing them.

Family history is not like a disposable item that we shop and dispose of. It is a lived-experience eminently useful for the present and the future.

This book seeks to remind people of the past in a very succinct, yet, morally instructive, historically revealing, and pedagogically satisfactory narrative and manner.

The sociological strength of this book is its timeliness and the agelessness of its central focus. Its special character is the simplicity in which it has been written and the concision of its presentation.
This book is important today and always, not only for the people of Ewohimi but for all and sundry. It is an imminent reminder of the beautiful past and also a testament of hope for the future. It is a timely contribution to the overall discussion on lineal family history which can never be overemphasized. I recommend it for all students and researchers and for those involved in teaching and appreciating History. Happy are you if you have this book in your hand!
Very Rev. Fr. Matthew Ovabor IHENSEKHIEN, Ph.D
Rector, Seminary of All Saints, Uhiele-Ekpoma, Edo State.

I have carefully gone through the over two hundred pages of this book on the life of an enigma and I am impressed with the work done.
From this record of the life and the times of John Okogun Omovuon, our children will be adequately informed of their lineage as it relates to Okaigben, Ewohimi; vis a vis the need for hardwork.
I, His Royal Highness, the Onogie of Igueben, a descendant of the Agbon-Osoh family of Okaigben is happy to be associated with this work.
The work will feature prominently in Igueben Museum currently being set up.
HRH Ehizogie Eluojerior, Justice of the Peace (JP).
Onogie of Igueben & the Okaigun of Esanland, Nigeria.

This work constitutes an important and commendable addition to what has been written by earlier authors about the culture and traditions of Esanland and Ewohimi in particular.
It describes events dating back to about 1900 in Ewohimi and the former Bendel State of Nigeria now Edo and Delta States including aspects of Colonial history of the area.
The dances of the people, especially the Esan acrobatic dance Igbabonalimin is given full treatment in connection with Okogun, who was a famous and great acrobatic dancer.
Okogun's courage, hard work, entrepreneurial and indomitable spirit, active community involvement for development, and unusual spiritual encounters serve as useful models and reference for contemporary youths and elders.
The book should be read by all interested in African culture and traditions and those interested in reading inspirational true life stories.
His Royal Highness Lord Peter Ogienefoh Usifoh II
The Onogie of Ewohimi Kingdom, Edo State, Nigeria

THE LIFE OF AN ENIGMA

A BIOGRAPHICAL ACCOUNT OF THE LIFE AND THE TIMES OF JOHN OKOGUN OMOVUON OF EWOHIMI (EBHOKHIMI), NIGERIA

JOSEPH I. OKOGUN

FriesenPress
Suite 300 - 990 Fort St
Victoria, BC, V8V 3K2
Canada

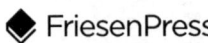

www.friesenpress.com

First Edition — 2021

The life of an enigma: Front cover images explained

- Blacksmith
- Canoe on Odu River loaded with yams for Onitsha market
- Masquerade: Esan acrobatic dance (available on YouTube)
- Crucifix
- Hand sewing machine
- Helix: Okogun held his indigenous culture and Western culture together

ISBN
978-1-5255-9148-8 (Hardcover)
978-1-5255-9147-1 (Paperback)
978-1-5255-9149-5 (eBook)

1. BIOGRAPHY & AUTOBIOGRAPHY, CULTURAL HERITAGE

Distributed to the trade by The Ingram Book Company

CONTENTS

VII DEDICATION

IX ACKNOWLEDGEMENTS

XI PROLOGUE

XIX FOREWORD

1 CHAPTER ONE: INTRODUCTION

9 CHAPTER TWO: EWOHIMI IN ESANLAND, EDO STATE

25 CHAPTER THREE: BIRTH, PARENTAGE AND BLACKSMITH HERITAGE

33 CHAPTER FOUR: OMOVUON'S FAMILY AND OKOGUN'S SIBLINGS

39 CHAPTER FIVE: OKOGUN'S BOYHOOD LIFE AND THE DEATH OF OMOVUON

45 CHAPTER SIX: ADOLESCENT OKOGUN

61 CHAPTER SEVEN: OKOGUN ENCOUNTERS A PROPHETESS ON THE WAY BACK ON FOOT FROM BENIN TO EWOHIMI

67 CHAPTER EIGHT: OKOGUN'S INITIAL PAYING JOBS AND EARLY ADULTHOOD

71 CHAPTER NINE: OKOGUN JOINS THE TIMBER LOGGING BUSINESS AT OBOMKPA AS A HANDSMAN

77 CHAPTER TEN: OKOGUN BECOMES A TAILOR: ONITSHA YAM SALE EXPEDITION

83 CHAPTER ELEVEN: OKOGUN RELOCATES TO AGBOR AND UMUNEDE AS TAILOR AND CLOTH MERCHANT

89 CHAPTER TWELVE: RUBBER BUSINESS

91 CHAPTER THIRTEEN: OKOGUN DECIDES TO BUILD HIS OWN HOUSE BY OFURI MARKET

95 CHAPTER FOURTEEN: TIMBER BUSINESS AS CAMP OVERSEER UNDER CHIEF PAUL E. ODIGIE

103 CHAPTER FIFTEEN: OKOGUN IS APPOINTED TRAINEE OVERSEER IN AREA B28 CAMP UNDER MR OMONRAMEN

107 CHAPTER SIXTEEN: OKOGUN IS FORCED TO PULL DOWN HIS OLD RESIDENCE TO REPLACE IT W ITH A NEW ONE TO FACE THE MARKET

119 CHAPTER SEVENTEEN: OKOGUN AS A TIMBER CONTRACTOR: HIS LORRY, AGBOR PROPERTY DEVELOPMENT AND OTHER BUSINESS ENTERPRISES

131 CHAPTER EIGHTEEN: OKOGUN AS A FAMILY AND COMMUNITY MAN

143 CHAPTER NINETEEN: OKOGUN'S INTEREST IN THE EDUCATION, MENTORING AND TRAINING OF YOUNG PEOPLE AND CHRISTIANITY

153 CHAPTER TWENTY: OTHER COMMUNITY ACTIVITIES: OKOGUN THE OGIE-ESE

163 CHAPTER TWENTYONE: THE BEGINNING OF THE END

171 CHAPTER TWENTYTWO: PA OKOGUN'S ORDERS THE SANCTIFICATION OF HIS PREMISES: JOURNEY TO IBADAN

177 CHAPTER TWENTYTHREE: LIFE AT THE UCH

187 CHAPTER TWENTYFOUR: "DO SUCH PEOPLE DIE?"!

193 CHAPTER TWENTYFIVE: BABA OKOGUN DEPARTS SMILING

197 CHAPTER TWENTYSIX: PREPARING FOR THE LAST RESPECTS AND BURIAL

203 CHAPTER TWENTYSEVEN: THE BURIAL CEREMONIES AND THE BURIAL

213 CHAPTER TWENTYEIGHT

222 EPILOGUE

225 REFERENCES

234 APPENDIX I: DICTATED NOTES IN THE OLYMPIC EXERCISE BOOK

255 APPENDIX II: MINUTES OF TWO-FAMILY MEETINGS

260 APPENDIX III: EZE FAMILY TREE...........

261 APPENDIX IV: PA JOHN E. OKOGUN OMOVUON ACADEMIC PRIZE WINNERS AWARDS; FIRST YEAR AND 16TH YEAR 2017/18, OKAIGBEN PRIMARY SCHOOL

JOHN OKOGUN OMOVUON (circa 1905-1993), circa 1967

DEDICATION

I dedicate this work to the following children of Okogun who, we pray, have gone asleep in the Lord:

Felix Osatohamhen Okogun aka FO2 (1942-2018) who from our childhood till he slept was my able, diligent, devoted, and dynamic brother, friend, and assistant in Okogun and Ibhi-Eze family. He looked forward to seeing this biography; but God knows best, he has fallen asleep and did not stay to see it. He is dearly missed by us all.

Late Akhigbe, Okogun's first son born 1931

Late Mrs. Mary Ogiadan Akpolo, Okogun's first daughter

Late Oyugbo, Okogun's third daughter

Late Mrs. Egbeke P. Aguele nee Okogun

Late Mrs. Irene Omisi Omole nee Okogun

Other children born after 1942 but died in infancy; most before they were named.

Our beloved sisters, Madam Lucy Ebatele A. Odigie Enosegbe, the mother in Okogun family and one of her deputies, Reverend Pastor Felicia Ekeagboniyokpa E. Ailende slept in the Lord in 2020. They also share in this dedication.

And to the living:

Robert Peter Okogun, our prayerful dreamer and loving brother who for reasons, considers himself as a sacrificial lamb for the unity built in John Okogun Omovuon and Ibhi-Eze families. He has offered us respect, support and love.

Amuda R. E. Enato our gentleman brother of the Enato of Ohordua dynasty who also encouraged the writing of this story and who also was very much loved by Baba John Okogun Omovuon.

And to you all, my brothers and sisters of all the branches of Ibhi-Eze family. You have been supportive and cooperated with your prayers, time and resources

ACKNOWLEDGEMENTS

John Okogun Eguaereona Omovuon provided most of the materials that has been used to produce this unique presentation of largely what was in Esanland and to some extent in the present Edo and Delta States of Nigeria. I thank him for his foresight in passing much of his history to me and schooling me in the culture and traditions of our people. I must also thank his relatives and others in the village who also taught me. It became my task to pass on this legacy to all.

Reverend Father Dr. Anselm Adodo of the Benedictine Monastery, Ewu-Esan, Edo State and of Pax Herbal Clinic & Research Laboratories of the same Monastery has for a long time been encouraging me to write in order to leave some of my knowledge, especially in natural products research, behind for posterity. I made very many research journal and conference publications in natural products chemistry and related subjects which I hope will be read by people. I thank Father Adodo for his encouragement, and I hope that this book which has little chemistry but gives an insight into the operations in Esanland of his concept of Communitalism will please him. I also thank OFIRDI Publishers through him for accepting to publish the Nigerian edition of this book.

My wife Lady Justina I. Okogun nee Odigie, my children, brothers, sisters, and cousins encouraged me and prayed that I completed writing to get this book published. Their interest was a source of strength for me to complete the task of writing. I am grateful to them all.

The first draft and proofs of this book were read through by Engineer John Enomen O. Okogun using a searchlight approach. He made over two hundred notes of queries, corrections, and amendments which I found most useful. I thank him. Enomen is namesake of his grandfather John Okogun and son of the author of this book.

Reverend Father Dr. Charles Imokhai and Dr. Osahon Chris Eigbike read through the book, made useful suggestions for improvement of the work, and respectively wrote the Prologue and the Foreword. I thank them for doing me the honour and accepting to do what they did.

Mr. Oriabure S. Otoigiakhi, my Research Assistant and a former journal editor who has an excellent command and use of the computer, working with Mr Augustine Obi of Pax Herbal Clinic and Research Laboratories helped to format and finalise the arrangement of the document. Mr. Otoigiakhi also helped to construct the Eze Genealogical tree (Appendix III). I thank him and Mr Augustine Obi for their assistance.

I thank Mr. Igotie Ogieyan aka Ice Water and Mrs. Dora Emuagbon for making Madam nene Uhomonye Ogieyan's picture accessible to Mr. Odeh Ebhogiaye who kindly retook and sent the picture to me, Dr. Victor A. Ilegbodu and Engineer Kelly Ilegbodu for Madam nene Omolafe Ilegbodu's pictures and Okogun's picture by Ofuri Market. I thank Mr. Michael Ik. Omovuon for Madam nene Arhetuemen Omovuon's picture.

I thank my inlaw Dr. Solomon Iguanre who suggested the term "enigma" to modify the title after listening to what I intended to write about Pa Okogun.

Professor Dan S. Izevbaye, despite his very busy schedule, undertook to read through the finished draft of the manuscript. He edited and made very useful comments and suggestions for amendments. His comments coming from a giant in the field of writing the English language helped to enhance the presentation of this work. I thank him.

I thank Engineer Osahon Okogun for drawing the sketches of ukpee, the drums and musical instruments.

The Front cover was designed by the author with inputs from Dr. Osahon C. Eigbike, Idia L. Aijanyain, John Peter Aijanyain and Erabor A. Okogun. It was put together by the Graphic Artist, Oluwanmi Israel and made by FriesenPress.

I thank FriesenPress for the design of the Back cover using Enomen and my inputs. FriesenPress has done a great job taking me through the process of publishing the Northern American edition of this book. I thank them for showing understanding and for the good job.

I take responsibility for any errors and inadequacies that may still be in the book.

For everything I thank our Lord through Jesus Christ. To God be the glory.

PROLOGUE

The decision to write this book is that of Professor Joseph Okogun the son of **John Okogun Omovuon**, who was inspired by the tapes and dictates recorded by him from his father, as the treasure trove he inherited from his father, Okogun John Omovuon.

Professor Joseph Okogun was spell-bound by the wealth of information his father left behind; not only for him, but for humanity. This information ranges from Okogun's philosophy, social stratification, social mobility, kingship systems, to spirituality.

Okogun left this information in his native language – Esan. Okogun's eloquence and erudition can only be matched by Cicero of Roman Empire and Saint John Chrysostom (the golden mouth), Bishop and doctor of the Church.

For this reason, I highly recommend that Okogun's tape be reserved in its origin for posterity. The tape is germ in oratory.

Having said this, I like to draw the readers' attention to some of the highlights in this book, that I consider unique: "The need to have a family house to which the daughters and children returned yearly during celebration of the ancestral feast, led to the creation of the stay-at-home female child as "man" (*arheobhuwa)* out of one of his sisters. For the same reason, Okogun's sisters did everything to make sure that Okogun did not acquire Western education. The belief was that with Western education, Okogun would take up white collar job and there would be no one at home to run their father Omovuon's leading and aristocratic family estate. Okogun's unfulfilled appetite for Western education was later in his life manifested in his sacrifice to ensure that he educated all his over twenty children, his advice to parents to do the same and his part in the founding of Okaigben Memorial School now known as Okaigben Primary School, Ewohimi.

For the same reasons of ensuring continuity of family lineage, a prosperous childless woman performed all the marital rites and "married" a young girl to have children through cousins in the name of the prosperous woman's family. The young girl was referred to as "woman's wife" This practice of having a woman's wife had its problems. There was the saying "One can take a man's wife, but one cannot take a woman's wife" (*Arhe amhen okpea, airhe amhen okhuo).* The 'women husbands" used all means to protect ownership of their wives so to say and would fight to finish any male trespassers. Okogun had courage and love which got him entangled in this system." (pages 16-17).

The second highlight is the origin and the link of Ewohimi to Benin Kingdom: "The late sage Honourable Joseph O. Odigie related examples of the brave and spiritual services of Ewohimi warriors in the Benin Kingdom era and of Ewohimi native doctors to the Obas of Benin in the past on the occasion of the visit of Omon n'Oba n'Edo Ukuakpokpolo Erediauwa to Ewohimi shortly after his ascension to the throne in 1979. The facts were stated in the address read by Honourable Joseph O. Odigie, on behalf of the then Enogie of Ewohimi, His Royal Highness Omon S. Usifo Enosegbe II and his people at the Enogie's Palace. "(pages 24-25).

The third highlight is: "Okogun was born when his mother was expected to have reached or about to have reached menopause. Okogun was the last of seven children five of whom were living females. The only male who would have been his immediate senior died as a baby."

The fourth highlight is the betrothal of Maria at birth to Okogun as future wife: "Maria was betrothed to Okogun immediately she was born as a baby in the traditional way of the time. Esekhor was the first to get a log of firewood to *Pa Ayangbe* (Maria's father)'s house immediately after baby Maria was born (*ohienran o bhor*). Esekhor followed up later by depositing two pounds as part dowry for Okogun's future wife Maria before Esekhor died. In those days, if a family was interested in getting a wife from another family, the family meticulously monitors pregnancies and births in the family of interest. Once news is given of a female baby birth in the family of interest, the interested families compete and the first to carry a good log of firewood and drop it with a loud thud at the back of the father of the new baby's house won. And so was the case with baby Maria."

The fifth highlight is the cultic iconoclasm ordered by Okogun: "The next day in the evening, we told Pa Okogun that we had to move early the next morning. He immediately requested us to go and bring in the Catholic Church Parish Priest at Ewatto.

That evening he had *Pa Aghughu* with him. Pa Aghughu, an Odion-egbe was his customary and traditional godfather and longtime colleague from their early days. They were also famous acrobats and danced together. He came to visit and console him on his illness. Pa Okogun excused himself and signalled Pa Aghughu to leave as the Reverend Father arrived.

At that time October 4, 1993 Ewohimi was under Ewatto Parish. The Parish Priest was *Reverend Father Ambrose Alumiasunya*. We went to him and happily he agreed to the old man's request. On arrival at our residence, Pa Okogun told him to help lead us to get rid of all the fetish objects and shrines in the premises starting from the main building and through the women's apartments. Before this day, Pa Okogun had asked me to take down a charm pinned with a staple to the lintel of one of the doors in his room saying, "they are tired" (egbe lo ale). I hesitated but prayerfully emboldened myself and pulled it down. We started from Pa's room to collect and assemble the charms and shrines.

Okogun said pointing to the *osun: "Take it, Joseph will not have time for these".*

We took the Reverend Father through rooms and places in the main house that had the fetish objects. Father Ambrose would sprinkle Holy Water on each object before we took them away. We did the same through all the women apartments[76].

We assembled all the objects at the back of the premises. Under supervision of Reverend Father Ambrose, we dug a shallow grave into which we threw the objects. The Reverend Father once again sprinkled Holy Water on them, followed by kerosene and set them ablaze to burn out completely.

We went back to report to Pa Okogun that his will had been done concerning the shrines, charms, and fetish objects and how the objects were disposed of. He then asked *"if the said water will no longer be poured"* referring to his being baptized into the Catholic Church. We informed the Reverend Father of Pa's request.

Father Ambrose said that Pa still had two wives namely: Madam Maria Imanrhokanbhor and Madam Julie Agbonizebeta. He could not therefore baptise Pa unless he wedded one of them" This demand to wed one of his two living wives was later at Ibadan conceded to by Okogun, and he was baptized a Catholic and he was given the name John, (the beloved Apostle and Evangelist): "One of the first steps Justina and I took on 7 October was to go and invite *Reverend Father Mulumba Oguogho who was then the Parish Priest at Saint Michael's Catholic, Yemetu, Ibadan and our friend* to visit and pray for Pa Okogun. Father Oguogho who hailed *from Opoji in Esan, Edo State* had become well known for his healing Masses and practice of exorcism. He was a very busy Priest but readily graciously accepted to visit the old man in the Hospital at his earliest opportunity. Father Oguogho eventually was able to visit Pa Okogun at the Hospital. Father Oguogho was at the Hospital when none of us was present. Father Oguogho prayed for him and preached to him. Father Oguogho however did not wish that Pa Okogun respond immediately. Father Oguogho asked him not to be in a hurry to react to what he Okogun had heard from him but to take his time to reflect and send his reply through me when he had thought about all they discussed and made up his mind. When I showed up afterwards in the Hospital, *Pa Okogun instructed me to go tell Reverend Father Oguogho that he was ready to be baptized.*

He added that if given the opportunity to return to Ewohimi and able to manage an awkward posture, he would take one of his remaining wives for a wedding." (chapter twentythree).

The odyssey of enigmatic Okogun, an herbalist, **seer,** a renowned fetish-priest journey to becoming a Catholic was about 90 years. This is the longest catechumenate ever known.

The mother of Okogun, Esekhor, was said to be advanced in age, perhaps way past her childbearing age. However, she had no trouble giving birth to Okogun at this ripe old age. It is generally believed that children born in this type of circumstance have a divine mission and they are born by divine intervention. We believe that Okogun was no different from any of these children of advanced parent.

This is the story of Isaac, the son of Abraham who was born when Abraham was hundred years old and Sarah was ninety (Gen. 17: 1 –15). In the Book of Jgs. 13: 2 – 5, the story of Samson, the son of advanced age childless parents was born in the same circumstances as Isaac, with a mission to save the Israelites from the oppression of the Philistines. Also, in the book of Samuel, the story is told of Samuel the son of Elkanah and Hannah (I Sm. 1: 2 – 8, 10 – 11, 19 – 20), how Hannah was barren and childless, and by divine intervention through prayer Samuel was born to Hannah who was advanced in age and without hope of ever having a child. Samuel was one of the greatest Prophets who anointed David as King. David whose dynasty provided the King of kings from whom the Messiah God was born Jesus Christ the Saviour.

In the Gospel according to Saint Luke we have the story of Zachariah and Elizabeth, who also were passed childbearing age, when Zachariah through a vision was told he will have a son whom he should name John (Lk. 1: 5 – 7, 13, 18, 24 – 25, 36 - 66). John the Baptist was the precursor of the Messiah whose role in Salvation history was to prepare the way for Jesus Christ the Saviour, and point Him out at last when He came, John was the last of the Prophets. By the same token we have reason to believe that the birth of Okogun by a mother who was advanced in years was not an accident. It appears to be by Divine intervention.

Note how before Okogun died, he transferred his dynasty to his successor, Joseph Okogun. The following is the actual investiture ceremony: "On November 21, our sisters Lucy, Uwamusi and Mammy and I were by Pa's bed. At about 12 noon, he summoned me to get closer to him.

He then asked me in Esan Language "*Have you finished weeping*?" (*We e vie fo?)* I told him that we had decided to leave things in the hands of God. He then continued "*When the Uzebu people join and they start the discussion, you should leave the Idinrio people whom I had discussed with to inform them about the arrangements and my decisions about my household. If they do not say, you should tell the Uzebu larger family members yourself*"

I was not sure what exactly he was talking about but one of the daughters caught in to say what she thought the old man meant. Pa nodded in agreement and it was about the hierarchy in his household. Pa had held family meetings on the issue in the early 1970s and in 1978. The minutes of one of the meetings were even signed by Pa Okogun himself *(AppendixII*).

The hidden wisdom portrayed by the life of Okogun is the cultural importance he placed on motherland and fatherland. This is generally referred to as the place of origin mostly known as place of birth. But a careful reading of this book, shows that the expressions "place of origin" and "place of birth" as synonyms for motherland and fatherland are misleading.

Okogun illustrates the marked distinction between the two concepts by his classic kingship analysis. According to him, motherland bestows on the individual his cultural identity. Whereas, fatherland, on the other hand, bestows an occupational or professional identity on the individual.

One's cultural identity is bestowed at various times from when one is born until one becomes the eldest in one's own community.

For example, when a child is born in traditional Uzairue clan, the placenta is taken to the abode of the mother. A hole is dug right at the entrance to the mother's room and the placenta is buried in that hole, and a stone is placed over the top of that hole. This stone is known as the child's birth stone. The children of the compound into which the child is born are called upon to escort the mother and child into the bedroom in a processional fashion.

Mother and child remain in seclusion for seven days. After the seventh day, the child is presented publicly to the family in a reception ceremony. This is the first of several initiation ceremonies of enculturation to the motherland. Age group initiation ceremony follows when the child becomes an adult.

As an adult, the individual is inducted into the occupation by which the individual will earn his livelihood. Okogun's occupational versatility took him from Ewohimi to Agbor, to Umunede and Benin in the search of wealth with which to raise his family of procreation and orientation. One's motherland is geographical location as was described at the first chapter of this book.

The fatherland is the professional economic orbit, in which the individual uses his creative talents to create a world to serve his pleasure and leisure. This orbit can be as close to home (motherland) as the farm, or as far away as the rubber factory or as chemistry laboratory in Germany, where Okogun established his claims to this fatherland.

Finally, I like to close my remarks about this book by pointing out another major contribution to our understanding of Okogun's dynasty, namely, the concept of family.

Ewohimi is strictly a patrilineal society. Inheritance is passed on from father to son, as demonstrated at the deathbed ceremony of Okogun at which he passed his dynasty to his son, Joseph Okogun with meticulous accuracy to custom and with scrupulous fidelity to tradition.

Because of the importance of this custom and tradition, Okogun went out of his way to explain the provision Ewohimi traditions made for the case of a family that has no male offspring to succeed to his father. In such a case, to maintain the sanctity of patrilineality, Ewohimi adopted a system of woman's wife (*amen okhuo*) and stay back home daughter (*arhe obhu uwa*). This kinship novelty is Ewohimi's contribution to our understanding of descent and kinship systems.

In traditional Ewohimi society, teenage pregnancies were virtually unknown, because premarital sex was tabooed. Virginity was highly priced and rewarded. The reward went first to the parents of the bride who are considered responsible for proper upbringing of their daughter, as a pure and chaste virgin. Then the virgin daughter was rewarded for being docile and faithful to her parents' guidance.

If a daughter became pregnant while under her parental guidance, the child so born was considered her parent's child except the biological father-of-the-child arranged and married her. In an era of abortion and prochoice debate, this book provides a highly instructive roadmap.

The life history of Okogun which the author of this book entitled the life of an enigma: the biographical account of the times and the life of John Okogun Omovuon of Ewohimi Nigeria, West Africa profoundly elucidates the cultural riches and wealth of human relationships. The web of human relationships described in this book as brilliantly exposed by Okogun the cultural icon of Ewohimi, is highly educative for those who are interested in understanding African philosophy and traditional religions (paganism, hedonism, and animism).

Thus, the lesson of this book is that the dynamic of social change does not originate from the capitals of world civilisations nor from the great names that rule the famous empires of the world. The dynamic of social change originates from obscure communities as Ewohimi and from unknown persons as Okogun.

Rev. Fr. Charles Imokhai, M.Sc., Ph.D.
(ordained Catholic Priest December 21,1968)
Author and Anthropologist
Past Parish Priest, St. Paul's Parish, Benin City, Nigeria
Past Secretary General, association of the episcopal conferences of anglophone West Africa (a.e.c.a.w.a.)
Past Parochial Vicar, Blessed Sacrament Church, New York.

FOREWORD

In usual literary tradition, mouth-watery expectation visits picking up the historical work of a history scholar to read. We say, with convinced conclusion "here he comes again with his spark of stories and anecdotes!" And, in the predetermined fashion of default excitement at *the mere appearance* of a veteran comedian before hearing him talk, we take a comfortable position to begin a relishing of the work of the history scholar. Not so, reaching for a history book by a professor of chemistry to read. We wonder; what, with his *lonely* laboratory confinement stocked up with acids, bases, symbols, formulas, pipettes, beakers and dry-confounding chemical equations, does he have to say about *history* to make a reading that tickles the mind – historically...

This work by Professor of Chemistry, Joseph Okogun, is a game-changer in that conventional thinking. From an instructive surrealist angle, I argue that he wrote this history book as *chemistry.* Speaking to its etymological rooting in *alchemy* which relates to *black earth* (al khemia), the *chemistry* of this work is, technically, about *earthiness*! An unmistakable representation of Pa Okogun as a profoundly *earthy man*, the story is an unfiltered whole-meal for slow rumination about genealogy, suffering-and-hoping (faith), falling and getting up(determination-resilience), simplicity-humility, integrity (wholesome inner core), passion, compassion, culture, cross-culturality, spirituality, interfaith, relationships and communitalism, all steeped in awe about life that dwarfs yet emboldens us all. In amazing fashion, Pa Okogun's life is a didactic permutation of relationships which, cutting across a very broad area, calls us to mindfulness about our human interconnectedness. The chemistry blends Ewohimi town with tons of towns and villages in Esanland (talk of the Borha's of Ubiaja, the Aghenta's of Emu, the Esangbedo's of Igueben, etc.), Ika area of the Niger Delta, the Agbontaen's of Benin as well as faraway Idah (Kogi State) and Ibadan (Oyo State) into one dynamic family. John Lennon's song got us imagining *the brotherhood (and sisterhood) of man (and woman)*, Pa Okogun's life exemplified it!

This book could not have been more appropriately titled; Pa Okogun was, indeed, an enigma. What, with his long and winding life's journey – practically a candle in the wind that never went out! He was an orphan, and then a quasi-houseboy at some point, both speaking to acute vulnerability. Rejecting the implied default to nothingness about his life and determined to put his feet on the ground as a man, he was a tailor, a clothing trader, a farmer, a yam seller, a rubber merchant and a timberman. In the process, he strategically relocated to different places as conditions dictated. However, his inner core of integrity would not break under pressure from the detours and the embedded nuances. Thus, when the *lucrative* timber trade required his membership of a secret society for some promised *progress and fame* he tactically declined. They had to leave him alone! PA followed his heart, the values of his inner core.

As the book notes, Okogun spells Oko-Ogun and translates "son (Oko) of an ironsmith (Ogun)." An instructive insight about "Ogun" is fitting here. In Esan spirituality, Ogun is also a deity to be revered around farming as a viable economic enterprise because the necessary tools (cutlasses and hoes) come from ironsmith, an equally viable economic enterprise in metallurgical engineering. Thus, Oko-Ogun is a mindful two-edged penciling for economic success. Pa Okogun knew himself deeply by knowing his name deeply hence he could not be swamped in the muddy and winding trail of his life. He aimed to succeed in life **just as himself** – and he did. His integrity went as far as his instituting a tenancy law that anybody wanting to rent a space in his house must agree never to bring in stolen items. Spartan rigorousness!

As already hinted, this work is also about interfaith and cross-culturality in the life of Pa Okogun. As appropriate for all societies, Pa Okogun embraced the indigenous spirituality of his people. Following his heart, the system made sense to him in context, even in the face of European Missionary Christian advent and expansion. Yet, he practised his indigenous spirituality in the manner captured by Gandhi: *I am a Christian Hindu*. That he was popularly referred to as *Papa Original* and *Ogie-Ese* (king of crowds) speaks his genuine and compassionate heart that authentic and fear of God are all about. After many years in that unsung space of holistic interfaith, he would formally embrace Christianity at an appropriate *Kairos* moment; he asked to be a fully baptised Christian in his old age. He had used his deep sense of humor (which had been his catalyst and navigating tool in life) to describe one of the gods of his indigenous spirituality as "tired!" Pa Okogun was a man of stellar wisdom for embracing change when appropriate. Again, he was all tuned into his inner core: his integrity.

Of import, also, about this story is the sublime bond between Pa Okogun and the author, Joseph. It was one of mutual love, appreciation, and respect of deeply spiritual dimension. Joseph told Pa Okogun that he had been such a strict disciplinarian, the old man replying calmly, see what it made of you – and a deep mutual understanding struck there and then. Behold a bond in which Pa Okogun told Joseph the dream he had in faraway Germany which he did not even disclose to the old man! The mystery of how he knew about it can only be captured in incarnational terms! Pa Okogun was therefore not mincing words when he later addressed Joseph as *edionmhan* (old man). In a culture of strict hierarchy in the relationship between father and son, the former calling the latter old man can only be transcendentally incarnational; Joseph caught it as the ultimate transfer of power to him as father was now in transition to yonder life.

I must acknowledge my privilege of having an acquaintance with Pa Okogun and Professor Joseph Okogun which informs my writing this note. Growing up in Ewatto (colonially disfigured from Ebho-Ator or Ebho-Akhator), I met Pa Okogun many years ago through my father while accompanying him to places as a little boy. My father worked for the local colonial Public Works Department (PWD). To make ends meet especially when seasonally laid off, he did petty trading for which he had a shed inside Ofuri Market in Ewohimi (colonially disfigured from Ebho-Ikhimi). Pa Okogun's house is near Ofuri market. I believe that through one or both economic endeavors, my father became acquainted with Pa Okogun, known for friendly and encouraging chats with PWD workers in his neighbourhood, and nearby traders in the market. Traditional Esan acrobatic dances as well as Pa Okogun's genealogical connections with Ewatto may have also ignited or reinforced their acquaintance.

My father talked passionately of the warmth, integrity, and wisdom about Pa Okogun as his attraction to him. He soon found out that Pa Okogun was a deep lover of education, committed to training his children and others in his community. He also found out that his son, Joseph, was a university student, and he was brilliant! The whole information was a fitting package for my father to appropriate: he would draw closer to Pa Okogun as his mentor as well as sing and drum the brilliance of Joseph (whom he called "Big Brain Son of Okogun" for effect) into my siblings and I as inspiration to apply ourselves at school. My father was younger than Pa Okogun; that worked perfectly in cultural nuances for his learning from him. A beautiful and warm friendship grew between them.

Though I heard about "Big Brain Son of Okogun" all through my schooling years, I never had a chance to meet Joseph. Yet, my father's drumbeat of "Big Brain Son of Okogun" was locked in my inside as an enduring inspiration. I was later to hear of his feat in chemical discoveries particularly the famed "okogunic acid!" That was an *aha* for me about my father's "Big Brain Son of Okogun" maxim. Finally, my desire to meet him was fulfilled; thanks to a conference organized by Paxherbals Ewu at the University of Ibadan where Professor Joseph Okogun is a revered Emeritus Professor of Chemistry. It was a deeply cherished moment! It was magic, not in the conventional sense of the word but in the sense of earthiness; I saw profound simplicity in the man. It goes without saying: an apple does not fall far away from its tree.

This is the spirit and message of this story: earthy living. It is about earthy relationships. It is about holism. It is about love. It is about trust that reads true spirituality. It is about commitment to the family and community. It is about authentic knowledge which is simple and practical. It is about growth and the potential for growth. It is about possibilities. It is about the future: the greater future of us all because it is beyond us all... Accordingly, it is about holding the future in awe! It is about self-correction speaking to ongoing learning. It is about the simplicity-humility duo. It is about a sense of humour for navigating life, especially humor pointed at ourselves. Pa Okogun's life embraced all these and their homologues! In one of his heart-to-heart discussions with my father, he teased "Okay, now that you shared your financial challenges with me; I guess I cannot ask you to lend me money!" He probably did not mean or intend to borrow money from my father. He was just in one of his humorous elements. He and my father then went into one of their laughing sessions that I watched with deep admiration for their passion and friendship. Watching them relate, I yearned to have good quality friendship as they did in each other. This power of friendship and of life is what this book is all about.

Africa needs the message of this book; the world needs it. The world is not likely to be blown up in a nuclear war; it will be wasted away in chronic aversion to holistic relationships. This story of Pa Okogun's life is a seed-story about integrity and mindful warming of our hearts to others. Pa Okogun stood out in warmness of heart in his relationships. Interestingly, his good looks (yes, he was a good-looking man) was particularly enhanced by his good spirit. We are more good-looking when the spirit within is beautiful. On the other hand, our putative external beauty stands no chance to glow with an ugly inner base. This story of Pa Okogun; The Life of an Enigma is an earthy treasure to its readers. Enjoy reading it!

Osahon Chris Eigbike, MA, MSc, PhD
of Asst. Professor Interfaith Theology, Interculturality and Indigenous Studies.
Visiting Senior Research Fellow, PaxHerbals-OFIRDI, Lagos, Nigeria (2018 to 2019).
Senior Research Scholar, PaxHerbals-African Action Research Community, Lagos, Nigeria.
Founder, Baobab Vita-Natura Community Development, Surrey, BC Canada.

CHAPTER ONE

INTRODUCTION

This book has been written from materials in an audio recording by Pa John Okogun Omovuon, written notes[1] he dictated to the author about his life and times starting from about 1905, verbal history as told by Okogun himself and corroborating verbally transmitted knowledge that I received from others who were his friends, relations and contemporaries. I had to write fast to take down, as much as possible, what was being said. Okogun was born when there was no country called Nigeria. Nigeria in West Africa was formally created by the British in 1914. Okogun died a Nigerian in 1993.

The story is not a catalogue of what Okogun did or did not do. It is a story of the structure of the society, its values, cultures and traditions at the times covered in his life and his efforts to navigate the changing times over the period of his over eighty years on earth to rise from being an early orphan to become a legend in his community.

The story also gives a small glimpse into the period slightly past the mid-1800s when it describes the circumstances associated with the betrothal of his mother to his father at a time when royal and aristocratic families kept slaves in Ewohimi. Some aspects of Ewohimi history are described.

To get a complete picture of the times when Okogun lived and his life, the reader is encouraged to read the structure and history of Ewohimi. The references give details which could have disrupted the flow of the story. I encourage all to read the information as contained in the references. The researcher and other interested readers will find the references helpful.

He was born about 1905 when the Colonial Government began opening Nigeria's hinterland to the Niger Delta ports and in preparation for the 1914 amalgamation of the Southern and Northern parts of Nigeria. One of the major roads to link the North to the Delta passed through Ewohimi. The road from Agbor through Ewohimi to Ubiaja and the North was commissioned[2, 3] for use in 1908. The road was surveyed and cleared when Okogun was born and at a time when his parents were anxious to have a male child. Okogun came when his mother had reached the menopause age.

The need to have a family house to which the daughters and children returned yearly during celebration of the ancestral feast, led to the creation of the stay-at-home female child as "man" (*arhe obhu uwa)* out of one of his sisters. For the same reason, Okogun's sisters did everything to make sure that Okogun did not acquire Western education. The belief was that with Western education, Okogun would take up white collar job and there would be no one at home to run their father Omovuon's leading and aristocratic family estate. Okogun's unfulfilled appetite for Western education was later in his life manifested in his sacrifice to ensure that he educated all his over twenty children, in his advice to parents to do the same and in his part in the founding of Okaigben Memorial School now known as Okaigben Primary School, Ewohimi.

For the same reasons of ensuring continuity of family lineage, a prosperous childless woman performed all the marital rites and "married" a young girl to have children through cousins in the name of the prosperous woman's biological or marital family. The young girl was referred to as "woman's wife" (*amhen okhuo).* This practice of having a woman's wife had its problems. There was the saying "One can take a man's wife, but one cannot take a woman's wife" (*Arhe amhen okpea, ai rhe amhen okhuo).* The "women-husbands" used all means to protect ownership of their wives so to say and would fight to finish any male trespassers. Okogun had courage and love which got him entangled in this system. The practices of stay-at-home daughter as a "man" and "woman's wife" clearly show how the people addressed pre-modern issues that are still challenges today in modern societies. The society in which Okogun grew up gave women some rights and freedom to continue patriachial lineage and have inheritance while recognising their natural roles as wife, mother, and childcare provider.

His parents intended that he should become an indigenous divination doctor perhaps to get back to the profession of native doctors for which

Okogun's *Iya/Aigbiya* dynasty was famous. During the final rites to initiate Iya's first son Ehimin, Okogun's great-great- grand father as the natural heir of his father's native doctor profession, Ehimin confessed that he could not prophesy or see beyond the ordinary. As a result, Ehimin's father and family decided that the heir apparent of the family Ehimin be initiated not just as a blacksmith (*Ogun)* but as a chief blacksmith (*oka-igun*, oka means be in the group that takes precedence at the guild meetings, plural of *ogun* is *igun*) while Ehimin's immediate junior half-brother was successfully initiated to take over their father's native doctor profession. Okogun means the son of blacksmith (Okolo-*ogun*). Okogun was given as a mentee to a famous native doctor, *Oghunmu* who was to train him to become a native doctor. Okogun's training as a native doctor was terminated abruptly when his father died while he was away with his mentor in Ugieghudu and Ehor in Benin Division but not before he had experiences arising on the one hand from colonial rule and on the other hand, from the Oba of Benin's customary powers.

Okogun's life became fully enmeshed in community organizations and life: mentorship to become a farmer, Enogie of Ewohimi Palace page as a protective arrangement, participation in community duties according to his age grade status and growth to become a courageous and famous acrobatic dancer. In all these, the norms, values, expectations and ethics of community life and development are exemplified. The operation of *Communtalism*[4] is evident in the times and life of Okogun.

At a very early period in his life, Okogun started to develop his entrepreneurial skills. He began by keeping poultry and working as potter of tobacco crates from Onitcha Ugbo to Ewohimi on foot. He engaged in traveling to Benin on foot, because vehicles were not yet available, from Ewohimi to work at building sites to earn money and to Onitsha on foot to buy articles of trade. The distances to these towns were between 70 and 100 kilometers. Later in life he would make these journeys first on bicycle and later in vehicles. These journeys had interesting and strange episodes and we learn about the first vehicles that operated between Onitsha and Agbor and between the Delta ports through Benin to Igueben in Esanland.

The British merchants had interests in palm produce, rubber and timber in Okogun's area of Southern Nigeria, West Africa. They organized the people as contractors, camp owners and labourers for the purpose of harvesting, collecting, and exporting these commodities. Okogun got involved in all these. He went through all the ranks in the timber industry starting as a labourer in Obomkpa in Delta State, rising to timber camp overseer and eventually becoming a timber contractor at Ewohimi. Okogun's timber business experience is itself an intriguing story that gives a glimpse into the operations of the British timber merchants, the people and Enogie of Ewohimi and his chiefs and the friendly interactions between the Ibos, Esans from Ewatto, Ohordua, Uromi, Irrua, Ekpoma, Igueben and others.

Life in Esanland in Okogun's generation was organized around activities assigned to each day of the native week of four-day cycle. These activities concerned the farms, feasts, dances and entertainments and community. There were core community values, norms, and ethics.

Igbabonanrimin/Egbabonelimwin/Igbabonanlimin is one of the best-known characteristic acrobatic dances of the Esan people. Okogun became a great acrobatic dancer and his story gives an insider and interesting experience of the organization of the dance cult. The dance was fraught with dangers and demanded the use of protective charms and support from powerful diviners (*obo* in Esan dialect meaning doctor). It should be pointed out here that Colonial anthropology call such diviners witch doctors. The word witch doctor is a misnomer because witch/wizard translates as *azen* in Esan dialect while doctor translates as *obo.* The people of a community do not in general deal with revealed witches and wizards for solution to their problems the way they do with the diviners. Diviners were summoned to reveal the witches and wizards in a community presumed to be afflicted by evil arising from witchcraft. The dance was used to socially link villages and towns from Ogwa through Ewohimi, Ewatto, Ubiaja, Okhuesan, Oria, Udakpa, Ohordua, and Emu in parts of Esanland.

The Urhobos are an Edo-related ethnic group that inhabit the Niger Delta towns and villages around *Sapele, Okpe, Abraka* and Warri. Canoe rowing and fishing culture are part of their life. Their presence in Ewohimi at the time provided opportunity for Okogun to make the journey to Onitsha on the river to sell yams.

Okogun commenced his entrepreneurial life by learning to become a tailor and cloth merchant. The demands of community life made it difficult for him to carry out his business at Ewohimi. He migrated first to Agbor but settled finally at Umunede where he spent many years trading and raising his early family before returning finally to Ewohimi. From Umunede he traversed Ika, Esan and Bini towns and villages on his bicycle to do his tailor-cum-cloth merchant and rubber businesses. He visited Onitsha market and engaged in rubber plantation business in Urokosa (Urhokuosa) zone bushes and forests of Benin. At Umunede he converted briefly to a Christian sect probably the Jehovah Witness and was to be installed an elder in that Faith.

In later life, Okogun engaged in transportation business after acquiring a Bedford lorry jointly with *Mr. Toba,* an Ijaw from Patani and finally as a kerosene depot retailer at Ofuri market, Ewohimi. He bought land and built a house at Agbor near the Boji Boji Owa market for commercial purposes as investment that proved very helpful in maintaining his large family till his death.

Okogun was well respected in community, in Ewohimi and beyond as a courageous man of integrity. He was relied upon to tell the truth on any issues and to be fair-minded in giving judgement on issues. He turned down offer of chieftaincy and village elder titles but took the deputy village elder title (*okaigbama)* when the pressure was on him to take by right the highest village elder title (*odion egbe).*

He systematically and gradually disposed of inherited gods, ancestral symbols, and fetish objects even to his last day at home before leaving for what would become his deathbed at the University of Ibadan Teaching Hospital in 1993. He asked to be baptized as a Catholic Christian on the eve of his departure for the hospital, but the Parish Priest could not because he still had two wives. He eventually got baptized at Ibadan by *Reverend Father Murumba Jem Oguogho* and was a communicant before he died on December 4, 1993.

Okogun's story is filled with stranger-than-fiction incidents. That a man who grew up and lived much of his life using protective charms could decide to be a Christian sends a strong message about the transcendental qualities and fundamentals of the ancestral worship and spirituality of most African communities.

Okogun's acrobatic and dance prowess involving ambition and efforts to overcome natural forces of gravity, space and time can be interpreted to have partially influenced his decisions and courageous travels and journeys through difficult and challenging terrains on land and water. His participation in the cultural dances made him important in positive social interactions not only in his community but in building interactions between his community and neighbouring communities. His abilities were also exploited politically by traditional rulers who also wished to have him in their entourage.

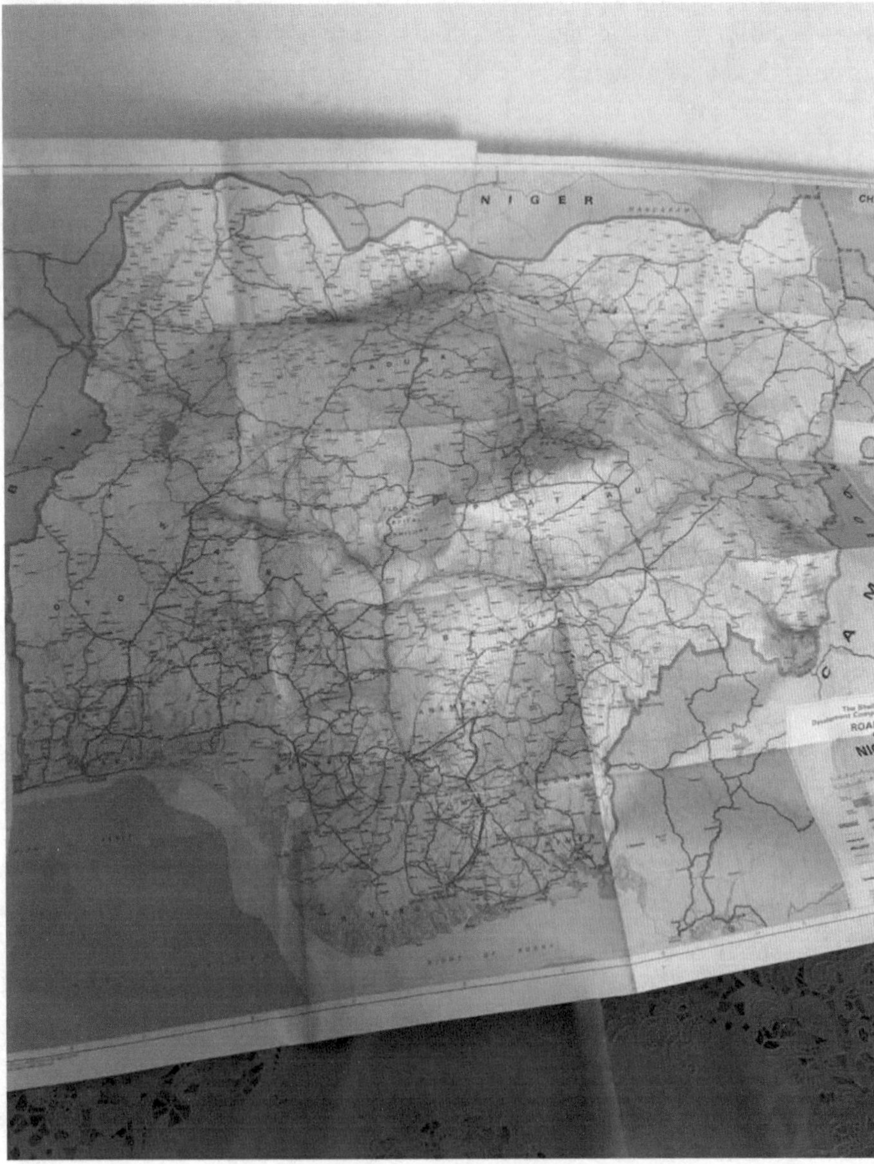

MAP OF NIGERIA, WEST AFRICA

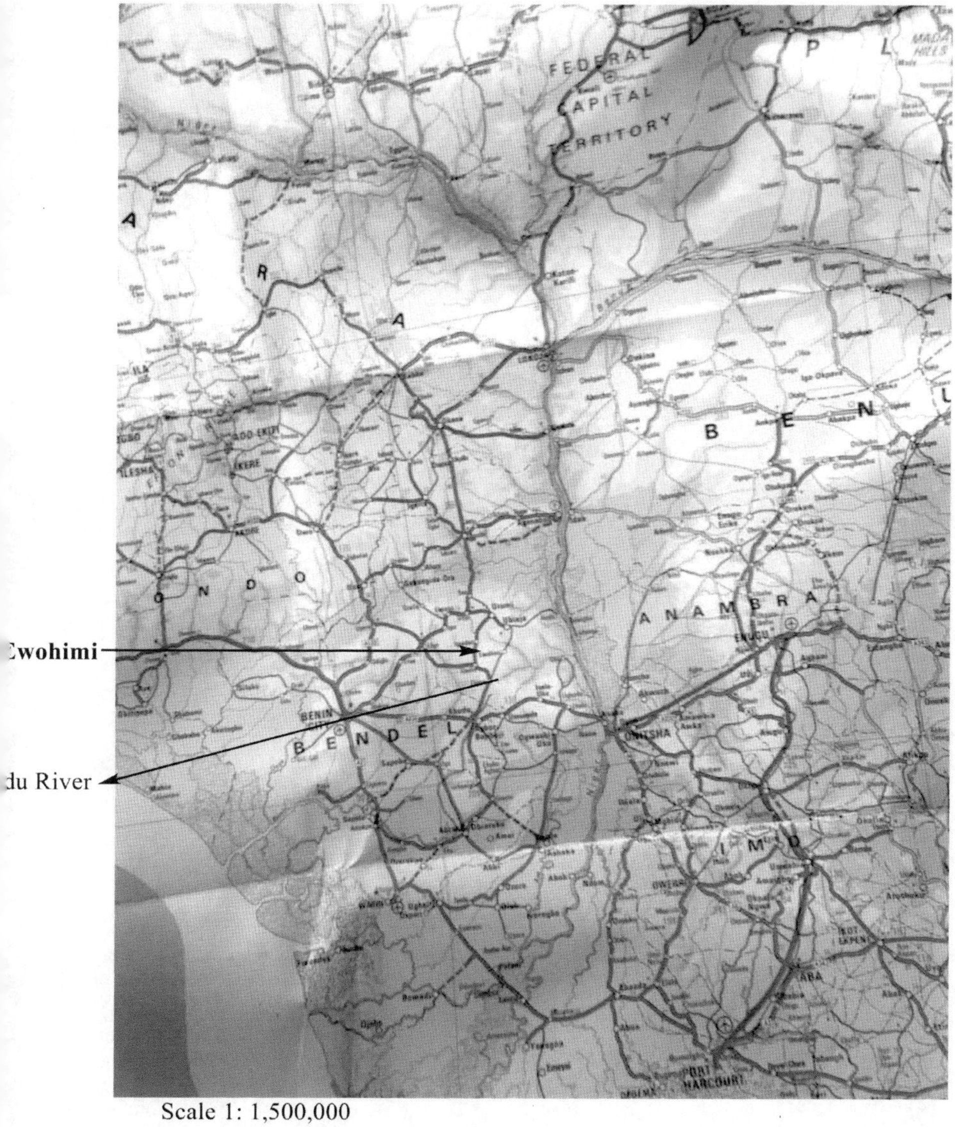

Scale 1: 1,500,000

MAP SHOWING LOCATION OF EWOHIMI AND ODU RIVER. Scale 1:1,500.000
Ewohimi, towns and villages mentioned in this book are located on these maps2 of Bendel state (Edo and Delta States), Nigeria West of the River Niger

CHAPTER TWO

EWOHIMI IN ESANLAND, EDO STATE

EWOHIMI (Ebhokhimi/Ebhokimi)

Ewohimi is a town in Esan South East Local Government Area, Edo State, Nigeria. It lies about 6° 29' 0" N and 6° 19' 0" E. It is on the Southeastern lower part of the Esan Plateau. It is in Edo State which was part of Nigeria known as Bendel State in the map. It is on the North-Eastern road from Agbor through Ekpon to Ubiaja.

Dr Christopher G. Okojie has published probably the most detailed work[3,4] on Esanland including Ewohimi and his work is a major source of information about Esanland.

The 1963 Census in Nigeria puts its population at over 15,000 inhabitants. Assuming the correctness of the 1953 Census figure for Ewohimi, the minimum population growth rate of 2.5% and all other things being equal, Ewohimi should be about 40,000 in 1993.

The Structure of Ewohimi

Ewohimi consists of the following villages: *Eguae*, the seat of the *Enogie* and paramount ruler of Ewohimi, *Okede, Agadaga, Oghu, Ikeken and Okaigben* with *Iselu* as a quarter in Okaigben. Each of the villages has several quarters.

Okogun hailed from *Idinrio* in Okaigben. Okaigben is subdivided into Okaigben senior and junior and Iselu. Okaigben senior consists of

Ikemenzelomon, Ubie, Idumuguokha, Idumeho, Idumekhae all as the four Ologhe (*Ologhe ne enen) and Idumu-agho* while Okaigben junior consists of *Uwi-Idinrio* with *Iselu, Uzebu* and *Idumobo* all referred to as Idinrio. The fathers of Okaigben senior are *Ogun* and *Ezelomon* while the fathers of Okaigben junior are *Ogbe, Ohen* and *Edion*. Ogbe, Ohen and Edion were junior brothers of Ogun and Ezelomon; all being sons of Okatu the founder of Okaigben. Edion, the founder of Iselu was joined early by migrants[5] from *Okhuesan* near Ubiaja. There were shrines for these fathers of Okaigben. Many elders in Idumu-agho including the late Odionegbe of Idumu-agho Reverend John E. Ilegbedion said many of their ancestors migrated from Ika ethnic group of Delta State. It is relevant to note that Idumu-agho may be linked with *Prince Erediauwa* who became *Oba Osemende of Benin's* sojourn in Ewohimi and hence with *Chief Obaseki's* family of Benin Kingdom.

Amedokhian, Efandion and *Ukato* in Uromi, *Okpaja* in Ubiaja, and some settlements around Emu, *Ogwashiukwu* area in Delta State and *Idah* in Benue State were founded[2,3] by Okaigben people who fled from Ewohimi because of violent retaliatory reaction by Okaigben against the Enogie, in their time, whom they accused of being involved in the assassination of their father while they were away as warriors sent by the Enogie to fight in the Oba of Benin's army.

The supreme authority in Ewohimi is the Enogie but there are two types[5] of village administrations subordinate to the Enogie in Ewohimi. While the village executive authority respectively in Okaigben and Agadaga is the *Odionwele* in the village council, the village authority in the other villages respectively is the head chief (*Okhaimon* of the village).

At the beginning, Ewohimi started as a federation of *Ewohimi, Ewatto* and *Ewossa* (*Ebhoikhimi, Ebhoatto/ Ebhoator* and *Ebhossa*).

Ewohimi as at today has loose boundaries with Ewatto and Ewossa because the people inhabiting these towns are brethren with Ewohimi people. The other boundaries are with Ohordua, Udo, Igueben, Ebelle, Igbanke now through Ekpon, Igbodo, Idumuje – Ugboko and Idumuje – Unor. Ekpon is now full owner of the land on which they have settled, and which land was given to them by the Enogie and people of Ewohimi, when long ago they migrated through Ekpoma to the area.

Three princes, sons of an Ogiso or Oba of Benin were commissioned by the Benin Palace to go and found a sanctuary, Orikhimi for the Benin Kingdom which was also to serve as a war camp. A version of the story says that the princes were *Alan*, the most senior, *Oron* and *Oisa*. For this reason, for a long time the villages operated as one under the leadership of the Enogie of Ewohimi who installed and gave authority to the Enigies of Ewatto founded by Oron and Ewossa founded by Oisa, as it were then, on behalf of the Oba of Benin. This practice stopped first in the case of Ewossa about 100 years ago while it stopped with Ewatto relatively recently during the reign of HRH *S. Usifo Enosegbe II* and with the current Enogie of Ewatto His Royal Highness *Sylvanus Osagie Ikhumhen*. Ewohimi, was at the beginning, regarded as far enough from Benin City to be granted partial autonomy by the Oba of Benin.

With time Orikhimi became Ebhorikhimi, then Ebhokhimi/Ebhokimi and finally anglicized by the English to Ewohimi because they could not pronounce Ebhokhimi.

Professor Ademola Iyi-Eweka once wrote on a website[6] about Ishan and Ewohimi as follows: "ESAN/Ishan-for the immediate neighbour to the north are people living in around Irrua, Orhodua, Uromi, Ubiaja, Ewu, Ewatto, Igueben and the almighty Evbohimwin (Ewohimi)) the city by the big river " or " the city of Ikhimwin trees " etc. Thus, Ewohimi was also associated with its nearness to the River Niger *(Ohinmin)*. Note that Ewohimi was called almighty among the towns and villages of Esan. Ewohimi was also a military outpost of the Benin Kingdom. No wonder, the people had so much land around them at the beginning that the Colonial Government created an extensive Ewohimi Forest Reserve[7] in 1931 that had boundaries with Ekpon, Igbodo, Idumuje-Ugboko, Idumuje-Unor, Ohordua, and Ewatto.

Recent research publications[8a, 8b] reveal that Ewohimi, Ebho-Ikhimin was founded during the reign of the Ogiso Igodo reign (40BC – 16AD) when Benin was called Igodomigodo. Ikhimin was the son of the Ogiso Igodo who sent him to establish the Ewohimi Kingdom and hence the name Ebho-Ikhimin for Ewohimi thus contradicting the land of Ikhimin translation and other stories regarding the name Ewohimi.

Ewohimi's military prowess and spirirtual powers are still being talked about today and people still regard Ewohimi people as being tough in divination and the use of charms. Many ignore the fact that the people are now mostly Christians and produced the first Esan-born Catholic Diocese of Uromi Bishop, *Most Reverend Dr. Donatus A. Ogun*, OSA. The oldest Religious from Ewohimi is *Reverend Sister Gladys Osagie*, OLA., who in the year 2012 celebrated her 25 years in her Congregation of Our Lady of Apostles.

Ewohimi for reasons best known to our ancestors, but which are not unconnected with the events at their first encounter, in 1908 rejected a Government School allocated by the colonial masters to Ewohimi because of its importance. Ewohimi people continued to be hostile to the presence and activities of religious missionary organisations until the late 1930s. Consequently, Ewohimi remained relatively undeveloped[9] in the Western sense compared with their "northern cousins" which are the Esan people in Uromi, Irrua, Ekpoma and others in those areas.

Initially the three founding fathers lived together in Ewohimi until they decided to separate with Oisa moving to the South to found Ebho-Oisa now Ewossa and Oron moving to the North to found Ebho-atto (Ebho-Ator) now Ewatto possibly because of the semi-Savannah or grassland vegetation in parts of the area. It can be deduced that the people of Ewohimi came mostly from Benin. However, the present Ewohimi people through migrations from other areas notably the Ikas and through intermarriages have people of other origins. Evidence for this exists in Okaigben and in Oghu that claims to have been fathered by a man of Ika name, Ezewanghu dropping from the sky. There is an unauthenticated story[10], from a source that should know, which recounts that when the Arochukwu native doctor and his entourage including the escorts from Benin, were returning from Abeokuta after spending some time in Benin, they passed through Ewohimi and left some of their men to live and integrate with Ewohimi people. Ewohimi was to ensure a safe passage for them through to the River Niger. There are also people of Ewohimi descent in Uromi, Ubiaja, Idah, Ugun, Ieren and the Ika areas to the East as already mentioned.

Ewohimi and the Benin Kingdom

The late sage Honourable Joseph O. Odigie related examples of the brave and spiritual services of Ewohimi warriors in the Benin Kingdom era and of Ewohimi native doctors to the Obas of Benin in the past on the occasion of the visit of Omon n'Oba n'Edo Ukuakpokpolo Erediauwa to Ewohimi shortly after his ascension in 1979 to the throne. The facts were stated in the address read by Honourable Joseph O. Odigie, on behalf of the then Enogie of Ewohimi,

His Royal Highness Omon S. Usifo Enosegbe II and his people at the Enogie's Palace. These episodes have been partially described in Prince Eweka's book[11,12].

One of these services to the Oba of Benin was that when the Bini people did not support the erection of the perimeter wall around the Oba's palace by causing heavy rains and floods to destroy erected walls, it was Ewohimi rain doctors who were invited to Benin to standby and do whatever they did to ensure that the wall was successfully erected without the rains falling to cause floods.

Other Ewohimi history

It is not possible to discuss Ewohimi history in a short presentation.

Abomination that Ogbebor carried out in Edo Land (*Akhailu no Ogbebor lu bho oto Edo*) episode happened as Ewohimi led a vital section of the Prince Erediauwa forces into Benin to oust Ogbebor the usurper Oba from the throne.

The abomination was that Ogbebor set the Oba's Palace on fire as he was forced out by Prince Erediauwa's forces.

One of the corollaries of this episode is reported to be the *Ogie-Iliki* creation as reward for the Iliki Chief whose charm (*ekhuae ofan din) was effectively deployed against Ogbebor's forces.* It is remarkable to note that the name Osemende was the name of an Iliki man who died in the 1990s. Prince Erediauwa took the title Oba Osemende when he ascended the throne.

Ewohimi appeared to have become a haven for aggrieved princes of Benin who used Ewohimi as base from where they caused problems for the Oba. Prince Ogbewekon did so in his efforts to unseat Oba Adolor. Prince Orokhoro was rival to Oba Ovonramwen. During the period of uprising by rival princes, forces led by Ewohimi during the reign of His Royal Highness Aigbe as Enogie, that appeared to have included Ohordua, Ewatto, Ewossa, Ebelle, Ogwa and Amahor engaged an Oba Ovonramen's army in the Ezen/Ibilli war. Ekpon's refusal[13] to join forces with Ewohimi who provided land for their ancestors became a sore point in the relations between Ewohimi and Ekpon. The Oba's forces lost the Ezen/Ibilli war[13,14]. The canon usually displayed during Ukpeze feast in Ewohimi is said to have been captured by the Ewohimi-led forces at that war. To curtail the powers of Ewohimi, Oba Ovanramwen introduced[15] the controversial Okaigiesan title.

Ewohimi people had thriving economy – the UAC (United Africa Company) facing the triangle in Eguae, the John Holts in Okaigben facing Ofuri market, the then main Ewohimi market, when it boomed with traders from neighbours and far away Agbor, Benin, Sapele, Warri, etc. The Royal Mail Post Office run by kind Pa Jacob Ogholoh, the Dispensary with a devoted staff Pa Okhuebor, the Government staff barracks (ibaleke), the UAC, the District Oficer (DO)'s Rest House and Madam Otamhanyehor Aigbe nee Pa Ogun Ifebhor's popular local restaurant around the Eguae triangle with Pa "Free Lawyer" (Freeliar) from Ohordua entertaining listeners with his anecdotes and satires constituted a beehive of interactions, administrative and economic activities in Ewohimi. Ewohimi people used canoes with the involvement of Urhobos to take their farm products to Onitsha market starting from the Odu River through river Iyagun. Odu River was also used to float timber logs to Warri via the River Niger. Ewohimi had a thriving timber industry in its Forests run by the UAC, Chief Odigie, later by Chief Paul E. Odigie and then by four of its leaders led by HRH the Enogie S. Usifo Enosegbe II. There were the Western Nigeria (later Midwestern Nigeria) Development Corporation Plantation and Mills for oil palm tree fruits and the Asaboro Rubber Plantation.

Ewohimi has been a giant political force in Esan, Benin Province, and the old Western Region though the past appeared to have been relatively more glorious than the present. Ewohimi currently does not host a Local Government Headquarters. From 1918, Ewohimi was the Headquarters of the District Council comprising Ogwa, Ebelle, Amahor, Ekpon, Ewossa, Ewohimi and Ewatto. Igueben was once part of a District Council with Ewohimi as Headquarters. Ewohimi was later the Headquarters of the Ewohimi, Ewatto and Ewossa District Council. The Court and disused barracks and Colonial Rest House at Eguae are reminders of important Ewohimi eras. Ewohimi had a direct motorable link to Asaba and the East from where the Colonial Officers first came to Ewohimi and the rest Ishan. The Enogie of Ewohimi, *His Royal Highness Ifebhor* was one of the leading Chiefs that represented Esan people at the Mapo Hall Ibadan consultative conference organized by the Colonial Government. Chief Odigie represented the Enogie at the Ibadan meeting. In the late 1950s to early 1960s before the creation of the Midwestern Region, HRH S. Usifo Enosegbe II was one of the chiefs that represented Benin Province (present Edo State) in the House of Chiefs in Ibadan and was a Minister in the Midwest Region. Honourable Joseph O. Odigie represented Esan in the Western Nigeria House of Assembly in Ibadan and was later Parliamentary Secretary to Government (position like assistant Minister).

Ewohimi had festivities in addition to *Ukpeze* which united its people and families in celebrations. The name[3, 4] Ukpeze for the feast arose from the relationship between the ruling house in Mbiri, Delta State and the ruling house in Ewohimi. The ruling house in Mbiri (*Ibi* as Mbiri is called in Ewohimi) was founded by an excommunicated Prince from Ewohimi who told the people then at Mbiri, when he first arrived perhaps with some princely paraphernalia, that he was wandering, *mon bi bi khian*.

Ewohimi people organized igbabonanrimin which, as earlier mentioned, took them to villages in Ogwa, Ebelle, Okalo, Emu, Ohordua, Okhuesan, Udakpa, Oria, Sapele, etc. and its youths organized friendly football matches with their counterparts in Igueben, Ohordua, Ekpon and Ewatto.

Towns, Rivers, and streams in Okogun's narratives[1] on the Bendel State map[2]

Odu River has about five sources South and South East of Ewohimi. It joins *Rivers Uto*r and Iyagun beyond *Ohordua* and *Emu*. River Utor's major source is in Udo area between *Ubiaja* and *Igueben* and it is called River Elah where it is crossed, North of Ewohimi, on the road from Ewohimi to Ubiaja. The Odu and Utor Rivers combine with the Iyagun River to flow into the River Niger after Ebu town. Ubiaja, Ebu, Igueben and the Rivers can be located on the maps.

Umunede and *Issele Uku* are on the road linking Benin and Asaba beyond Agbor. *Uromi* is beyond Ubiaja from Ewohimi. *Ehor, Urhuokosa, Ekpoma, Irrua and Ewu* are on the road heading North from Benin while *Illushi (Ozigolo or Ega)* is by the River Niger on the road from Ubiaja. *Idah* is on the bank of the River Niger across from Illushi. They can also be located on the maps.

Age grades

At Ewohimi, there are the following age grades and communal duty groups for the males: *egbolughe* (street sweepers), *igbama* (mature adulthood), *oka-igbama* (leader of the igbamas and deputy senior elder), *odion-egbe* (senior elder in the quarter) *and odion-wele* (most and head senior elder in the quarter).

The communal duty groups are *otu* (group of young men) who carried out security and communal tasks, *egbe-ede* (bridge-builders or literally: stream tiers). The women had their own categorisation which was not as many as that of males. The overall head of the women in the community was known as *Ogiadan (queen of the daughters of the community* which is based on seniority).

Egbolughe

The *egbolughe a*ge grade comprises teenagers, adolescents, and young adults most of whom are bachelors. Some older men may continue to be reckoned as members of this grade if they are unable for whatever reason to perform the rights of elevation from the grade. This group sweeps the street every fifth day known as *Edewor.* When the farm path is to be weeded, the group weeds to the ground. The group digs the grave during burials. Sanctions against defaulters who fail to report for duties, include fines and seizing fowls in the village which the defaulter must pay for. Every member of this age grade as with others keeps his ears to the ground and goes without being summoned to any duty that arises. It should be noted that this is the only age grade that has no initiation rites.

Igbama

The *igbama* age is the promotional grade from the egbolughe group. The usual qualification for admission to this age grade is to be married with children and have a proposed residential property site for one's family. The man must already at least be farming independently for his family upkeep. The ceremony for initiation into the igbama group in the various parts of Ewohimi has the same core process but the demands or outlay by the candidate varies among the quarters in Ewohimi. The rite is almost the same in all Ewohimi. It is a purification, and the elevation implies not doing certain things perceived as sinful or against God's commandments and offensive to the spirits of the ancestors. It is for this reason that young persons are discouraged from elevation to Igbama until it is considered that they are mature enough to obey the prescribed commandments. Also, for safety reasons, only a short notice is publicly given about the day set apart for the elevation ceremony and the day must be the Ofuri/Agbado market day which is one of the Guardian Angel's Day(*ede ehi)*.

The rite of elevation is carried out by the priest representative of the *Odion egbe* supported by the *owaimhin (meaning sharer of things)* seated as priest by the effigies, *ukhure* representing the male ancestors of the family of the candidate. Two calabashes of palmwine are provided by the candidate along with kola nuts. The body of one of the calabashes of palmwine is made white with chalk while the other one is left in its natural colour: brown with stains from use. After the prayers for blessings and protection from evil for the candidate, a symbolic hand-woven white cloth measuring about fortyfive inches by eighteen inches, is tied, as underwear by the priest around the candidate's waist who tactically completely undresses to have the white cloth tied.

Earlier, the candidate collected the white cloth from its traditional custodian in the village. The candidate presents token small gift of kola nuts with or without small drink to the custodian to collect the cloth. The following are some of the commandments which the fresh igbama must obey and the commandments are publicly given to the new igbama:

> *One: if he sees a woman fleeing from her marital home, he must tell the woman to return to her husband,*
>
> *Two: if he meets two children fighting or quarreling on the street, he must adjudicate justly and punish the guilty with a few lashes of the cane even if the guilty child is his own child,*
>
> *Three: if he finds that a trap set in the bush has caught an animal, he must disengage the dead animal and take it to the owner or put a sign by the road to indicate to passersby that a trap along the bush trap trail has caught a wild animal,*
>
> *Four: if he meets a tree fallen across the farm path, he must remove the fallen tree from the path or wait for fellow igbamas and otu to join in removing the fallen tree if he could not do it alone. If the trunk is too large for easy removal, he and his colleagues must create a detour along the blocked farm path away from the fallen tree,*

Five: he must avoid a situation that could lead him to fall during the five days that he must have the white cloth on,

Six: the white cloth can only be temporarily untied from his waiste throughout the five days only for the purpose of having a bath and so on.

A cup of the palmwine in the whitened vessel is prayed over to bless the candidate and then given to the candidate who drinks it or takes a sip from it. Only the igbamas drink the palmwine from this white body container to remind them of their purity. The males below the rank of igbama drink from the other ordinary palmwine calabash.

At the end of the ceremony, all present, then hail the new igbama with the same salutation for a woman who has just successfully delivered a baby: the greeting is *amonghon* roughly translated as congratulations. The new igbama then first genuflects to greet the following persons in turn:

the priest and the elders, his father if alive, his mother and his wife. *The igbama's wife is warned: "your husband is now to genuflect for you: if after this occasion, he threatens to genuflect for you, you must run away from him"*

Token gifts may be named by these relatives for the new igbama to mark his elevation.

The new igbama signs himself profusely with emulsion of white chalk and is accompanied, that night, by the rejoicing crowd to knock on every door in the village and to dance in celebration before the residents who come out to the door to congratulate the igbama saying *amonghon*. They also sign themselves with the chalk to share from the blessings and prayers. The residents give token money thrown to the ground for the igbama.

One of the songs by the entourage is:

Bo okhin? Eghonghon non!
Meaning what is it? It is rejoicing/joy.

The new igbama may loan, with token gifts for the custodian, a special golden decorative raphia cloth tied over his dress to visit the Enogie, chiefs, other friends, and relatives to announce himself as igbama during the remaining four days of celebration.

On the fifth day, the next market day (Ofuri and Agbado), the village assemble in the early evening for the ceremony to untie the small white cloth. The Igbama at this stage wears a pant under the white cloth. He engages in a mock wrestle with a selected man in the village. The man selected must be one whose first son is alive, and he defeats the new igbama in the contest and while still over him, unties the white cloth. The igbama now celebrates his new status that night. A dance (asologun) group usually performs and there is entertainment of guests by the new igbama. It must be stated that since about 1987 when most Christians accepted to perform the rite of elevation to the igbama age grade, ancestral effigies in the form of ukhure are no more used during the ceremony. Most homes no more have these effigies at least in public view.

One of the duties of the igbamas apart from those already implied is to clean and dress corpses and lay them in the grave during burial. An igbama has the right to break kola nuts at gatherings if he is the most senior or if the most senior person has not performed the rite of elevation to the igbama age grade. When an igbama dies, he is buried in his plot of land built or yet to be built as distinct from egbolughe who are buried in the bush with no celebration or other formalities. Men who qualified to be igbama but did not perform the elevation ceremony while alive, are elevated posthumous before burial.

Oka-igbama

The Oka-igbama age grade is attained with age. An Igbama is supposed to rise to the oka-igbama age grade with age. The oka-igbamas are old males who have been active in the affairs of the village. They are usually from about age 75 years. The prospective oka-igbama must "receive" an *oror.* An oror is the equivalent of godfather in Christian baptismal rites. An oror is chosen for the oka-igbama candidate by divination using some objects which Christians have objected to as being fetish. Two males who are orors are to regard their families as having become one in all aspects of life. From the eve of the oror assignment, the two men sleep on the same bed, eat from the same dish, and live together in the senior oror residence for five days. The junior oror is escorted back home on the fifth day with specially cooked pounded yam and soup with a designated number of chunks of wildlife meat, preferably antelope meat and gifts. The meat of the antelope is preferred for this and many purposes in Esan and Edo rituals. The oror practice certainly helped to unite families in the village.

The rites of elevation to the oka-igbama age grade are relatively simple and it is also performed on behalf of the odionwele by his representative known as his *owaimhin*. A designated number of kola nuts and coconuts are used. The number of coconuts was probably up to twentyone or more. The new oka-igbama are prayed over and blessed using some of the kola nuts and some of the coconuts during the ceremony. The ceremony is also performed on Ewohimi market day. One of the roles of the *oka-igbama* is to direct and conclude burial ceremonies for families when the head of a family dies. The oldest Oka-igbama leads his colleagues on the last day by addressing the children and families of the deceased to advise on the need for unity and love in the family. They formally inform the children that their father has gone home but their father is still alive. They point to the first son as their living father.

The first son is advised to be true father to all his siblings just as the deceased was father to all in love, patience, and guidance. The siblings are advised to accord all love, cooperation, and support to their living father.

Odion-egbe (senior elder in the quarter)

Odion-egbe attained through performing a rite, literally means *the oldest male* in the quarters or village. They are also referred to as *odion-opia* to distinguish them from those who may be of the same age or older in the village but for one reason or other have not performed the rite to ascend ("eat") to the odion-egbe grade. Such an older person is usually asked to give his approval and blessings for the installation of a junior old man in the quarter as odion-egbe. The rite in Okaigben, Ewohimi is performed in two locations where *the symbolic two cutlasses of Okaigben* are kept respectively: *Aile's family compound at Uwi-idinrio for Okaigben junior (Idinrio) and Ikuenobe's family compound at Idumuguokha-ugbolobhede for Okaigben senior.* These two families are also supposed to be the custodians of the white cloth used at the igbama ceremony. The ceremony to create an odion-egbe is normally performed by the *odionwele, the head odion-egbe himself. During the ceremony, the odionwele and the new odion-egbe walk along the street together, several times to and fro away from the rest of the people with the odionwele talking in whispers to the new odion-egbe*. The odion-egbe after consulting takes the final decision on any issue confronting his quarters. They are supposed to consult with the spirits of the ancestors and have share in burial materials and some sacrifices. Odion-egbe is expected to stay home and carry out no more farming. An odion-egbe walks around carrying a special long walking stick as a symbol of his position and authority. Oka-igbamas and odion-egbes on waking in the morning do not immediately emerge from their bedrooms. They lock themselves in and first pray and bless themselves and men and women of the village wherever they may be and for the peace in the village. The odion-egbes and Okaigbamas formally greet the past ancestors odion-egbes of the village as if the dead were by them. They rinse their mouths with water and then open for members of the family to stand at the bedroom door to give the morning greeting to them.

The special community duty groups: Otu and Egbe-ede

The communities have special duty groups other than the indigenous doctors for men and the *ogiadan (*queen of the daughters) and her group for women.

Otu means a group or band of able-bodied young men selected from egbolughe and igbama age grades whose duty is to carry out tasks like communal building and defence of the community. The head of such a group is called *odion-otu.*

Egbe-ede

Egbe-ede literally means "those who tie stream". In Okaigben, Ewohimi the people must cross the *Odu stream* to get to their main farms in the area they call *ugbo-odu* translated as "Odu farm".

The egbe-ede groups in the various quarters of Okaigben are made up of able bodied igbama. Their duty is to construct and maintain bridges across the Odu stream. They use logs of felled trees to construct the bridges. There were five main bridges in Okaigben across the Odu River. The bridges were located at Odu bridge at Idumu-agho farm road, motorable Okhonmhen (okhonmhen means will fight for me) constructed by the colonial powers also at Idumu-agho – Idumuje-Ugboko road, Ogbeni bridge at Idumu-osun cum Idumu-oleghe farm road, Odu and Ihiezi bridges at Idinrio farm road located on their respective farm paths. It should be mentioned here that shrines of the Okaigben water-goddess Odu were to be found along the course of the stream near the bridges. The main shrine is called uwa-nokhua (the large palace or large house) located in the forest area on the left of the *Okhonmhen* /Odu River bridge as one moves away from Ewohimi facing the Delta State. The name ogbeni means killer of elephant. The Odu River is deep and fast flowing at the ogbeni bridge point.

Market days[16]

In Ewohimi as in the rest of Esanland[2, 3], the days of the year were divided into a four-day week according to the markets and activities for each of the days. Days of the week were associated with markets and activities. Two of the four days in the customary week were associated with God's Angels and guardian Angels. Ogidigbo now called Agbado was named after a god while Ofuri was named after a courageous daughter in the history of Okaigben. It is necessary to briefly recount the events that led to the change of name and market day from Ogidigbo to Agbado and from two days after Ofuri market day to Ofuri market day. When the Colonial Government and Esan traditional rulers assigned market days, the main market in each town was used. Ofuri Market was gazetted about 1918 as Ewohimi market day. In the mid-1960s, His Royal Highness the Enogie of Ewohimi Samuel Usifoh Enosegbe II for various reasons including his opinion that a town's main market should be in Eguae near the Palace told Ewohimi people to hold Ogidigbo Market on the same day as Ofuri Market and changed the name Ogidigbo to Agbado (like a market in Benin City). Naturally, there were court actions challenging the change during the tenure of Chief Okotako of Uromi, Chief Anthony Enahoro and siblings' father, as the Customary Court Judge in Esan. Many were imprisoned for violating the law gazetting Ofuri Market and its day as all Ewohimi market day. Agbado is on the main Ewohimi highway and more central in Ewohimi than Ofuri Market. Most of the rest Ewohimi people were pleased with the move of the market from Ofuri, so to say, to Agbado and Agbado won on the will of majority Ewohimi people. His Royal Highness the Enogie Lord Peter Ogienefo Usifo II who succeeded his father told the people that nothing stops Okaigben people from continuing to hold Ofuri Market on its historical day now also assigned to Agbado. Most Okaigben people, over time now attend Agbado Market.

Ede-aki

The word *Ede*, the two e's sound as in egg here means day and it is the word also for river.

Ede-aki means market day. At Ewohimi, it meant Ofuri market day before the change and now means Ofuri and Agbado markets day. On market day, most of the men are at home and the women take the farm products to the market to be sold. People could go to farm just to collect items for the market and check their traps or go to the small farm near the village as distinct from the farm up to 8-10 kilometers from the village across the Odu stream or River on the Okaigben side. Some of the other Esan markets on Ewohimi market day are Uromi, Iruekpen, Emu, Ogwa and Amahor

Edewor

Edewor is the traditional Sunday. The environmental age grade sweeps the streets, visits are exchanged and there is recreation including staging the various dances.

Market days in Esanland on Edewor are Ewu, Illushi (Ozigolo), Igor, Ewatto, Ugbegun, Ewossa, Egoro and Amahor Waterside. Ewohimi people, women and traders attend Ewatto market called *Ombinobor* or Ewossa market.

Ede-amhien-edewe

Ede-amhien-edewe literally means the day the dawn is seen. It is also called the small farm day (ediwe ni ikhere). Early at dawn on this day, the people hurry to go to the farms especially during the period of much work in the farms. They had gotten all materials together the previous night to ensure early departure at dawn to the main farms far from the village.

Markets in Esan on this day are Ekpoma, Ibore, Okhuesan, Ugboha, Igueben, Ekpon, etc. Ewohimi women and traders go to Ekpon mostly or to Igueben for Agadaga villagers.

Ede-esese-ede

Ede-esese-ede means the day of the middle of the day and it is still spent in the farm until late afternoon. The tradition was that most men and male children spent the previous night in the farm during times of intensive farm activities and return home late on this day. Market days on this day in Esanland include Irrua, Opoji, Ebelle, Ubiaja, Ohordua etc. Ewohimi women and traders go to either Ebelle or Ohordua.

The next day is again Ede-aki, market day in Ewohimi.

Ede-ehi, Guardian angels' days

Two days, Ede-aki and Ede- amhien-edewe, in the traditional week were regarded as the days of the guardian angels. Certain activities like traditional marriages, celebration of age grade elevation and burials of mature persons could be performed only on these days.

CHAPTER THREE

BIRTH, PARENTAGE AND BLACKSMITH HERITAGE

The key professions in Ewohimi

It is relevant at this point to briefly describe the key professions of Ewohimi people during most of the time Okogun lived.

Farming was general though the expert farmers were called *owee* pronounced o as in odd and e as in egg. Every child was expected to acquire the art of farming and rearing domestic animals.

Hunting using traps for wild animals was also general but had to be learnt from experts. The celebrated hunters who could kill dangerous animals like the elephant were called ozeden. The use of guns with or without hunting dogs for hunting was more a family profession which was learnt in families. These were the real hunters called *ohue* in Esan. Until the Nigerian Government banned the possession of guns, almost every family had at least a dane gun. Sadly, this disarming of the people appears to have prepared the ground for the current situation in Nigeria where the people's community self-defence capability is weakened.

Health problems were managed by the *Obo/Oboh* which translate as doctor for men or *obo no okhuo* for women doctors though every child in the village knew the treatment and plants that were used for common ailments. The doctors were approached when the common knowledge fails to cure. The doctor profession was based in families and passed from generation to generation. There were two types of doctors. *Obo-udo* referred to those versed in the use of herbs and usually grind plant parts using stone *(udo)* as grinder. The other type of doctor used divination and herbal remedies to treat patients and were referred to as *obo-ise (ise* is the name for the diviner's tool of objects cast, read, and interpreted by the doctor). These divination doctors also dealt with other issues concerning witchcraft accusations, rain making and inter community attacks and wars. The doctors had their guild to regulate the practice. The head of the doctors at Ewohimi is/was at Idumu-isaba at Oghu.

The *owen nan (women)* included surgery, midwifery, and infertility problems in their practice.

Blacksmiths called *Ogun* made cutlasses, axes, knives, hoes, and guns. The trade was based in families which passed the knowledge to their heirs. The blacksmiths like the doctors also had their guild to regulate the practice.

The head of the blacksmiths' guild in Ewohimi is at Idumu-agbor in Oghu.

The tapping of palmwine could be learnt by every male but usually certain families acquired fame in the trade. They were called *okpe/okpeh.*

Some village gods had priests or priestesses which were recruited from certain families. For example, the chief Priest (*Ohen-Odu*) of the goddess Odu in Okaigben must come from families in Idumu-Odu, part of Idinrio. To ensure that the brotherly link between Okaigben senior and Okaigben junior (Idinrio) is maintained, their ancestors have Idumodu inside the Ologhe part of Okaigben senior. The Priests and Priestesses were referred to as *ohen.*

Before the advent of sewing machines and imported fabric and other goods, the main items of trade were farm products, local food items, hunted or trapped dead wildlife, clay pots and various types of handwoven cloths, mats, and baskets. It was the duty of the wives to sell most of the items. Thus, the populations in markets were essentially women. The men usually took positions around the markets as observers and sometimes to have opportunities to interact with future wives and lovers at corners of the market. When an old woman died, the final burial involved war dance around the market to celebrate her with praise songs, dances, gun, and cannon shots. For these reasons, announcements of scheduled forthcoming feasts and celebrations were made by the respective representatives of priests at locations around the market, on market days. Such announcements always had a final part of an announcement requesting women to inform their husbands (*okhuo kha hon, otama edo le)*

Okogun's parentage

John Okogun Eguaereona Omovuon was born about 1905 to *Omovuon Okuoebho* (literally meaning peoples' war) and *Esekhor*, eldest daughter of *Emuze, the Chief Ebalogbhen of Idumigie*, Ewohimi, Edo State, Nigeria. Esekhor's mother Aitolo was the daughter of Chief Idogun of Idumebo, Ewatto and Aitolo's mother was Airegbeogun of Idumarhu also of Ewatto. Omovuon was a blacksmith and a hunter. Esekhor was famed to be tall and stately. She was a very fair skin woman.

Okogun was born at the time the Agbor Ewohimi Ubiaja road was surveyed.[1, 3, 4]

He told the story as his mother related it to him. The circumstances of his birth included the parents's fear of danger for his life as shall be related later. His body just after birth was covered with rashes and the parents decided to secretly take him to safety and get treatment somewhere in Ewohimi away from Okaigben. As his mother, Esekhor took him away in search of safety and healing, she suddenly came to a surveyed road path and she had to run to cross the path which she said was frightful to view because it was so straight that she described it as being like a street in the world of the dead (*ukpughe arimin*). The surveyed path became the Agbor -Ewohimi-Ubiaja Royal Mail and telegraph and telephone road. The road was opened for use in 1908.[3,4]

Taking into consideration the fact that there were no bulldozers and machines for road building at the time, the initial survey track must have been about 1904. The complete construction to put the road into use for vehicles could have taken three to four years. Okogun must have been born about 1905. The other event that supports the year of his birth comes from records[15a] of the Owa, Agbor war in which Captain Crewe Reade was killed by an Owa warrior named Okunbor Osagie in 1906. Johnson Okokhue Odigie , second son of Chief Odigie, and Okogun from what they were told were age mates. A record of Johnson Okokhue's birth showed that he was born in 1905[15b].

Chief Odigie, the Ologbosere of Ewohimi was said to have participated in the Owa war. Honourable Joseph Ahimingiese Obhiebo Odigie of Ewohimi was born immediately after the war. The belief was that Honourable Joseph O. Odigie's albinism was because of the dead Captain Reade's spirit that reincarnated in the Honourable. Okogun was born about one year before Joseph

O. Odigie's birth. The mothers of Okogun and Obhiebo were from Idumigie, Eguae, Ewohimi and both men belong paternally as cousins to the same larger Aigbiya family of Idinrio, Okaigben, Ewohimi. The parents of Okogun and the Joseph Odigie must have been aware of the relative ages of their sons.

Okogun was born when his mother was expected to have reached or about to have reached menopause. Okogun was the last of seven children five of whom were living females. The only male who would have been his immediate senior died as a baby.

Omovuon was a blacksmith and a great hunter. He was rich by the yard-stick of his time for he had slaves. Esekhor was the first daughter of the then very important chief in Ewohimi, Chief Ebalogbhen of Idumigie. Because she could not as a female inherit the chieftaincy title, Esekhor was married away to Omovuon with a number of her father's slaves at her service. The Ebalogbhen family children were not as a rule to carry anything on their heads as other people did. That meant they did not carry loads on their heads. They could have things in their hands and light objects on their shoulders but never on their heads. They had servants to carry loads for them. One of their nicknames or praise names was "children of those whose heads do not carry loads" – *Ibhi uhuomon ne i he ihe*. Okogun never carried loads on his head.

Okogun related an incident that gave some insight into the relationship then between slaves and the families to which they belonged. It happened that the heir apparent of one of the Chief Ebalogbhens was not liked by the slaves of the chief because of the way he treated the slaves. The slaves started plotting against the heir probably to harm him. One of the meetings of the slaves took place when they were alone all by themselves in Chief Ebalogbhen's farm. Chief Ebalogbhen decided to visit the slaves in the farm. As he approached the farm through the forest path, he noticed that the slaves were together in a kind of meeting. Chief Ebalogbhen as a hunter had a gun in hand. He moved stealthily unnoticed by the slaves through the bush under forest cover to a point behind the farm nearest to the gathered slaves. He was able to decipher the purpose of the meeting and identified the ringleader whom he shot with a perfect aim. There was immediate alarm that Ewossa had attacked Eguae, Ewohimi in the farms. Chief Ebalogbhen had to move fast to dissuade Eguae, Ewohimi people many of whom were already heading armed into the bush, from going to war with Ewossa.

Omovuon was the son of Okuoebho, the great grandson of Ehimin or Ihimin. Ehimin was the first son of the father, probably called *Iya,* who was of the head of the Aigbiya lineage of Idinrio. The king of native doctors' title (*Ogie-obo*) that now runs in the Osagie-Ilegbedion of Idumobo line was to be inherited by Ehimin but Ehimin lost it to the second son of their father. The second son was his half- brother who was the father of Aigbiya. That was why Pa Asuerinmen Abhukhegbe[17]once reminded us that Ehimin's son Eze was the senior brother of Aigbiya. That was how he understood the relationship.

The blacksmith heritage and the name Okogun

It happened that as the father of Ehimin and siblings, Iya felt that he was nearing the end of his sojourn on earth and he decided as a famous native doctor to initiate his eldest son Ehimin into the profession as to take over from him. The practice was to assemble a meeting of all the native doctors at Ewohimi led by the head native doctors from Idumu-Isaba in Oghu, Ewohimi. It was usually a festive occasion as the initiate was introduced to various potions and taken through much ritual amidst singing usually in idioms, drumbeating (*okede was a special drumbeat for native doctors)* and dancing.

One popular song on such occasion goes thus:

Imhan eba le nan mhon Obo eeeh!

Imhan eba le nan mhon Obo eeeh o o!

Imhan eba le nan mhon Obo eeeh!

Imhan eba le nan mhon Obo eeeh!

(The call four times is significant[18] in Esan culture).

Airebale non obo le non obo khaite

The song and meaning are roughly translated as follows:

"Imhanbale (meaning I plan a forbidden thing), Is the name of the native doctor's wife. Imhanbale, the doctor's wife answers Eeeh or Eeeeh oo. She answers each of the four times that she is called.

> *Don't feed forbidden food to the doctor so that the doctor does not get disgraced"* (apparently, eating the forbidden food would be a sin that would make him lose his spiritual powers.)

To finalise the initiation Ehimin had to carry the usual rectangular cane basket with wooden bottom (*ukpee*) laden with charms. At that point he should prophesy and see visions, run through streets and paths followed by the rejoicing and drum-beating crowd. The recruit initiate would touch or pull plants along the way from the bushes. Any plant so touched would be collected as a future herbal medicine component. When it reached this stage for Ehimin, he shocked the crowd as he confessed that he saw no vision.

The initiators quickly took the load from Ehimin's head shouting

> *Ekui i sira Obo de!*
>
> *Ekui i sira Obo de!*
>
> *Meaning "tricks or secrets (Eku) don't get exposed (fall) in the presence of the doctor (Obo)!"*

Eventually Ehimin's brother who was by a different mother was successfully initiated and he inherited the position of their father as a native doctor keeping it for the Ilegbedion of Idumobo lineage through his son Aigbiya's father. As expected, this episode led to various developments.

Some thought that the wealthy mother of Aigbiya's father had arranged that Ehimin be charmed and made spiritually blind. A few felt that the outcome was divine and should be accepted.

Despite that, it was accepted that Ehimin and his heirs are the natural owners of the native doctor instrument of his father as will be seen later in Okogun's life. Ehimin's headship of their father's family was also not to be contested[17] and the heritage was passed onto his heirs in succession to this day among the Aigbiya family of Idumu-iya, Idinrio, Okaigben in Ewohimi.

The name Okogun

Ehimin's father was sufficiently embarrassed that his first son could not successfully go through the initiation to enable him to inherit the position as a native doctor. He felt that it was unacceptable that his first son did not belong to a profession other than the normal as farmer and hunter. Being a man of substance, he performed all the rights required and summoned all the blacksmiths of Ewohimi led by the head blacksmith from Idumu-agbor regarded as the headquarters of Ewohimi blacksmiths for the purpose of initiating Ehimin as a member of the head blacksmiths: *Oka-igun*.

Ehimin's first son Eze, whose Esan name is now unknown, became a very good and ingenious blacksmith. His fame reached beyond the confines of Ewohimi. Ika-Ibo speaking neighbours across the border in the then Asaba Division now in Delta State would come looking for him. They would say "*Eze ogun ayin na cho*" meaning "we are looking for the king of blacksmiths". With time people simply referred to him as Eze and that took over his name. No one has bothered to know what his real name was. Ehimin's line thus became blacksmiths. Therefore, the name Okogun (son of blacksmith) was given to the baby after birth. This outcome has played out in Okogun's life.

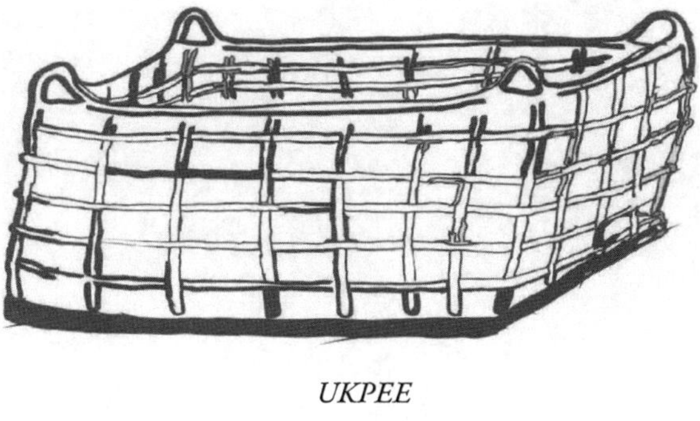

UKPEE

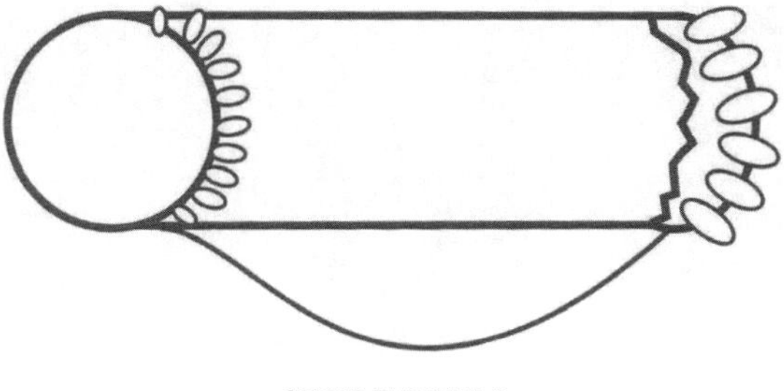

OKEDE DRUM

CHAPTER FOUR**

OMOVUON'S FAMILY AND OKOGUN'S SIBLINGS

Okogun had five sisters all of whom were senior to him. They are in order of seniority, Uhuomonye, Omolafe, Arhetuemen, Okun and Owobu.

Madam Uhuomonye Ogieyan was married to Ogieyan of Uzebu, Ewohimi. She had a son Mr. Ehikhamen Osalumense Willie Ogieyan (Ojieyan). Ehikhamen raised a large family from his marriage to Ubhiminiye and Iluosemenla.

Madam Nene Uhomonye Ogieyan

Madam Egiamanyo Blackie Magdalene was her beloved non-blood daughter. Magdalene was born to her by her "wife" so to say.

Man's wife and woman's wife

It is necessary early in this biography to distinguish between a man's wife and a woman's wife. In those days there were two types of traditional marriages: the usual and majority marriages involving a man and a girl and the unusual special marriage involving a prosperous usually childless woman and a girl. Thus, there was a man's wife and a woman's wife. The saying that "one can take a man's wife, but one cannot take over a woman's wife" shows respect given to the unusual type of marriage by the people. The unusual woman to girl marriage involved the prosperous woman performing all the marital rites of marriage to the girl who was then called her wife. The prosperous woman installed her so-called wife in her home and linked such a wife to her marital family or her own family distant cousin male to procreate children for either of the families of the prosperous woman. The prosperous woman had no sexual relations whatsoever with "her wife". The purpose of the woman's wife arrangement was to ensure continuity of lineage. It was the people's most popular version of adoption of children for a childless woman and family. Okogun got directly involved in this woman's wife system.

Madam Omolafe Ilegbodu married to Ilegbodu of Idumu-agho, Ewohimi. She had four sons. The sons were Esezobor Joe Ilegbodu, Ahanegbe Stephen Ilegbodu, Egialegbele Patrick Ilegbodu and Ekaniyere Benson Ilegbodu. Esezobor, Ahanegbe and Egialegbele each had children from two wives. Benson died before he could get married.

Madam Nene Omolafe Ilegbodu

Madam Nene Arhetuemhen Omovuon

Flanked by Deborah Ilegbodu and Anthony Ogieyan.

(note the posture which she unconsciously took reflecting her status as a man in the family. Compare with the postures of her senior tough sisters who were married)

Madam Arhetuemen was not married out for cultural reasons as will be explained. She had several children two of whom survived. They are *Uubanmhen* a man who died before he could get married and *Ihensekhien Ibuku*. Uubanmhen will also feature again in this story. Ihensekhien had many children.

Madam Okun was married to a famous native doctor Itaman of Uokhuen, Ohordua. She did not have surviving children but adopted and brought to Ewohimi two sons, Iwenakhamen Jacob and Abumere both of whose mother was Madam Aluge apparently "married" to Okun.

Madam Owobu married Mr Ikekhide of Idumu-agho. She had two daughters that survived: Obeto and Enogialeguan Anna each of whom had many children.

The male born after Owobu, *Ogbaimen* did not survive. Okogun was the last child from Esekhor their mother.

For various reasons, these six Omovuon children from Esekhor were very much united on important family issues under the strong leadership of Uhomonye, assisted by Omolafe. They made sure that Omovuon family house was set up and fully supported and defended by them all. Omovuon's first son was *Ebikade* but was apparently junior to the senior Omovuon daughters.

Ebikade was born to Omovuon by one of Okuoebho's wives customarily inherited by Omovuon on the death of his father. In those days, if a man died leaving young wives, the man's first son took over the young wives. The old wives stayed in the family and were looked after by the first son of the deceased man if such older wives have no male children. This was very much like the old Jewish practice as recorded in the Holy Bible and used by Jesus Christ in one of His parables. Ebikade had older brothers who were fathered by Omovuon's father Okuoebho and were thus Okogun's uncles. Ebikade had a daughter Aituagie who was married to a man at Iselu. The man's name was Momoh. Aituagie's children died young. They probably had sickle cell anaemia based on what I observed of the children.

The decision was taken by Omovuon's larger family that Arhetuemen should stay home (*arhe o bhu uwa* meaning kept at home) and have children in the name of Omovuon virtually making her take up the role of a male child to propagate the name of Omovuon. The decision was taken using the argument that Okogun should not be the only male child from Esekhor in Omovuon's family house. Thus, Arhetuemen did not marry and her children are Omovuon's lineage. Her special status among her siblings led to her being the only one among her sisters that was allotted a plot of land in the Omovuon family land. The land was inherited by Ihensekhien and her "Omovuon" children. Ihensekhien, being the only child of Arhetuemen that survived to adulthood was for these reasons not formally given out in marriage. She was to have children to propagate the Omovuon lineage. Ihensekhien had five children that survived her. Rose Imanrenrior's blood father was a handsome man named Joseph from Uzebu. The other four were fathered by *Ikekhua,* a distant cousin of Okogun within the Aigbiya family. Okogun was very much impressed by Ikekhua's qualities as a man and Ikekhua's services to him. Okogun therefore decided that Ihensekhien's eldest son Uuazamain and eldest daughter, Alice be left as Ikekhua's children while the younger son Michael and younger daughter Gladys along with Rose remained in the Omovuon's line. When Gladys died, some members of Ikekhua's family wanted Gladys buried in their premises and Joseph as head of Okogun's family and his siblings and cousins demanded that Dorcas was a member of Omovuon lineage and should be buried in Omovuon lineage premises. To resolve the issue, the bigger family headed by *Odionwele Isikhuemen Agbonselobhor* of Idumobo gathered at Joseph Okogun's residence to resolve the issue in favour of Omovuon's lineage. Dorcas was thus buried in Rose's Omovuon premises. The Enogie of Ewatto's son and widowed husband of Dorcas had erroneously sent necessary services to the Ikekhua family but Omovuon family decided not to demand a return of the services to Omovuon family. During the various arguments, *Pa Asuerinmen Abhukhegbe* asserted[17] that Aigbiya was Eze's junior brother. This explains why Mr. Michael Omovuon was in 1994 chosen by the elders of Aigbiya's family as the head Administrator of Pa John Okogun E. Omovuon's estate when Okogun died. Mr. Michael Omovuon is one of the grandsons of Madam Arhetuemhen and was then a minor. There were Okogun's nephews who were already grandfathers to choose from as administrator of Okogun's estate, but they were not chosen.

This is an example of the working of daughters "kept at home" system that was practised in Ewohimi area. The system has died through the rebellion of daughters who wished to have the dignity of marriage rather than be looked at as concubines and children who wished to be identified also with their blood fathers while still enjoying their special positions.

Arhetuemen having the status of a male in the family with her Omovuon heirs is the only one of Okogun's sisters that has part of Omovuon land assigned to her and her Omovuon heirs.

Arhetuemen died in 1988. She must have been over 90 years at death. Okogun was very emotional as he attended to her on her deathbed. He was said to have shouted in tears saying to her in Esan "Are you leaving me alone?" implying her position as a "man" in Omovuon's dynasty. She was the last of the sisters to die. Okogun was happy to have outlived his sisters and given the grace to pay his last respects to all of them.

CHAPTER FIVE

OKOGUN'S BOYHOOD LIFE AND THE DEATH OF OMOVUON

Okogun sent to native doctor Oghunmun on training

Omovuon sent Okogun to the native doctor Oghunmun Aluyor to serve as one of his boys to be mentored in the herbalism and divination profession and eventually to become a native doctor. Omovuon must have wished to make Okogun a native doctor to achieve what Ehimin or Ihimin failed to achieve. *Oghunmun* belong among Pa Aile's family ancestors of Idinrio, Ewohimi. There was another *Oghunmun non rho obo re at Izumen*[19], *Oghu* in Ewohimi and it is not clear whether the two were in any way related.

Oghunmun's son, Ofuri Market and Ogidigbo (Agbado)) Market issue

The revered native doctor *Anyangbe* (*aka obhiarinmin* meaning the child of the spirits or the little spirit), Aile's relation was Oghunmun's son. Pa Anyangbe was very much involved in the struggle to stop Ofuri Market from being deserted by traders following the change of Ogidigbo (*now Agbado)* market day by His Royal Highness then *Enogie of Ewohimi S. Usifoh Enosegbe* II from its traditional day (two days after Ofuri market day) of the native week to the same day as Ofuri market. The market struggle in the spiritual realm was linked with an incident that happened in the late 1960s on Ofuri Market day when a whirlwind developed, lifted a woven flat tray (*otete)* used by women to exhibit their wares and cover large bowls from the market and carried it in the direction of

Ogidigbo market. People interpreted the incident as signifying victory for the opposing native doctors fighting on the Enogie's side for Ogidigbo market.

Ofuri market was gazetted in 1918 by the colonial Government to assign Ewohimi market day on the same day as Uromi and Iruekpen in Esanland. Ofuri is in Okaigben and not Eguae, the Ewohimi village where the Enogie resides. HRH Samuel Usifo Enosegbe II decided that the situation whereby the town's recognized main market was not at Eguae was unacceptable. He therefore ordered that Ogidigbo market rechristened Agbado should hold on the same day as Ofuri market. Most of the rest of Ewohimi supported the change which drastically reduced the patronage of Ofuri market even by Okaigben people themselves. The disaffection caused by this episode lingers on mainly because of the disruption of the economic, social, cultural, and administrative activities which revolved round the Market in Okaigben.

Okogun earlier in the early 1940s built his own residence facing OfuriMarket and, as will be later seen, benefitted from the courageous location of his residence by the Ofuri Market.

The role of native doctors in the community: Okogun at Ehor

Native doctors have also been wrongly referred to as "witch doctors" by non-Africans who could not rationalize the practice of the native doctors to themselves.

Good and tough native doctors moved around far afield in those days to make their powers available to clients and interact as well as compete with other native doctors. Such professional tours were their own kind of missionary journeys. The native doctors combined divination, sacrifice to ancestors, warding off evil spirits and healing therapies for the sick using mostly herbs, incantations, and divination. Sometimes and less frequently, animal parts and soils were used by the doctors for their disease management regimes. The native doctors were also invited to detect evil persons or wicked witches and wizards who were held responsible for observed evils, epidemics, drought, and other undesirable events in the land.

They would also prescribe solution through divination, appeasements of spirits, gods, and sacrifices. The cult of native doctors held court when there were disputes bordering on witchcraft accusations between individuals or wrong or evil use of powers in prohibited places among their own members. The court also put-on trial anyone who performed the role of a native doctor without being initiated into the native doctor cult. *Their knowledge of herbs, circumstances and the environment, spiritual discipline, customs, and traditions made them what one may call the leading scientists in their communities. This was Omovuon's planned profession for Okogun.*

Oghunmun with little Okogun aged about 12, in his team left on one of his professional tours. The journeys were on foot. They travelled through *Igueben, Ekekhen, Ugbegun ne Ebudin, Usi* and villages along their course and arrived at *Ugieghudu* in the old Benin Division where they spent some time working for clients. From Ugieghudu they operated up to as far as *Ehor* about 70 kilometers from Ewohimi, located on the Benin – Ekpoma – Auchi road.

One day while they were at Ehor, there was a pandemonium as people rushed to form anxious crowds along the road through Ehor leading to Benin to have a glimpse at some spectacle. On inquiry, Okogun learnt that the then Enogie of Uromi was being taken by the authorities on exile to Ibadan via Benin City[3, 20]. The year was 1917.

Okogun is temporarily recruited as Oba's sword bearer at Ugieghudu, 1917

At Ugieghudu, one of the towns visited by Oghunmun and his troupe including Okogun, there was an interesting incident that says much about how *the Oba of Benin Palace aids and officers* were recruited. Okogun, while moving around was captured by the Oba of Benin's men, who wanted to recruit Okogun to serve as one of the Oba's ceremonial sword standard- bearer (*Omuada*). Okogun was regarded as handsome, strong, well-built, and suited for the job. Oghunmun used his influence to make it clear to the native doctors and chiefs of Ugieghudu that he could not, for several reasons, allow Okogun to be recruited for the Oba's Palace and that he would remain in the town until they produced his boy. He felt insulted by the act. It should also be stated that Oghunmun would not have peace on return to Ewohimi without an only son of a woman given to him by the aged father as a trainee native doctor. In the end Okogun was returned unharmed to Oghunmun certainly out of fear of threats by Oghunmun.

Ordinarily, it would have been regarded as an honour to be one of the Oba of Benin's standard-bearers. Okogun's circumstance as an only son of two important families in Ewohimi made the position in the Oba's palace unacceptable.

One day without warning or previous indication Oghunmun told Okogun and his mates that they must go back home. *They had spent about two years* on the tour. On arrival at Ewohimi, they met that Omovuon had just died three days earlier. It became clear to him Okogun that Oghunmun somehow mysteriously knew of the death of Omovuon. In those days there were no telephones, and nobody came from Ewohimi to bring any news and no one would have known where Oghunmun and his team were. Oghunmun had to break his tour to return the young and now fatherless Okogun to his mother and family so that Okogun could participate in the final burial rites of his father.

According to Okogun, his father Omovuon would probably have not died when he died if he had not been partially weakened from healed wounds from an accidental gun shot that he received during a hunting expedition with Ekhukhu.

Omovuon was the head of a very important family in Idinrio, Okaigben where he headed the lineage of the head-house of Aigbiya's group referred to as Idumu-iya. The name Idumu-iya suggests that Ehimin's native doctor father may have been called Iya. Omovuon also had slaves as the important families did in those days. Apart from being a blacksmith, he was a hunter. On one of his hunting expeditions, Omovuon was accidentally shot by a fellow hunter. Okogun said Omovuon, using herbs and means of those days, recovered from the gunshot wounds. The effect of the gunshot was considered instrumental to Omovuon's death earlier than would have been though he died quite old.

Omovuon (ovuen ne Ega): the sun than shines at Ega (Illushi)

Omovuon was a respected prosperous and well-known person. He used to style himself as *"the sun that shines at Ega (Ewohimi name for IlIushi): the one unseen abroad but who receives gifts from abroad"*

In those days both men and women in Ewohimi travelled on foot to trade with neighbours. The furthest for many people were the Ika markets at Onitcha Ugbo, *Issele Uku, Igbodo, and Igbanke. They also went as far as Illushi (Ega* or *Ozigolo, Esan names for* Illushi).

Uhuomonye and Omolafe who as young teen girls were said to be beautiful, courageous, strong, and bold, used to go on foot as petty traders and probably as practising indigenous midwives cum fertility doctors (*owena)* to Illushi. Madam Uhuomonye was a popular traditional midwife and herbalist well known for her infertility treatment. Those who admired Uhuomonye and Omolafe used to send gifts through them to their father who had such beauties as his daughters. He thus described himself as the sun that shines at Ega and one who receives gifts from those he had never met.

Omovuon's first son Ebikade left home to seek greener pastures abroad in cities outside Ewohimi much to the chagrin of Omovuon who had become old and could not effectively maintain his subsistence farming culture. Omovuon in his old age and family survived by selling his collection of rich coral beads and other treasures to have funds for feeding and other subsistence items. He complained a lot that Ebikade left him in his old age when he most needed Ebikade's assistance in the farm. Ebikade had not returned to his father when the man died.

There were two branches or factions in Omovuon's family. Ebikade was the first son from Omovuon's father's wife whom by tradition Omovuon inherited.

Ebikade, his mother and his uncles and mother's children who were Okuebho's sons and his own siblings were on one side while Esekhor, her five female daughters and Okogun constituted the other side. There was fear and alarm on Ebikade's half of the family when Omovuon decided to marry Esekhor, the first daughter of the prominent and influential *Ebalogbhen of Idumigie*. Ebikade's side were further intimidated when Esekhor being the first daughter of her father was accompanied to her husband's house by several slaves to minister to her needs. Ebikade had a half-brother and uncle Ogbeide who was reputed to be wicked and was taken to be a wizard. Ogbeide and group were said to have vowed to do all in their power to ensure that Esekhor did not have a male child for Omovuon, as such a male child born with a silver spoon would dominate the family and render Ebikade's position powerless. This was believed to have been partly responsible for Esekhor delivering only girls.

Ogbeide died in a miserable way. When he died his eyes were not closed and courageous or innocent children had fun going to peep at the corpse to view the dead man with eyes open. Ebikade left home and left his old father partly to avoid farming to feed his half-sisters and their mother. Omovuon thus felt betrayed and abandoned by his first son. Omovuon died about 1917 lamenting his situation.

Mentorship for Okogun circa 1919 - 1928

Omovuon's death brought the issues in his family to bear on Okogun's life in a way that Omovuon could not have allowed to be.

Okogun had not reached the adolescent age when his father died. He needed to be nurtured and guided by a man as his guardian and mentor. The native doctor training was no longer the way to go for him without the wisdom and experience of his father to help in the training.

The family had to decide to whom the young Okogun should go and live with to get appropriate mentorship while growing to adulthood.

Ozabor, a cousin of Omovuon was chosen as the foster father so to say for Okogun. Esekhor always rubbed on Okogun's body white chalk from her god (*ake olokun),* as her way of protecting him from harm. Ozabor was uncomfortable with this practice and after one year, he rejected having Okogun among his mentees. Okogun was then given to Aki, one of Omovuon's brothers. Aki took ill after two years and was no more able to control Okogun who then became troublesome and was growing out of control.

After consulting a diviner, Okogun was transferred to be under the tutelage of *Khaizamamen*. Okogun was under Khaizamamen for three years. In the fourth year, Khaizamamen took ill and died from a flu epidemic. Okogun, who was now an adolescent, successfully took over management of Khaizamamen's farm on which they had worked together before the man's death.

At about this time, Uhuomonye who was pregnant with her son, Willie Ehikhamen pleaded that Okogun should come to her at Uzebu to assist her husband Ogieyan. While there, Okogun accompanied *Ugbozeba*, Ogieyan's junior brother who was much older than him to the farms.

CHAPTER SIX

ADOLESCENT OKOGUN

Attempts to go to school thwarted

Okogun made several attempts to leave home and go to stay with friends where he could go to school. He very much wished to receive Western education. All his efforts to be in school were thwarted by the sisters. The sisters were convinced that if Okogun received Western education, he would take up a white-collar job and leave home. There would be no one to establish their father's estate and home for the family. In those days, during the annual village feasts[21] (*Ukpe)* to venerate the ancestors, married daughters returned from their marital homes on one of the days with their children to their father's home to join in celebrating their forefathers. They prepared mounds of pounded yam and soup usually with specified number of sizeable pieces of antelope or bush pig meat to serve their ancestors though the food was essentially eaten and shared by the extended family members or village men who moved from house-to-house praying, eating, singing, dancing, and drinking during the four days that the feasts lasted. The practice of eating sacrificed food from family to family was called *iku-uhie* in Esan language.

The sisters decided that Okogun should not go to school but remain at home to have their father's house established around him as the only biological male. Okogun on several occasions secretly escaped from home to go with friends to register in a primary school. Each time Okogun escaped from home, the sisters led by Uhuomonye and Omolafe spread out in the sun their mother's god (*ake*) requesting the god spirit to get back their brother. People believed that the god was very powerful and vengeful. The relatives of the person in whose house Okogun lived abroad would send strong messages to their son hosting Okogun, to return Okogun to avert the danger from Esekhor's god spirit. No one was therefore prepared to have Okogun in his house without the approval of his sisters and so he was forced to remain at home without schooling.

Prince Eguabiogie who very much loved Okogun, was one of those who accommodated Okogun from home to help him into a school. The opposition from Okogun's family foiled Eguabiogie's attempt to help Okogun in his craze for Western education.

Eguabiogie later took ill in 1947 and returned home. Okogun visited Eguabiogie and Okogun was very sad when he guessed that the illness was terminal. On the night Eguabiogie died, Okogun reported dreaming and seeing him dancing amidst a large crowd. Eguabiogie in an unusual manner moved further from Okogun when Okogun tried to approach him in the dream. Okogun interpreted that to mean that Eguabiogie had died. He rushed early at dawn to Eguae to find out that Eguabiogie had died that night. Okogun returned home very sad on that morning.

Okogun had been at Uzebu for three years when his senior brother Ebikade, whom he did not know well before Ebikade left home, returned from outside Ewohimi. Okogun was curious to see his senior brother and decided to visit him. After meeting Ebikade, Okogun decided to live with Ebikade. Uhuomonye was then not happy that Okogun had abandoned her husband. Okogun was hitherto in charge of managing Ebikade's farm and continued to mature as a young adult while at Uzebu.

Ebikade grew too old to go to farm. Okogun's sisters decided to fulfil their promise made when they did whatever was possible to prevent Okogun from going into a school to receive Western education. They sent Akpasubi and Ihensekhien's senior brother Uubanmen to live with Okogun and assist him on his farms.

Okogun was now a full adult.

Spending time at Omon Enogie Ifebhor's Palace

The Enogie or Onogie title meaning king in Esanland is the historical title bestowed on the Oba of Benin dukes who ruled a town in Esanland. The Enogie ruled the town and owed allegiance to the Oba of Benin from whom he received his authority and military support if necessary, to rule in his domain. The title Enogie was introduced by *Oba*[22] *Ewuare of Benin* in the 15th century A.D.

Okogun was only about 14 years old when the father Omovuon died. Okogun was given as a helper to several relatives to be mentored as already related. The senior sisters felt that they could not all alone provide adequate protection for their junior brother. They decided to use their relationship with the Enogie of Ewohimi Palace as grandchildren of Chief Ebalogbhen of Idumigie. Chief Ifebhor was very close to Chief Ebalogbhen to the extent that he had interest in the daughter Esekhor. That interest went to the extent of getting Omovuon to decide to take an extreme action to get the Enogie to drop his interest in his wife. At that point HRH Ifebhor stopped his overt interest in Esekhor and her children.

After Omovuon's death, Enogie Ifebhor agreed to have Okogun as one of his Eguae Palace Courtiers. Okogun resided at Okaigben while playing these roles. The arrangement gave Okogun the needed protection without his father. The usual harassment from some Eguae people who did not know how Okogun got to the Palace was intense at the beginning. To arrest the situation, Enogie Ifebhor decided to give Okogun the name *Eguaereona* (*Eguae knows this one*). During Okogun's service at the Palace, he befriended many princes and palace officials. Among his Palace friends were the Prince Usifoh who later became the Enogie HRH S. Usifoh Enosegbe II, Ifebhor's son Eguabiogie and Imhenrion. Mr Ahior was much older and was his inlaw being married to one of Okogun's cousins Mary nee Omole and daughter of Okogun's aunt Omoze.

Okogun's first marriage

Okogun had everything going for him. He was handsome and from an important aristocratic and royal families both from his father's and mother's lineages. He had influential and powerful sisters who loved him and whom he loved. His dancing skills and acrobatic prowess together with the other attributes made him popular, admired, and envied.

At this stage he felt that he needed to have a wife. Eventually he fell in love with Enimaluole, daughter of Osemenilu of Chief Obasenyen of Omhen – Eguae, Ewohimi lineage. Enimaluole was regarded[23] as a rare beauty in

Ewohimi at her time. Okogun was said to have first noticed Enimaluole Iyawo when Enimaluole, on a visit, accompanied her cousin Mrs. Owobu Uzebor to Idumu-Agho. Owobu's husband Pa Uzebor is from Idumu-Agho and Owobu's first daughter was named Iyawo.

Okogun needed to take the usual courtships gifts of palmwine, bundles of yams, kola nuts and so on to his prospective inlaws as well as send gifts to his love. Esekhor had become very old and lamented that she was no more in a strong position to assist him adequately with materials and money normally needed for the courtship of Enimaluole. Eventually, Enimaluole was released to him as wife before he completed all the customary marital rites. His pilot in Obasenyen's family *(osun-omhan)* who was like an intermediary between him and Enimaluole's family was Ilekhomon[24].

Shortly after arrival at Idinrio, Enimaluole gave birth to Okogun's first and male child. The child was given the name Akhigbe which means "not to be killed". With Akhigbe's birth joy was returning to the family after the death of Omovuon.

Dances of the people in Esan at the time

Okogun was a very good and famous dancer who excelled in acrobatic dances. This ability influenced the course of his life in a very significant way.

Okogun and the people who knew him from youth made much of his dancing prowess and the effect of his dancing ability on developments in his life. It is therefore necessary to describe the indigenous dances at his time in some detail.

The main non-worship dances at Ewohimi in Okogun's time

There were five main dances that were not associated with gods. These were *asologun and aba-ayon, igbabonanrimin for men and oyeke and igieleghe (ikpegbe gbe) for girls and women. Oyeke was the female version of the men's asologun.*

Asologun is performed to celebrate events but aba-ayon was performed to spend time around alcoholic drinks usually late into the night and sometimes till dawn.

Asologun usually transforms to aba-ayon (handclapping of palmwine or wine) at late nights. They both consist of rhythmic dance to music made from handclapping, cast iron gongs and *samba drums,* and melodious songs. The songs may be composed from contemporary or past events or as satire or lyrics. Idioms may be used to disguise personalities involved in scandals or misdemeanor. Women had their own version of these dances called *oyeke.*

Igbabonanrimin was the Esan people great acrobatic dance of colourful masquerades for the young and old. It was an excellent model of how division of labour all working together achieved melody, rhythm, dance, and drama. It was a dance essentially for the men and initiated young males.

Young women, girls and boys watched the dance from safe distances but the older women of dignity or older daughters of the community or chiefs who had been inititiated to know what the masquerade was could be allowed seated as spectators. It should also be said that spinsters spied on the masquerades of their suitors at the igbabonanrimin arenas using tips privately given to them by their suitors. Good dancers usually won the love of girls in general and they had beautiful wives.

The music was produced together using five drums of three sizes, one or two cast iron gongs, well-ordered clapping of hands and songs and a horn. The two small drums *(alukpe)* started the rhythm, then came in the two medium drums(*ugheregheru*)[25], and finally the big drum *(iyenma)* which served to direct the rhythm and dance steps. There was also a trumpeter who used an animal horn made of ivory, cow, or gourd horn as a trumpet. A good trumpeter could create recognizable music, sentences and sounds to send messages, meant to invite a masquerade to the dancing arena and to accompany the songs and drumbeats. Such trumpeters also served in the Enogie and some of his chiefs' palaces where they blew their horns to relate coded messages to the Enogie and courtiers.

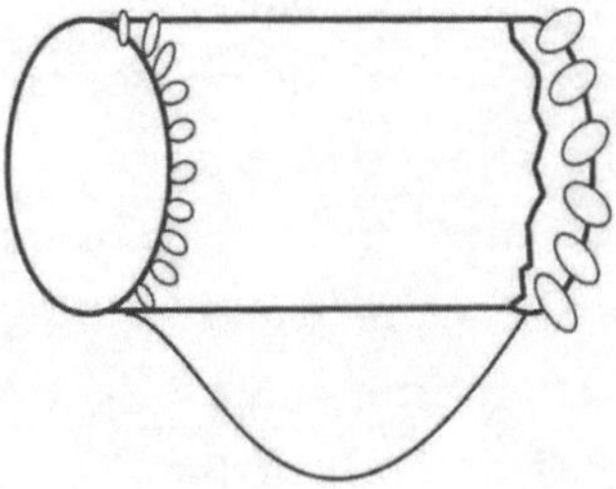

IYENMA

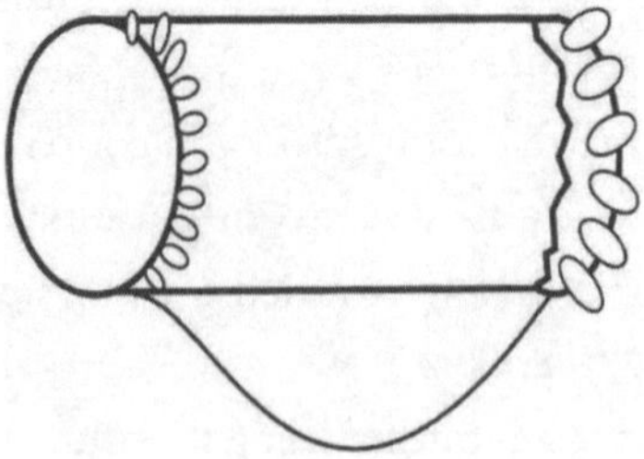

UGHEREGHURU

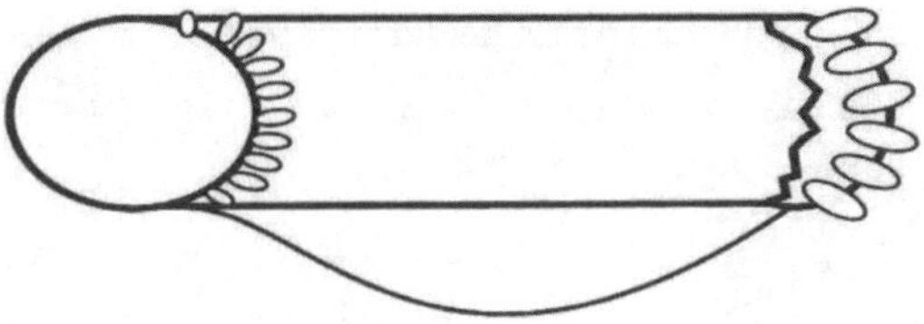

ALUKPEH

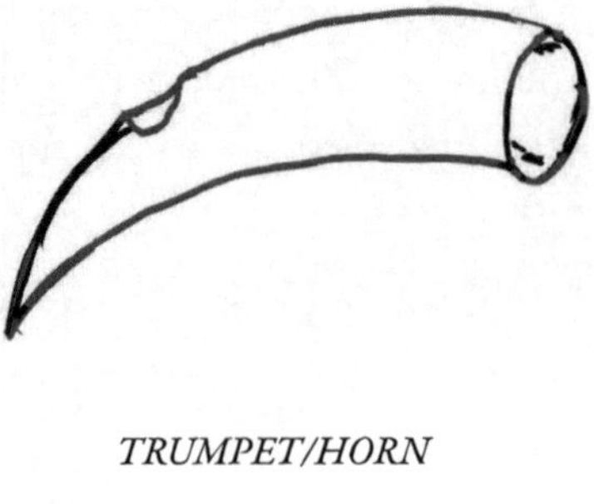

TRUMPET/HORN

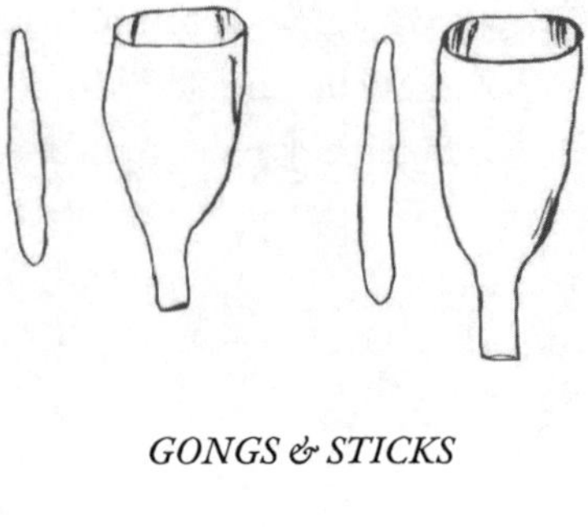

GONGS & STICKS

The song to be used each time was raised by someone with a good voice and the dance group chorused *(mu oye)* the song. The masquerades of healthy and athletic young and up to middle-aged men draped in colourful stripes of red, white, and black danced to the rhythms.

Usually there was a masquerade with old and overflowing regalia that did not dance but sat most of the time moving only when there was a crisis. This lone masquerade (*obo/Oboh meaning doctor)* was laced with charms and its duty was to defend the other masquerades against spiritual attacks that were not visible to the ordinary person. They also led the troupe even when there were physical attacks and violence.

An acrobat's masquerade performing, and other masquerades look on ready to take their turns. The drummers, trumpeter/Hornblower and singers produce music and rhythm to match the dance and the dancer ensures synchronism with the rhythm. Chief Adolor of Ewohimi, Chief (Engineer) Emmanuel Aguele's Igbabonanrimin Social Club performance December 24, 2009 at Okaigben Primary School Grounds.

The dance usually took place in an open arena that could be up to the size of a soccer field of play. The dance was normally held on the afternoon of the traditional Sunday *(ewor),* the same day on which environmental sanitation took place in the morning. The dance was always a celebration.

There were three varieties of dance at each celebration. The igbonanrinmin is a highly ordered and organized dance. The dance troupe, with a few masquerades, moved from the point of assembly with rhythmic music and dance to the arena. The masquerades perform in turns and if there are many masquerades on show, they are paired to perform.

The first stage is the dance around the arena by the performing masquerade who is accompanied by not more than four members of the troupe including the trumpeter.

The accompanying members sang, clapped hands, and interpreted the masquerade's steps and greetings. They also served as bodyguards for the performing masquerade. This dance round the arena is the masquerade's variation of the *asologun* type of dance. The masquerade paid special courtesy to dignitaries and fellow acrobats, from other villages, seated in the arena as it moved around by waving, bowing, and prostrating depending on the personality being recognized by the masquerade. The group of drummers and most of the singers together took up strategic positions where their views of the performing masquerade must be clear to enable the dancing masquerade and the drummers stay in resonance. By so doing the big drum, *iyenma* beat according to the dance steps of the masquerade while the masquerade matched its dance steps with the rhythm of the big drum and the trumpet. The dance and music were stopped in style as the masquerade completed the dance round the arena. The youngest masquerade danced first, and the rest masquerades danced according to their rank based on excellence in acrobatics. The best acrobats were reserved for near the end of the day's dance. The masquerades took acronyms to reflect their level of excellence and or spiritual powers.

There were pseudo-names that translates to aeroplane (*arhope),* magic (*maziki), okpagha (*okpagha was a fruit that exploded with loud noise when dry to release its seed), the tree belonged to the plant family Leguminosae), blacksmiths heavy iron piece(*idigun), oto de ba okhun (*ground joined to the sky), *Oguogho* (meaning complex and intimidating) etc. The aeroplane masquerade is usually the best dancer among the masquerades. Usually, the arhope masquerade flips into the air like an aeroplane taking off to move in the skies. Maziki for magic is another influence of European language to describe impressive dance styles that were difficult to follow or replicate. There is a saying in Esan '*okpagha i do va'*meaning the fruit of the tree *okpagha* does not open secretly or noiselessly to expel the seeds in the sun. The performance of the okpagha masquerade is so good that it draws spontaneous applause and admiration shouts from the spectators.

The second stage consisted of a fast pace music and songs introduced by the smaller drums. When the big drumbeats come in, the arena is set alight with various demonstrations and anticipatory signals to the performing masquerade. The masquerade concerned made movements to accept the call, readied itself using various mannerisms and performed the acrobatics. The spectators and members of the troupe reacted according to how impressive the masquerade's acrobatics dance had been.

These two types of dance are repeated in cycles until the last masquerade that was the oldest and on the verge of retiring from dance performed. The order of dancing by the masquerades was such that their abilities reached the maximum with the *arhope* and ended with the retiring masquerades. The masquerades *arhope, oto de ba okhun, okpagha* and *maziki* were usually the best dancers as masquerades.

At the end of the entire dance and sometimes as an interlude, the dance troupe together with some or all the masquerades performed a very graceful and relaxed dance that was similar in style and grace to the female dance. This was the third variety of dance (*oyeke*).

The older men past the age of acrobatic dances, performed drama mostly in mime around the arena. Such drama may be a satire or demonstration of farm activities or a play based on events in the community or town.

The dances were specially performed at annual feasts to serve the ancestral spirits and during special celebrations annually or bi-annually referred to as sweeping the "harvest street" (*gbolu ughe orho)* apparently celebrated just before the annual farm harvest season and when all the planting and yam staking had been done or at the end of farm harvests during the dry season when the seed yam harvests had been carried out.

The dance was also an inter-town social vehicle. The alternative name for the celebration, *ukpe-arinmin* translates to "feast of masquerades or spirits".

The masquerades were presented as spirits to the uninitiated and revealing the name of the masquerader was strictly forbidden. The violation of this prohibition led to serious consequences for the culprit. As would be expected young men privately disclosed the description and dance styles of their masquerades to the girls of interest to them. Many masqueraders won the love of their prospective wives this way. Several YouTube videos[26] of modern igbabonanrimin have been published.

MASQUERADES AND TROUPE

Igbabonanrimin group at the celebration of 25 years of Religious life of Rev. Sister Gladys Osagie OLA, the first Ewohimi Rev Sister. Present at the occasion, was the first Ewohimi Rev Father: Rev Father Donatus A. Ogun OSA who later became Bishop of Uromi Catholic Diocese accompanied by another Ewohimi Rev Father Dr. Matthew O. Ihensekhien who later became a Monsignor and Rector of the Seminary at Uhiele, Ekpoma : September 30, 2012

The inter-town socializing igbabonanrimin

The inter-town social interaction through acrobatic dance was quite interesting and helped to create friendship and fellowship between the people of linked villages. Okogun's village, Uwi-Idinrio of Ewohimi was for a long time linked with *Orhankhuan of Eguae, Emu* in Esan and at a time with *Abhurhu of Ewatto*. Ewohimi and Emu are about twenty kilometers (fourteen miles) apart. The link was maintained through alternating annual or biannual exchange of visits by the linked villages. The visiting village group comprised male children, young and old men who could make the journeys on foot. Those who with time owned bicycles rode. The visitors were hosted through an arrangement that was established at the first of such visits.

On the first visit, the visiting troupe performed a brief dance at a designated place on the street of the host village while the men of the host village assembled to watch. As the opening dance performance by the visitors went on, each of the spectators decided on who would be his guest friend during the visit. When the dancing stopped, there was a scramble and rush to pick the respective guest friends. The first to touch a man won. The guest friend ate, drank, and slept with his host friend. The host protected his guest for the duration of the visit. It is noteworthy that the choices were made on trust and often without prior knowledge of each other on either side. The visiting village troupe arrived early on the first day and left on the fifth day of arrival. On the last full day of the visit, both the hosting village and the visiting village performed their respective dances in a competitive atmosphere, which in a few cases may lead to violence when either village was outdanced by the other. Such violence happened at *Ikeken,* Ewohimi in the mid-1950s when Ikeken hosted *Ogbe-non-khua village* from Ohordua. There were good masquerade dancers on both sides but the famous Ogbe-non-khua masquerade, arhope of *Mr Ibomhen* outclassed all the masquerades on both sides. While the spectators enjoyed the celebration, violence suddenly broke out and we all sought safety and escaped from the scene. That was the last time to our knowledge that the two villages exchanged visits.

Idumobo, Ewohimi and Okede in Emu link experience – Aghenta, the drummer in Okede, Emu and a lion cult encounter

Idumobo in Ewohimi took their masquerade dance on the four-day visits to Okede in Emu such that the two villages annually or biennially alternated visits between themselves.

One drummer achieved great fame as a drummer on the big drum. He became known as the drummer in Okede, Emu (*okhue igede non rhi bhi Okede, Emu*). His name was *Aghenta.* Aghenta was the father a good acrobatic dancer, who became Professor of Education at the University of Benin, Benin City and was a Commissioner in Edo State: *Professor J. A. Aghenta.* Okogun was someone that most people wished to be with them to enhance their company. On one of the visits of Idumobo to Okede, Emu, Chief Paul Ebhohon Odigie requested Okogun to join him and he agreed. Part of the attraction of course was Aghenta's drumming skills and the great acrobatic dancers of Okede, Emu and of Idumobo, Ewohimi. Idumobo had great acrobatic dancers from the time of Obokhuemhen through Samson Osagie to the time of Jacob Odigie, Title Osagie Goodluck Iyoriobhe, and others. The great *trumpeter or horn-blower Mr Igiebor of Ikoko-Ogbe,* Idumobo must also be mentioned. He played a very important part in the igbabonanrimin troupe and used his horn to deliver messages to Chief Odigie as well.

Okogun experienced what he did not bargain for during this hosting of Idumobo by Okede-Emu. At night as they relaxed drinking and dancing (asologun and aba-ayon) in their host Ebhohon's friend's house, Ebhohon's friend left and went into a room in his house.

To everyone's surprise and fright, a lion emerged shortly after the host left the group. The lion proudly paraded round the audience sniffing at some people in turn. Okogun was worried but he maintained manly courage to stay in his position to receive the lion when his turn came to be greeted by it. This was one of the experiences he could not forget. The explanation then was, as they believed, that their host lived a charmed life, and he could transform to a lion at will.

The masquerade Ugbesea emerges from the roof onto the dance arena

Okogun was a great acrobatic dancer. His masquerade was called *ugbesea* (meaning *the crowd disperser or breaker).* The masquerade *Ugbesea* got the name for several reasons: Whenever the masquerade appeared, spectators moved around disrupting the ordered standing and sitting positions just to catch a glimpse of the masquerade's excellent performance at a safe distance. The masquerade *Ugbesea* moved at great speed, was uniquely able to dance backwards and could target and get to any part of the arena very fast. This was at a time when staged acrobatic dance could be dangerous both for the masquerades and the spectators who got beaten if met by masquerades along the masquerade's path. Charms were used for various purposes at such dances. Opponents could charm good acrobatic masquerades to make the masquerades incapable of exhibiting their talents.

Wicked charm makers, it was believed, also used such arenas as places to test the efficacy of their disease-causing charms (*utagba)* on masquerades and other spectators. Thus, the masquerades and most spectators had to carry protective charms on their persons. Additionally, persons armed with charms were appointed to guard the masquerades, detect, pick, and neutralize charms aimed at the performing masquerades.

The masquerade, Ugbesea had two such persons attached to it. They were Okogun's senior brother *Ebikade* after he returned home and *Omokhua of Chief Eholor of Uwi-Idinrio, the Ogi-ivie* (*Queen of corals)*'s household. *Ogieko* sometimes worked with them. With them around carrying a neutralization pot with liquid (elor), any charmed missiles, thrown at Ugbesea landed harmlessly on the masquerade, fell to the ground and were immediately picked up and dropped into the pot. Omokhua held the pot and Ebikade picked up the charms to deposit in the pot. The missiles would manifest as one object or combination of objects. Objects could be seeds*(akhue)* of the plant *Caesalpinia spp.* with red feathers of the parrot's tail, cowries, pieces of broken pots and stones. Ogieko of Uwi-idinrio was particularly feared by all and could do a lot of damage using his charms. Unfortunately, Ogieko died miserably, behaving oddly, in the bush and left no family trace behind.

There are two events related about masquerade ugbesea. *Princess Edandehi*, daughter of the Enogie of Ewohimi decided to see the then famous masquerade acrobats of Uwi-idinrio which featured Ugbesea along with other famous dancers. As a lady of dignity, Edandehi was given a special place where she had a seat among the spectators surrounded by her aids. When it was Ugbesea's turn to perform, the masquerade without warning somersaulted and landed on Edandehi's sit. The Princess was saved from harm by attentive dancers who as was the practice accompanied Ugbesea as it danced. Uwi-Idinrio Chiefs, elders and dancers were summoned to the Enogie's Palace for insulting the Princess by such a disgraceful and humiliating treatment. The matter was eventually settled with minimal costs after Okogun was implicated in the incident.

Aghughu was a great acrobatic dancer and friend cousin of Okogun. Later in old age Aghughu became an *odion-egbe,* village elder and Okogun's traditional godfather *(oror)* thus uniting their two families. His masquerade also attracted spectators when Uwi-Idinrio staged the masquerade dance and had a kind of sibling rivalry with Ugbesea. One day, during a typical well-attended Uwi-Idinrio masquerade dance celebration, the dance warmed up to a high pitch that set Ugbesea on course. It was Ugbesea's turn to perform. As usual the masquerade was summoned with special songs, drumming, and trumpeting. To everyone's amazement, Ugbesea emerged through the space between the thatch roof and the top of the wall and safely landed on the dance arena with great movements. Aghughu's masquerade being also a very good dancer tried to emerge through the roof. The masquerade as expected succeeded in emerging through the roof but was unfortunate as its regalia was caught on a peg in the roof. The masquerade had to be rescued from the trap by the peg to end that added drama to the performances on that day.

Okogun's masquerade's performance was so astonishing that Ugbesea was ascribed to having witchcraft powers rather than to Okogun's athletic nature and courage that many events in his life portrayed.

The Idah-Igala connection of the Esan (Ishan) masquerade

The masquerade, except on special occasions, was not expected to come out at certain seasons of the year. The season of non-appearance coincided with the wet season and the time for intensive activities on the farms. At those times of the year much of the work in the farms was weeding. During those seasons, the common saying was that the masquerade has gone to *Idah* (*arinmin rhe Idah).*

The regalia of the Esan masquerades are quite like those of the Igala masquerades. The Benin Kingdom - Idah war (1516)[27]and migrations brought the Igala (*Ighan* is Esan for Igalla) people and the Esan people close. There were inter-ethnic marriages between the two groups. The woman Chief Ihon (the *Ogi-ivie* meaning the queen of coral beads), the eldest daughter of *Chief Eholor* of Idinrio, at the time, was said to have an Igala mother. The masquerade spoke using a coded language that was a mixture of Esan and Igala through a contraption consisting of a short tubular stick sealed loosely at one end with a thin cloth or plastic material stuck in the mouth at the open end. The sound was weird and frightened people especially those uninitiated who heard it. The sound could signify a warning to those on the way of the masquerade to keep clear.

The special occasions that the masquerade came out were when a masquerade owner or dancer (*ogie-oku*) died and had to be mourned by masquerades and when special heavily charm-fortified masquerades surfaced at night to lead the older women through the streets to sanitise the village and pray for peace, health, success and safety of persons in the land. The elders decided upon such occasions, when too many deaths especially of infants, tragic accidents and epidemics were happening in the village.

The Idah Igala masquerades do not perform acrobatic dances. The acrobatic movements are peculiar and unique to the Esan people. Some have suggested that the people developed the dance from observing monkeys in the jungle. The somersault resembles those of monkeys, but the rest of the movements is not observed with monkeys.

Initiation into the masquerades' children

When a child became of age, the child was initiated to become a "child of the masquerade or spirits" (*la bho obhi-arinmin*). It was after going through the ritual that a person could safely stand and watch the masquerade dance or stand around when the masquerade was in the vicinity. Those uninitiated were referred to as *igbudu* probably meaning bold or courageous to be around when the masquerade appeared. Any Igbudu caught on the masquerade's path and so recognized by the initiated was usually harassed and beaten up.

The child was of age for initiation as child of the masquerade when the child was considered mature enough to keep secrets. Those who had been initiated usually told frightful stories of the initiation ceremonies. The initiated spread the information that the initiation ceremony included eating the long and fat variety of earthworms (*ikolo)*, chicken droppings (*ison okho-khor)* and doing odd things. They were to maintain that masquerades were spirits. Anyone revealing the identity of the masquerade was accused of having "killed" the masquerade. The consequences of killing the masquerade were grave. The culprit was taken to a masquerade meeting and fined and rough-handled in serious cases.

However, the initiation ceremony was usually performed at night in the house of the designated head masquerade (Ogie-oku) or chief in the village. Special spiced fish broth for the ceremony was made by the parents of the child to be initiated. The masquerade appeared in the dimly lighted room making weird sounds and speaking in special language understandable to the initiated but making the child to be initiated frightened as he or she waited to experience the alleged most unpleasant events. The last part of the rituals involved requesting the child to hold the masquerade's regalia in a prescribed manner. As the child held the regalia, the regalia fell to the ground lifeless. The crime of killing the masquerade was put into a song and the child was asked to wake up the masquerade.

One of the songs was

> "*Egwu bhe uu*
> *E e eh Egwu bhe uu, eh*
> *Egwu bhe uu o*
> *E e eh Egwu bhe uu, eh*"
>
> *Meaning the masquerade (Egwu) has died o, E e eh the masquerade has died eh.*

Some children wept at this point as they felt at a loss what they could do to revive the masquerade. The initiatee was asked to plead in various ways and taken through the ordeal. Eventually the masquerade rises and is revealed to the initiatee as being a person. The initiatee must never tell the secret to the uninitiated. The ceremony ended as a celebration with feasting by all on the spiced fish sauce and other snacks used for the ceremony.

The okpodu masked masquerade was usually part of the troupe but it did not dance as acrobats. It performed drama by the side and served to help maintain order at the igbabonarinmhin arena.

There were other sports in Ewohimi. An important one was the annual wrestling competition between the various villages of Ewohimi at the Enogie's Palace. Children and adolescents practiced wrestling on Edewor days and under moonlight. Wrestling was also often used to settle scores between children and young adults.

CHAPTER SEVEN

OKOGUN ENCOUNTERS A PROPHETESS ON THE WAY BACK ON FOOT FROM BENIN TO EWOHIMI

Okogun had established the practice to go on foot to Benin, about 100 kilometers, to do menial jobs when the dates for the feast of the acrobatic masquerades (ukpe-arinmin) were fixed if he felt he needed money to make a good celebration. The journey on foot to Benin usually lasted overnight. He was a star acrobat and would have to entertain many guests from all Ewohimi and beyond who would be around to join in the celebration as his guests and spectators at the dance of the masquerades. It happened that his village decided to celebrate a masquerade feast (*ukpe arinmin*) that year. He decided to go to Benin as usual and engage in manual labour to earn some money for entertainment and other resources during the celebration. The year was about 1929. At that time there were few Ewohimi people in Benin. *Igbenigie*, a relatively well-educated man and Chief Odigie's son was one of the few Ewohimi people in Benin City. Igbenigie was in the Postal Services and built a then modern residence at 23 Idahosa Street, Benin City. Okogun had his cousin, *Mr. Osagie Aki* who was a native doctor also in Benin. Okogun spent his days in Benin with Osagie.

In those days, very few houses in Benin were built with moulded blocks and roofed with corrugated iron sheets. Apart from Olowu, a few chiefs and the Oba of Benin part of whose Palace had corrugated iron roofing, most people in Benin City roofed their houses with woven raffia palm leaves (called *ibabo* in Esan) and used mashed mud to set the walls of their houses.

Okogun worked in the group that mashed the mud and got paid 8d, eight pence per day. Those that set the walls got 1 shililing (12 pence) daily for their job.

Okogun successfully arrived in Benin City and worked as usual. After earning enough for his purpose, he decided to return home. He bought a ready-made shirt for two shillings three pence at a *Thomopoulous* shop, a pair of khaki shorts, a white singlet, and a mat. He put these items together, said goodbye to his host and proceeded to the motor park.

Mr. Sanni Olelogieide Esangbedo of Igueben ran a business, at that time, which included the buying, processing, bagging, and carrying of palm kernels and oil for export to the ports in the Delta. He had a truck Okogun and Esan people referred to as *Alubion* (possibly Albion). The vehicle usually accepted passengers on its journey back to Igueben.

Okogun decide on this occasion to take the truck back to Ewohimi. The fare was two shillings which was equivalent to a three-day job at a building site. The driver on that occasion was Mr Tongo, a Bini man. There were palm kernel traders riding on the truck. One of them was Joel from Ora (Owan). Mr. Tongo accepted Okogun as a passenger on the truck. As the truck was about to depart, he flung his pack into the truck and held on to the truck to climb onto it as he had done in the past. Thrice he held on to the back of the vehicle to climb into it and thrice one of the men in the truck used a cane to hit at his hands to prevent him from entering the vehicle. He was surprised at the treatment.

It should be mentioned that Esangbedo, the vehicle owner regarded Ewohimi people in general and Uwi-Idinrio persons as his brothers and sisters. Okogun's reason for this surprise treatment was simple. Esangbedo's mother was a daughter of an Uwi-Idinrio woman from the Ighedosa Omovuon cum Osoh family and he took persons from Uwi-Idinrio like Okogun as his kith and kin. It should also be mentioned here that the *Okaigun, the Enogie of Igueben's mother at the time hailed from the same family at Uwi-Idinrio, Ewohimi.* A reigning Okaigun to this day cultures traditional relations with Idinrio and Ewohimi.

Be that as it was, Esangbedo was not on hand to control the antics of the un-cooperating man to allow Okogun to take a ride in his Albion truck. Okogun decided that having bid goodbye to his Benin host, he had to continue his journey to Ewohimi. He decided to make the hundred or so kilometers to Ewohimi on foot. He retrieved his pack from the truck and started his trek right from the motor park taking the Benin-Agbor road. When he got to

Ugonoba, he bought and ate *ukpor* (a delicious pudding made from either dried yam, plantain, or maize flour, he ate the one made from yam flour).

Thereafter he resumed his trek to Ewohimi. After passing through Ugo as he moved on, there was a light rain that made him wet. The road that had not been cooled enough by the light rain was then releasing thick smoke of water vapour. The road was quite lonesome and quiet. He got to a long straight stretch of the road. He had almost reached the turn on the stretch when he heard a shrill voice behind him. The voice cried out in *Bini*: "That man, come to me for a while" (*Okpea rin: le re ghe e*). The voice was commanding and persistent. Okogun looked back in the direction from which the voice was reaching him. He looked backwards along the gutter and saw the haggard-looking figure of a woman whose head was overgrown with unkempt hair that partly covered her face.

Okogun's first reaction was to run since he had her behind him. On second thought, he decided not to run convinced that the "witch" as he concluded would catch up with him. Summoning some courage, he cautiously approached the figure. He noticed that she had a dirty cloth or rag over her head. Okogun in his mind took her for someone banished from her community because of her evil deeds. She asked him for money in an assertive manner different from that of an ordinary beggar. He refused at first saying that he had no money. She paused gazing at him for a while, and then with a sigh said "Go home." She continued and went on to predict or prophesy Okogun's future life. She said in a mournful voice: "The world will harass you greatly" (*Agbon a kpokpo rue e e!).* She then added in a more cheerful tone: "Your dynasty or posterity will be very great" (*Ike rue kpolor gbe e!).*

Okogun then decided to give her one penny. She sized up the coin as if to ask that Okogun gave her more money but Okogun did not give her more.

She looked hard at the gift and accepted making a hum sound. She added, "Anyway, I have told you what will happen." After that Okogun felt released to continue his journey on foot but regretted that he did not have the presence of mind to give her more money and request her to tell him how the troubles or harassment from the world could be averted.

He got as far as Ossiomo and it was dark. He decided to sleep at Ossiomo among some Ika people. He related his encounter with the strange woman. His hosts were amazed that he met the woman about whom their fathers had told stories to them. One of the tales associated with encounters with the woman was that the woman was able to tell people who chanced on her, the way they could make riches. They called the woman, *Abhiomaen* meaning old woman sage. His listeners admired the courage he exhibited by trekking alone from Benin to Esan. Early the next morning, he left Ossiomo and safely arrived at home. He did not relate to anyone his encounter with the Abhiomaen.

Death of Esekhor

Okogun arrived home safely from the Benin job trip. The masquerade dance celebration went very well for him. He was able to perform well to the admiration of the fans and spectators and Ugbesea danced up to the high expectation. He successfully and satisfactorily hosted his guests during the celebration.

Shortly after the the following year's celebration, the storm prophesied by the roadside seer along the Benin – Agbor road took stage and started blowing in his life. Within the period of one year, his nephews Akpasubi, Uubanmen who had been sent by his sisters as helpers and his first son Akhigbe who was born in 1931, the year of death of His Royal Highness Ifebhor, the then Enogie of Ewohimi, all died under mysterious circumstances. Diviners were consulted over the deathswithin one year of the three males in the family, as was the practice. Accusing fingers were pointed at certain closely related individuals. What could be counteracted were counteracted through sacrifices according to the beliefs, but the great harm had been done. Within a short period and almost simultaneously Omolafe, Arhetuemen, Okogun, Enimaluole and their mother Esekhor were direct mourners along with other sympathising relatives. Esekhor felt embarrassed and confused: she was the chief mourner and wondered what would become of her children, especially Okogun, when she was gone from their life. She concluded that she was being ruthlessly and helplessly persecuted.

She became withdrawn and could not be consoled. She lost interest in life and stopped caring for herself. In the event, she took ill. She requested that she be taken to the residence of Eguaebor. Eguaebor had a reputation in the town. He was regarded as a powerful traditional doctor. He was also regarded as a dangerous doctor and some regarded him as a wizard.

While she was on her sick bed Okogun also took ill. On the day she died, Esekhor requested that Okogun be brought to her sick bed. Okogun met Ogieyan his inlaw with her. Esekhor lay down with her head resting on Ogieyan's laps. Okogun then sat close to her head.

She called him by the special name Eguaereona. She then looked up, lifted her hands to hold and bend Okogun's neck towards herself. She then made three profound statements[28]:

Firstly, that if there was reincarnation, she would not reincarnate as one of Okogun's children in order that those who gave her so much trouble and caused harm would not enjoy any drinks or entertainment at the marriage of the girl that would be from her reincarnation.

Secondly if she were holy enough, she would intercede with God in Heaven in order that Okogun's wives would have no delays and difficulties in begetting children. They would not need to consult diviners to beget children.

Thirdly, she declared that Okogun had acquired a wife and that if she Esekhor died, the wife, Enimaluole would stand in for Esekhor as his mother.

She drew him close and using her own head she hit Okogun's head and declared saying: "The death that will kill you, I have now taken over!" Okogun was led back to where he was staying. Not long after that he heard wailings: Esekhor had died and confusion ensued. The implications of her death were serious for the family. Meanwhile, Okogun who was still ill was taken out of Idinrio to reside with a traditional doctor for treatment and it was there he recovered from his illness. Esekhor was buried at her parental village Idumigie with all the necessary fanfare befitting her status.

More problems after Esekhor's death and refuge in Ebhogiaye's house

Okogun returned to Uwi-Idinrio, Ebikade and his farm on recovering from his illness. The atmosphere around him and his family was still unfriendly and full of hatred and suspicion. *Egiolamhen* of Chief Eholor family and others were accused of witchcraft against Okogun's family and were made to take oaths to cease further inimical activities. Eventually, Okogun decided to leave his family house.

The death of Akpasubi, Uubanmen, Akhigbe and finally Esekhor and other events in Omovuon's family including the deaths at different times of men to whom Okogun lived after his father's death, led many people to speculate at the reasons for such a chain of tragedies befalling the family in such rapid succession. He had to leave Omovuon's house but where should he go? *Pa Ebhogiaye* of *Iko-ogheghe*, Uwi-Idinrio offered him refuge.

At first things went well. After a while, Ebhogiaye started feeling unsafe as Okogun's host. He then started narrating stories to Okogun concerning families who gave refuge to persons that appeared to be under curses. Such hosting families, Ebhogiaye explained started experiencing problems themselves. It was obvious that Ebhogiaye was then beginning to be afraid for his own safety. To give rest of mind to kind Ebhogiaye and depart with gratitude, Okogun decided to find alternative refuge. Okogun's problem was where to go.

After consulting with his sisters, the best place to go was back to Pa Ogieyan and Uhomonye at Uzebu. He then took his family, now as a married man to Uzebu where he had earlier spent some of his life as a spinster.

CHAPTER EIGHT

OKOGUN'S INITIAL PAYING JOBS AND EARLY ADULTHOOD

Okogun had his own farm and Ebikade's farm to maintain. The farms were mainly at the sustenance level and produced very little for sales. Okogun had to do other jobs to earn a respectable living. He had also started plans to carry out some at least of what he needed to do, to complete the marriage rites required for full marriage to his wife Enimaluole.

Okogun harvested ripe palm nuts that were bought and processed for palm kernels and oil by women, collected and processed seeds of *Irvingia gabonensis* (Aubry-Lecomte ex O'Rorke) Baill. (*ohele, ogbonor*) family trees which he sold. He kept some poultry from which he sold from time to time.

Messrs. *Okanu, Egonu*, Okanu's brother, and *Izuku* were Nkwere and Awka men from Eastern Nigeria. They traded in and around Ewohimi on processed tobacco called European tobacco (*itaba-ebo)* for smoke pipes. They bought the tobacco at Onitsha market. The kit car, *olete* that was ferried across the River Niger carried the crates of tobacco up to Onicha Ugbo for the traders. Okogun joined *Igue, Oboite's father, Ogbeide Utute, Ikekhua's brother and Vincent Igidowan's father* both of Uwi-Idinrio and distant cousins to trek to Onicha Ugbo to carry the boxes of tobacco to Ewohimi for a fee.

When he had saved up to one pound ten shillings, he started accompanying Messrs. *Aitanu* of Omen-Idinrio, Ibuku Ihensekien's blood father; *Well* of Ekpoma and *Anore* of Iko-ogheghe, Uwi-Idinrio on their journeys on foot to Onitsha to buy cloths and other articles of trade. In those days, a piece of factory cloth was eight yards each and each yard[29] was one square yard material.

A piece of *obadan or abadan* cost[30] two shillings and six pence while one piece of *ankara* cost six shillings and six pence at Onitsha market. They sold these items for profit.

The treks and bicycle journeys to and from Onitsha about 1930 - 1935

The journey to and from Onitsha by foot usually took three days (about 130 miles/200 kilometers return journey). The route was Ewohimi – Idumuje Ugboko – Onitcha Ugbo – Issele Uku – Issele Azagba – farm road to Okpanam – Cable Point Asaba on the bank of the River Niger. To get to Onitsha, they were taken across the Niger by commercial canoes. Business-like, they bought the trading wares and returned to Cable Point later the same day. Before dawn, the next morning they embarked on the trek homewards and arrived at Ewohimi past midnight or slept at Ugboko to arrive Ewohimi very early the next morning. Okogun made three such journeys on foot to and from Onitsha. At the end of the first journey especially, his leg got swollen and sore. He had to stay in the house unable to walk around for some days.

Okogun bought pieces of cloths which he hawked in Ewohimi and surrounding villages.

Later when Okogun possessed a bicycle, he made the journeys to Onitsha and back in two days. His colleague on the bicycle trips was Mr Tommy who had his own bicycle. Mr Tommy later became a Chief in *Abudu, Oriomo Local Government Area,* Benin Division.

They used the same route as they took on foot to Asaba except that instead of using the Issele Azagba farm path, they rode their bicycles along the main road. Okogun explained that at the time they trekked to Onitsha, there were no vehicles. The only vehicle was the kit car, *Olete* in Onitsha. At Asaba, the Reverend Father had an auto-bicycle. These two were all the automobiles around at that time.

Okogun borrows two pounds and betroths his child in marriage to complete his marriage rites

Meanwhile, *Osobor,* Enimaluole's uncle and guardian kept up his pressure on Okogun to complete the marriage process for his wife Enimaluole. He kept demanding for money. He informed Ebikade of Osobor's demands. Ebikade gave him authority to get Ihensekhien married and use the dowry from her marriage to pay Osobor. Madam Arhetuemen, Ihensekhien's mother who was "a man" in Omovuon's house rightly objected. Arhetuemen reported the matter to Uhuomonye. Uhuomonye declared that it was improper for Ebikade to give out Ihensekhien in marriage considering all the diabolical persecution that Arhetuemen had suffered and the status she and her children had in Omovuon's family.

Osobor's demand became unbearable for Okogun and he felt that the simple solution proposed by Ebikade should have relieved him of the problem. Out of frustration, he engaged Arhetuemen physically over her refusal to give out her daughter in marriage while not helping him to solve the problem. It should be recalled that Okogun still gained from not marrying out Ihensekhien because Ikekhua, Ogbeide's brother to whom Ihensekhien became betrothed was Okogun's distant cousin. Ikekhua was very loyal to Okogun and served him very well both as a relative and a quasi-inlaw. He fathered four children through Ihensekhien including Michael Omovuon.

Okogun eventually solved his problems with Osobor by receiving two pounds from *Akpolo of Uhie*, Okaigben which he then gave to Osobor along with other service items. Osobor then let him off the hook. He agreed to give out his first little daughter *Mary Ogiadan*, when she became of age, to Akpoolo in marriage[31] and the two pounds from Akpolo served as deposit for the dowry on Mary.

CHAPTER NINE

OKOGUN JOINS THE TIMBER LOGGING BUSINESS AT OBOMKPA AS A HANDSMAN

Okogun was back to Uzebu now as a married man and adult. This should be about 1933. His first wife, Eninmaluole Iyawo who was late Akhigbe's mother was now with him. Akhigbe was born in 1931, the year of the death[3, 4] of His Royal Highness Ifebhor, the Enogie of Ewohimi. Enimaluole conceived and gave birth to a daughter that was given the name Mary Ogiadan and later to a second daughter Lucy Ebatele. He had his own farm in addition to helping in Ogieyan's farms along with *Ugbozeba Johnson Imenrion* who was much older than Okogun.

Okogun, being a courageous and brave person with strong faith in God as the Director of human affairs, decided to join labourers in the timber felling and logging industry to make more money. He left his wife and daughters with Uhomonye at Uzebu and traveled on foot to *Obomkpa near Ugbodu.* The timber logging industry was happening at Obomkpa.

He was first assigned to the *"osiko" gang*[32]. The Osiko gang comprise the men assigned to dress, plane and square the logs of timber before loading on to the trucks.

Felling of trees at Obomkpa and environs stopped after six months. The Headman with whom Okogun worked recommended him to join the chain gang that pulled the logs to the collection point. He was made second in rank to the Headman. The Headman had observed his "rascality", courage, and open-mindedness as Okogun put it and decided that Okogun would do well in the new position as second in rank to the Headman. The chain gang sang melodious songs in between the pulls. The Headman had to have a good commanding voice coupled with physical agility and strength to lead the gang. Okogun was not lacking in these.

The call to be ready to pull was made by the Headman:

Eso be e e!

to which the gang response with their hands on the chain in readiness was

he e eh!

Then the pull song from the leader alone was:

Hehe e e e heh

during which the log was pulled by the gang without joining in the song.

A relaxing song led by the Headman was

E e e Hee; Eee, Odo tu mennn

meaning he or she came to visit me perhaps referring more to her than to him.

The gang members would in unison follow with

E e e e h e e

At the end of another six months making a total of one year at Obomkpa, the camp was dissolved and closed. The timber Company then relocated to Okaigben, Ewohimi, Okogun's town to exploit for timber in Ewohimi forest. Many Ewohimi men then joined as co-workers in the timber company.

At this time, Okogun was considered knowledgeable enough in the timber logging work to be made a full Headman. To make up his gang Okogun received into the gang the boys who had worked respectively with *Josiah of Ohordua* and *Obi of Eguae- Oliha, Ewatto*. Josiah and Obi graciously gave Okogun their respective men(boys). *Ogudo* and *Amiendamen of Uwi-Idinrio* were among Okogun's boys. Eventually work extended from Ewohimi to the forest at *Akpoza in Ohordua* and a camp was then created at Ohordua. Okogun was transferred to the Ohordua Camp. While working from the Ohordua Camp, Okogun was able to visit home once a week.

Okogun takes Angelina Ailegbesuan as his second wife

It was while at Ohordua that Okogun met his second wife to be *Ailegbesuan Angelina.*

First, he dated her as friend. After a while, Okogun informed Enimaluole about Ailegbesuan in his life. Enimaluole did not object. She accepted his association with Ailegbesuan.

Okogun then decided to inform Uhuomonye. Uhuomonye, as was the practice, consulted an oracle through a diviner. The diviner revealed to Uhomonye that Ailegbesuan was a

"woman's wife" (amen-okhuo)[33]. Okogun was cautioned not to think of marrying her because of her status and was advised to terminate the association. Okogun told Uhuomonye that the friendly association with Ailegbesuan was just a temporary one.

Ailegbesuan decided to visit Ewohimi during one of the annual feasts with a baby girl she had through Okogun. The child later died. As usual the death of the child was attributed to witchcraft acting in the interest of *Prince Aikpagie, and heir to the Enogie of Ohordua throne* who with the support of *Aiyobase,* Ailegbesuan's "*woman husband*", was linked to Ailegbesuan. Ailegbesuan however did not like the Prince's advances since she already had friendly relations with Okogun with whom she had fallen in love.

Enivie, Ailegbesuan's senior sister over-ruled Ailegbesuan's stand and rejected Okogun's association with her. Ailegbesuan was then persuaded to accept the Prince. Okogun decided to let go and stopped his relationship with her. Ailegbesuan and Okogun did not fully dissolve their mutual love.

Floating and paddling logs from Ewohimi to the River Niger

Meanwhile, the timber Contractor at Ewohimi *Mr. Odiase* and the *European* in charge had a disagreement over the business of timber logging. Eventually, Odiase was forced out of the business. The European then brought a *Mr. Isaiah* to replace Odiase as Contractor. For six months under Isaiah, salaries were not paid. On inquiry, workers were told that the European was withholding salaries because no logs had arrived at Warri for export.

Isaiah summoned the workers to announce that timber logs were then to be taken to Warri through the River Niger starting from the Odu River at Ewohimi. The way to do so involved a man staying on a floating log of timber and guiding it through the waters to the point where the timber should float into the River Niger. At that point, the man should jump off the log and swim ashore. Mr Isaiah asked for volunteers. Several Ibos including Obadigbo and Moses an Urhobo man volunteered. Agbai who was co-Headman with Okogun at Ohordua volunteered. Okogun also volunteered.

The next day each of the volunteers including Okogun mounted a log each and with poles commenced at the *Idumu-agho end of the Odu River* to paddle the log towards River Niger.

The navigation was done in stages. Ogugu camp in Ewatto area was the first stop at the end of the first day. The next day, the journey went on to the bigger Odu River on the Ohordua side now named Iyagun. After the camp at Ohordua was closed, the next camp towards the River Niger was at Abumere in Ebu area. Abumere was beyond the point of the merging of Iyagun and River Uto which now was the name of the combined rivers and was a tributary of the River Niger. At about the point known as Ogege-Aigbe, the log paddlers jumped off the logs and swam to the bridge leaving the logs to float to the Ijaws waiting at the next point on the River Niger to take the logs to Warri. By so doing the logs were then arriving at Warri. Most of the volunteers resigned from the task of ferrying the logs when they reached the point where they had to take the logs on Iyagun onto the point near its confluence with River Niger. Just five persons decided to remain on the perilous duty, and they were then referred to as Water Boys.

The courageous five were *Agbai from Ohordua, Jacob (Ibo), Moses (Urhobo), Obadigbo (Ibo) and Okogun.*

Storm on the River and the floating log is forced to move upstream

On the first day of the log-ferrying, every other person progressed smoothly with their logs through the water but Okogun had problems. Okogun's log kept swinging across the stream instead of staying lengthwise along the stream. The others including Obadigbo, Okogun's friend took their logs successfully to Ogugu the first stop. Okogun struggled on with his log and reached the Idinrio end of the Odu River in the evening. He tied up his log there and returned to the camp. He informed Obadigbo of his unpleasant experience. The next morning Obadigbo accompanied Okogun to the tied-up log. The two of them with a pole each mounted the log, one person at each end. They then maneuvered the log to Ogugu, tied it up and returned to camp. Obadigbo gave Okogun tutorial on how to paddle the log with little or no problems. The next day, the waterboys took their respective logs to the final point at Ogege – Aigbe. Obadigbo had Okogun to be always next to him on the River. By so doing Okogun by using Obadigbo's technique was able to paddle his logs all by himself without problems. Okogun successfully took logs to Ogege – Aigbe on three occasions. On the fourth attempt to ferry a log to Ogege – Aigbe, he started out quite early as usual with his assigned log. He had just two colleagues on their respective logs ahead of him as he had learnt the trick. He had not gone far on the River when the sky suddenly became overcast. It became very dark everywhere and visibility along the River became poor. He managed to guide the log on the journey towards Ogege – Aigbe and got to the Abumere camp zone. Violent thunder and lightning took over the atmosphere and a storm ensued.

Suddenly, still under the stormy weather, the forward end of the log tilted upwards above the water. Then the log started moving upstream against the usual river current. Okogun became frightened at the unusual development. Using the pole, he vaulted off the log into the river and swam ashore. This happened in the middle of the forest.

He had no idea about where he was and for that reason, he did not know in which direction to head through the forest. He decided to head in a direction that he felt would lead him to Abumere camp. With a type of *army jack knife* on him he made his way through the jungle. As he roamed the forest, he came face to face with a herd of wild pigs. Wild pigs are known to attack and could kill people who confront them in the forest. He slowly and carefully moved in such a way that the pigs did not feel threatened by him. Even so the pigs made a signal pursuit, and he was able to escape from them. It was evening when he arrived on the road to Abumere quite tired, exhausted, hungry and with bleeding wounds all over his body caused by thorns as he made his way through the jungle. In that state he reached the camp and spent the night sleeping at Abumere. The next day he packed his bags and returned to Ewohimi camp where he reported his experience to Mr. Isaiah the contractor. Mr Isaiah was quite sympathetic to Okogun saying that Okogun was fortunate to be alive and that things could have been much worse. Mr. Isaiah then re-deployed him as a Headman and removed the extra two shillings and six pence paid monthly to each Waterboy. The Headman received five shillings monthly, carpenters and boardmen each received three shillings and labourers each received two shillings and six pence monthly.

After six months from his last visit, the European business owner returned with the sad news that he was quitting the timber logging business and therefore declared the camp closed. He paid salaries at half the agreed rates. The workers had no alternative but to accept whatever they could get as salaries. Okogun received one pound ten shillings. Okogun out of frustration decided to remain at Abumere living with some Uromi and Ibo young men. Meanwhile he reckoned that he would have saved three pounds jointly with Uhuomonye and Enimaluole.

CHAPTER TEN

OKOGUN BECOMES A TAILOR: ONITSHA YAM SALE EXPEDITION

After a short time at Abumere, Okogun returned to Uzebu and decided to learn the art of sewing clothes to become a tailor. This should be about 1935. He decided to make some investment in the tools he needed for the trade. He put together the money he saved with Uhuomonye and Enimaluole as part of his initial capital. He bought a bicycle for one pound five shillings and a manual sewing machine for one pound five shillings. He learnt the profession of tailoring with *Mr. Joel*, an Ora man of Ora quarters[34] and *Mr. Salawu* of Yoruba Quarters[35] both in Ewohimi. He focused on sewing female dresses. He became a resident women's tailor at Uzebu.

Okogun and Lamise decide on a canoe trip to sell Ewohimi yams at Onitsha

His tailor business was going quite well. He sold his cloths and dresses at Ewohimi and border towns using his bicycle as a means of transport. He kept thinking about ways of deriving more economic benefits from his environment.

The Urhobos[36] from the Delta around Warri and Sapele in those days settled in camps along the course of Odu River. They had one of their chiefs at the Idumu-agho end of the river and his name was *Otan or Otah*. There were others at the Uzebu end of the river.

Lamise, an Urhobo man and father of *Ugo* as he was referred to, was in a camp at the Uzebu end of the river. He used to go with his brother's canoe on the Odu River to and from Onitsha on the River Niger. He was Okogun's friend. The moon was shining bright one night and they were engaged in one of their usual interactions discussing life. Lamise had just returned from one of his trips to Onitsha. After Okogun welcomed him with the traditional kola-nuts presented to visitors, they settled down to discuss. He reported how yams were selling very well at good prices in Onitsha because of the high demand for the commodity.

Lamise lamented the lack of money to buy yams from farmers and take the yams by canoe on River Odu through Rivers Utor, Iyagun and the Niger onto Onitsha for sale. Okogun and Lamise decided to put a project together to take yams by canoe to Onitsha.

They would need about three pounds worth of yam to fully load a canoe. They would have to get a canoe and hire two paddlers *(ulowe)* in addition to Lamise who was himself a paddler. Okogun was to provide the three pounds and buy the yams. In addition, Okogun was to pay the fee for one of the two hired paddlers *(ulowe)*. Lamise was to use his brother's canoe free of charge and pay the fee for one of the two hired paddlers *(ulowe). The deal was sealed that night.*

Okogun with his bicycle on his shoulders crossed the Idinrio Odu local bridge made by the Idinrio men called *egbe-ede (*literal translation could be river-tieers or river-overcomers or river-breakers). He and Lamise worked to make it possible to use the bicycle on the farm paths by clearing bushes and removing stumps with cutlasses along the path. Lamise used his contraption for carrying palmfruit bunches *(Ekpeh)* to carry yams. Okogun prided himself on the fact that he was the first person to use a bicycle on the farm paths made on crossing the River Odu from the home side.

Farmers'sale of yams to Okogun

The farmers were overjoyed at the idea of selling their yams from the barns at their farms without the need to carry the yams on their heads to the markets. In those days, the women used large calabash bowls *(ugba)* to load materials that they carry on their heads. The pad on the head over which the load was placed was made from leaves or rags from old clothes. The men had rectangular basket *(ukpee)* with a wooden base woven with cane strands made from a plant climber. Selling their yams in the farms saved the task of transporting the yams to the nearest markets that were several miles away. They sold a yam-barn row of very large tubers for one shilling and three pence, medium sizes for one shilling and the rest for nine pence to Okogun. Some of the farmers were quite kind and cooperative. *Pa Akhibi* of Uwi-Idinrio for example gave Okogun his yams without insisting on immediate payment when he noticed that Okogun had no more money left on him to pay for yams.

Akhibi told him to take the yams and pay when he returned from the Onitsha yam market. Others from whom they bought yams included *Ebaobomhenifo and Imhanrhiagbe.* The farms were located mostly in the derived Savannah area of Ewohimi land near idumuje-Ugboko and Idumuje-unor beyond what was *Ewohimi Forest Reserve.* The Ewohimi Forest Reserve was deliberately[7] created to include the timber populated forest and exclude the Savannah parts for the farmers. Twice daily Lamise and Okogun went to the farms to collect yams for their canoe on the River. They completed the transfer of yams and the loading of the canoe in four days.

The navigation to Onitsha

Thus, they filled a canoe with yams to make a full load. Okogun employed *Akpofure* as a paddler (*ulowe)* and Akpofure also brought in the third paddler (*ulowe)* for Lamise as earlier agreed. Okogun's nephew, Patrick Egialegbele Ilegbodu (Patrick Ilegbodu later in life returned to settle in Onitsha as a Public Works Department artisan) pleaded to accompany Okogun on the journey so he could know Onitsha. His request was granted and so he joined the group. Early the next day, which was the ninth day since Lamise returned from Onitsha they set off on the journey along the same water course that Okogun and colleagues used to ferry the timber logs to the River Niger while they worked with the timber logging company. As the River tributary approached the River Niger, canoes encountered a point on the river where water appeared to be rushing noisily into a deep gorge to the left of the River course. The paddlers (*ulowe)* had to keep close to the right bank of the River to maneuver through the waves rushing towards the gorge. As the paddlers (*ulowe)* struggled to keep the canoe on course, someone in the canoe, at strategic points, threw tubers of yams with force into the river on the left side of the canoe. This practice probably created powerful ripples and certainly the momentum[37] in the direction away from the thrown tuber that helped to keep the canoe away from the current going into the gorge though some interpreted the practice as a sacrifice to river gods. The canoe happily was navigated successfully, and it safely reached the River Niger at nightfall the same day. They decided not to get into Onitsha, which was now on sight but still a distance from them, at night. They moored the canoe at a sandy point mid-river to spend the night.

At Onitsha

Early at dawn the next morning, they resumed their journey and arrived at Onitsha at about 1PM. Okogun and his colleagues noticed that when the traders on the riverbank sighted their canoe and its cargo of yams, a lot of agitation and pandemonium ensued among the traders. The traders on the shore were frantically signally to the paddlers *(ulowe)* to row the canoe into the various spots on the shore where they respectively were standing. There were so many such invitations from different groups. Okogun and Lamise had to decide on the best spot on the bank to disembark and sell the yams. They successfully got to the chosen spot on the shore. The yams sold out very quickly at good prices like the then hot *Madam Igbennake ikpeke oka* at Ofuri Market. (Madam Igbennake who is the paternal grandmother of Chief *Josiah E. Izevbaye* in those days made very popular chunky corn flour pudding cakes fried in palm oil called ikpeke.) They sold most of the yams on the first day. At the end of that day, Okogun received his project capital outlay of *six pounds*. The next day, he left Lamise to sell the remaining yams and asked Patrick to stay with Lamise. Okogun who had been used to visiting Onitsha, though first on foot and later bicycle from Ewohimi, then went into the market to buy various articles of trade. He bought twelve large metallic basins, six easy chairs with tables at nine pence each and three dozen (36) eating plates which he gave to Lamise to take back and hand over to Uhuomonye at Uzebu on arrival back to Ewohimi.

Okogun and Lamise were overjoyed with their successful business of taking yams from Ewohimi for sale at Onitsha. They paid the paddlers *(ulowe)* their fees for labour, accounted for the debts owed to the farmers who gave them yams without collecting their charges and all other debts arising from the business. They then shared the profit amicably.

Okogun decided to use his share of the returns from their venture as capital to expand his petty trading. He bought several commercial items as cargo for the canoe. The canoe was dispatched to return to Ewohimi with his cargo. Patrick returned with the canoe and with instructions to discharge his cargo and take them to Madam Uhuomonye at Uzebu.

Okogun and Lamise each made five pounds and fifteen shillings in addition to small items like singlets as gain. Okogun stayed back in Onitsha to make further purchases of trade and gift items. He bought special baskets, earrings, plates, spoons, multiple yards piece of shirting cloth, three yards of khaki cloth, Hausa caps and slippers. He then took these back to Ewohimi. On arrival, he met that Uhuomonye had organized the sale of most of the items that he sent through the canoe and had a total of twelve pounds from the sales. This journey may have taken place about 1936.

CHAPTER ELEVEN

OKOGUN RELOCATES TO AGBOR AND UMUNEDE AS TAILOR AND CLOTH MERCHANT

Okogun and Lamise's successful business journey to sell yams at Onitsha yielded good capital that gave Okogun a stronger foothold as an entrepreneur. He had to operate his business which revolved around Esan market days and simultaneously carry out his duties as appropriate to his age grades and groups.

Community life in Esan revolved around age groups and the days of the traditional week which were associated with market days(Chapter Two). These concepts were so ingrained that every person who reached the age of reasoning knew without being reminded what his or her duties were whenever situations developed or there were duties to be carried out. They also knew what activities they should engage in on each of the days of the week. *Every person who had reached the age of reason woke up each day of the traditional week of four days with full awareness of what his/her duties and activities of the day should be.* It was thus not normally necessary to remind anyone to go about his or her duties for the day. The culture and practice in this regard was communitalism[38] at its best. The structure brought development to the community, encouraged heroism, made no room for laziness and with strict sanctions, discouraged stealing.

Okogun relocates to Agbor and then Umunede

On returning from the very successful journey to sell yams at Onitsha, Okogun became a relatively big-time tailor who also traded on cloths. His trade was growing, and he enjoyed good patronage. He was visiting the markets in *Ohordua especially, Ewatto, Ebelle, Ekpon and Igueben* in addition to Ofuri, the then main market at Ewohimi.

As a member of the young men of the environmental age grade (egbolughe) and as Igbama at Uzebu, Ewohimi, Okogun had to be with his age group to serve the community as their duties arose. Such duties included fetching water for mixing and mashing the mud and carrying the mud on wood planks on their heads to those setting the walls when houses were being communally built then as was the practice, digging the grave when there was burial, weeding the farm paths, sweeping the streets every fifth day, taking part in the dances and so on. He had to join when there were dances especially as he was a sought-after excellent acrobatic dancer. Okogun would have by this time elevated to the igbama status since he was married with children and had his own family landed property. Even as an igbama, he still had to participate in the many communal duties of the igbamas. He had to attend to the farms.

On the days he could not participate in communal duties because he had to attend to his market business, he would send kola nuts and palm wine with apologies to his colleagues who were at the communal duty posts. His colleagues appreciated his gesture but absenteeism from communal duties became frequent. He felt that the situation was unhealthy and could not continue for long without naturally bringing about issues with some members of the community.

He soon realized that he could not have enough time and freedom to practice his business from Ewohimi. Eventually, He decided to leave home and go abroad as was the parlance when people left their villages to go to the more developed towns outside their own areas. He decided to go to Agbor to meet *Mr Josiah Ajieh*. Josiah welcomed him and helped him to get an accommodation that he rented for himself. He continued his tailor and cloth business at Agbor. After a short time at Agbor, he was advised that he would be better off doing business at Umunede which was then the United African Company (UAC) headquarters in the area. At that time, the UAC Manager was Mr Butter (or Butler). At that time Chief Christopher Ebhodaghe Abebe of Iruekpen, Esan West Local Government Area was a Clerical Officer in the services of the UAC. So, he packed his things from home at Uzebu and left to settle at Umunede. This movement should be about 1936. During the time he was at Umunede, Okogun got a letter of introduction from *Chief Odigie, the first Ologbosere of Ewohimi* to a Company, probably the John Holts Company, so that the Company could patronize him if he made purchases. Odigie in the letter described Okogun as his fifth son. Chief Odigie Osaguona Ilegbedion who was a good man interested in mentoring young people took to Okogun as belonging to the same larger family as himself and admired Okogun for his good looks, courage, boldness, integrity, and acrobatic prowess. He would always wish to have Okogun in his entourage. Chief Odigie took him as a son to the extent that he requested him to judge a case in his harem involving *Madam Oshioaye*, mother *of Otiti* and grandmother of *Messrs. Moses Anore* and *Gregory Onakhinor*. Okogun passed judgement, found Madam Oshioaye guilty and imposed a fine of a goat on her. The verdict and fine were upheld by Chief Odigie and the family elders.

At Umunede he met *Egbeaba* from Igueben just like *Ebhohimen,* Okogun's relative also from Igueben. Egbeaba assisted him to get a place to rent in *Aigbogie's* house at Idumu-Oba quarters in Umunede. *Okonobo*[9] from *Ogbokpa, Ewatto* and his two wives *Evaimague* and *Owobu from Okhuesan* who was childless lived in the same house that Egbeaba got for him.

Life and business at Umunede

He used Umunede as his base. On his bicycle he went to Onitsha to buy cloths some of which he cut up to sow clothes for women and children. He hawked the clothes and dress materials in markets at *Umunede, Agbor, Ute, Igbanke, Ubulu Uku, Ewohimi, Ohordua, Igueben* and others traveling to each place with his wares on his bicycle. Sometimes he made it back to Umunede on the same day at the close of market even from Ewohimi.

He lived initially like a bachelor cooking his own food and cleaning his accommodation and doing other necessary things all by himself. He decided to bring Enimaluole to Umunede. She objected to leaving Uzebu to accompany him to Umunede. Meanwhile, Angelina Ailegbesuan had decided not to live as a woman's wife and left Ohordua for Ewohimi against all opposition but with her immediate senior sister Madam Ailuhi as overt supporter.

The woman husband so to say Madam *Aiyobase* of royal lineage at Ohordua was greatly incensed that she left Ohordua to join Okogun at Ewohimi. Aiyobase decided to do all in her power in darkness and in light to eliminate

Okogun and Angelina. They did all in their power to protect themselves from her evil plans. Okogun then brought Angelina to be with him at Umunede to end his bachelor-like life there. After about one month stay at Umunede, Ailegbesuan became very ill with serious headaches. He then decided to return her to Ewohimi for care. Okogun then pleaded with Enimaluole to reconsider her stand on accompanying him to Umunede and she then agreed to go with him to Umunede.

Change of residence at Umunede

Okonobo and Okogun were engaged in the same business. They could be away from home for up to four or five days at a stretch. One day, on return from their business outside Umunede, they met that the women were not in their usual cheerful mood. They settled down to take their meals and decided to inquire from the women about their condition and what the problem was. There was a misunderstanding between the women. It turned out that Evaimague and Owobu for some reasons were persecuting Enimaluole. The matter was settled. After two months, to get the women busy, Okonobo and Okogun bought axes for their wives so that they could together engage in the wood splitting and sales business. Enimaluole refused to work together with Evaimague and Owobu.

Evaimague and Owobu then started imputing and guessing at Enimaluole's motives in her rejection to partner with them. A serious quarrel which led to violence developed between the women. In the event Evaimague and Owobu had combined to fight with Enimaluole. In the fracas, Enimaluole tore the other women's clothes.

Since the two husbands were away, Ika neighbours kindly quelled the fight until Okonobo and Okogun returned from their business tour. The women each related their part in the matter. Okogun was silent and allowed Okonobo to settle the matter and to give judgement. Okonobo found his wives guilty on the grounds that they were two against one. Okonobo's wives were not happy with their husband for finding them guilty and kept grudges against him. Apparently under pressure from his wives, Okonobo raised the issue of cloths some months after the incident. It was obvious to Okogun that the two families could not live together in peace under the same roof. Okogun decided to change accommodation without discussing it with anyone else other than his wife.

The new accommodation along Mbiri road

Okogun prepared his exit from his accommodation at Idumu Oba quarters where he and his wife lived with Okonobo and his wives over a period of two months. He did not confide in Mr. Okonobo until everything was set. He met a house owner *Mr. Okuerie at Ugbobi – Eguae* along Uzor Mbiri (Mbiri road). He negotiated with Mr. Okuerie to move into the house. He also got Mr Okuerie's consent to renovate the house. He bought doors and installed in the house and re--roofed the building. The Ika people were glad that he had decided to move into their midst.

When the building was ready for him and Enimaluole to move in, he informed Okonobo. Okonobo did not like the idea and opposed his moving from the house. The discussion was such that no definite decision was agreed on between them. Two days later at night Okogun decided to pack and leave with Enimaluole. He loaded and tied most of the loads on his bicycle while Enimaluole carried the rest of the loads on her head. Evaimague and Owobu woke up to their surprise to see what was going on. They started asking why they were leaving raising issues again. Both sides exchanged uncharitable words and they left. Okogun returned the keys to the landlord Mr. Aigbogie. Ailegbesuan joined Okogun at Umunede. Okogun brought in his third underaged wife *Maria Imanrhokanobhor* after he had been at Umunede for about four years. Because she was still too young to execute marriage Maria was attached to Enimaluole who took her as a daughter and mentored her as wife-to-be until she came of age. Okogun and family[39] spent the rest of their stay in Umunede in the Ugbobi - Eguae house carrying out his business.

The betrothal of baby Maria as Okogun's future wife

Maria was betrothed to Okogun immediately she was born as a baby in the traditional way of the time. Esekhor was the first to get a log of firewood (*ohienran o bhor*) to *Pa Ayangbe* (Maria's father)'s house after Maria was born. Esekhor followed up later by depositing two pounds as part dowry for Okogun's future wife Maria before Esekhor died. In those days, if a family was interested in getting a wife from another family, the family meticulously monitor pregnancies and births in the family of interest. Once news was given of a female baby birth in the family of interest, the interested families competed and the first to carry a good log of firewood and drop it with a loud thud at the back of the father of the new baby's house won. And so was the case with baby Maria.

CHAPTER TWELVE

RUBBER BUSINESS

Okogun's business prospered at Umunede and he had made good savings and could expand his business. At that time, rubber became very important as article of trade. Okogun decided to engage in the rubber business and informed his wives.

He started out and rode his bicycle to Benin to *Mr. Osagie Aki,* his first cousin who was then still living in Ikpoba, Benin to discuss the rubber business. After exploring opportunities in the rubber business, he decided to hire rubber plantation in the *Aduhanhan* area near Benin on the Benin – Ekpoma road and recruited tappers to tap the rubber trees for him. He would pay the plantation owner by sharing the profits from selling the rubber lumps. He returned to Umunede and explained the new deal to his wives. He decided to rent and take over three rubber plantations.

He rode to Onitsha to buy cloths which he carried to Benin to continue his cloth and tailor business there near the rubber plantations. He recruited rubber tappers. The first tappers he recruited from Ewohimi were *Josiah, Madam Aghe's son* of Idumu-Oleghe, Okaigben *and Iribhor* his own cousin. He made two recruitment trips to Ewohimi. The rubber sap yield was poor at Aduhanhan. He left the initial plantations and moved to *Urhokuosa* to rent better plantations. Urhokuosa is on the same road as Aduhanhan further away from Benin.

He met Mr. Joseph Imansuangbon, his cousin on the Chief Ebalogben children link at Oken (or Ohen). He transferred his tappers to Urhokuosa and then visited Umunede to visit his family. He returned to Urhokuosa via Ewohimi where he again recruited more tappers. This time the recruited tappers included *Okogun Aigbe,* and *Ayemere, Igbede's* brother both from Idinrio. He was still not satisfied with the performance of the plantations at Urhokuosa. He decided to move *to Idemudia's* camp at *Eko-Ahue.* Idemudia after whom the Camp was named was a native doctor. Okogun Aigbe refused to follow him to the new location and escaped from camp.

At first, the plantation owners at Idemudia Camp did not want to deal with him because they said an Esan man from Irrua had duped them. He convinced them of his genuine intentions, and he promised to do better than what they said his fellow Esan man from the Irrua did.

He again went on his round trip to Umunede and then to Ewohimi to recruit more tappers for the third time before returning to the plantations. On his third recruitment drive, he recruited *Oyugbo from Idumu-agho, Omozokpea Ilegbenehi, Pa Osogiahon's* son through *Ikhuohuomon* of Idinrio *and Iboi* of *Iselu, Aiya's brother.*

Okogun had fifteen tappers at Urhokuosa that he moved to work at Idemudia Camp. At the end of the first full month of tapping the rubber plantations, he had five pounds net gain after paying all overheads. He then settled to the routine of operating from Umunede where he carried out his cloth business and visited the rubber plantations fortnightly. At the end of the year's rubber business, his total gain was sixty pounds. By this time, he had started taking back some members of his family from Umunede to Ewohimi. He was satisfied with the returns from the rubber business and continued with it. Shortly into the second year, *Isaac, Omonakhin's* brother organized a rebellion in his camp of tappers. *John Utubor* who by 1971 was well established and prospering in Northern Nigeria *(Kano)* gave him details of what transpired in the camp and the plans of the ringleader of the rebellion. Isaac had decided to be on his own.

He summoned his boys to *Edionwe's house* to show gratitude to them and as was the practice entertained them. The party drinks then featured native gin[40] also called illicit gin as it was not approved by government for consumption or trade at that time.

Owaemi then became the leader of his camp. After Okogun had a brawl with Isaac over his disruptive actions, he decided to fold up his rubber plantation business in that area.

He took John Utubor away from the camp to Benin City as a protective measure. *Mr. Okonobo, Chief Okogie Imanyelea's* relation was in Benin. He was a tailor. Okogun handed John Utubor to him so that John could train to become a tailor.

CHAPTER THIRTEEN

OKOGUN DECIDES TO BUILD HIS OWN HOUSE BY OFURI MARKET

Okogun then felt that he had enough funds to build his Ewohimi residence. He was uncomfortable building in Uwi-Idinrio for fear that he could revive the harassments that he had from some persons in the village before Esekhor's death.

He could build at Eguae, Ewohimi where his mother came from. He feared that if he built at Eguae, his Okaigben people would resent him and they could arrange his premature death. He therefore dropped Eguae out of fear for his safety from consideration as a possible location for the proposed building. He therefore decided to take the risk and build by Ofuri Market. At that time nobody lived near and around Ofuri Market which was then surrounded by uninhabited jungle. Chief Odigie Osaguona Ilegbedion, the first Ologbosere of Ewohimi told Okogun that Ofuri Market zone was a meeting zone for robbers, witches, and wizards. Chief Odigie advised him against his decision to build by Ofuri Market which was also the meeting point of five roads. Okogun said that he had a clear conscience that would protect him from evil since he was neither a robber nor a wizard. He would work and go by his clear conscience.

Okogun sacrifices a goat to free Idinrio people from the prohibition to build beyond Ogbe and Ohen shrine

As an Idinrio man, Okogun should not build beyond *Ogbe and Ohen* shrine[41]. Idinrio people must go pass the shrine area to go to the Ofuri Market. Okogun put his case before the elders of Idinrio. The Elders then apparently were a progressive group and able to see the future. They then requested Okogun to take a goat to Ogbe and Ohen shrine as appeasement sacrifice to Idinrio ancestors so that the rule could be abrogated for Okogun and future Idinrio persons who desired to build their houses on locations beyond the shrine. Okogun was happy to produce the goat and he was then permitted to build by the Market.

He cleared a site by the market and as usual by communal effort mashed the mud to set his house.

The native doctors' sacred tree problem and Chief Odigie's solution

After clearing a portion of the bush and felling some trees by the market to build his house, Okogun had a surprise formal visit by a delegation of the Okaigben Ebo (plural for Obo/diviner and healer) summoning him to appear before them. He was accused of felling a native doctors' sacred tree (Eran obo) in the area he cleared around his building area. The consequences of such an act were very serious. Okogun would have to be subjected to some oath-taking possibly involving drinking some concoction and eating kola taking from a heap of the native doctors' shrine of assembled effigies and symbols of gods. He would be heavily fined and could be cursed. The consequences of such a ritual on Okogun could be grave and dangerous. His future life would be adversely affected. The venue for Okogun's trial was at *Chief Odigie's Palace* because Odigie by then had become not only a member of the native doctors' group but also a senior elder (*Odionwele)* in Idinrio. He also belonged to the same larger family of Ibhiaigbiya as Okogun. Okogun's sisters led by Uhuomonye who was still at Uzebu at the time accompanied Okogun to the trial.

At the trial, Okogun was at first made to sit on the bare dusty floor surrounded by the offended native doctors each with his god's symbol. The others sat on chairs or on the raised mud benches (*ukpekhere)* by the walls or stood around. The case against Okogun was presented in very strong terms laced with curses. The matter went on and on as the native doctors considered what punishment and fine to impose on Okogun. After a long session of the court, Chief Odigie took a deep breath followed by a noisy sigh as if he was being relieved of some heavy load on his mind. He then asked those gathered if they knew that Okogun, as a matter of fact, owned the native doctor's god and practice in the larger family. He was reminding them of the Ehimin episode that took the native doctor inheritance from Okogun's lineage. After this and without saying more, the other elders and native doctors who had forgotten history or pretended not know the fact, in unison and with some reviling words asked Okogun to get up from the floor and sit in a more respectable place. They then asked him to produce some palm oil, white chalk, and a piece of white cloth. He should go to the nearby bush and tie the white cloth on any appropriate tree of his choice to replace the one he cut. Such a tree was then to be recognized as a sacred tree for the native doctors. He added minor entertainment materials for the elders and native doctors and that ended the matter on the physical. Okogun related his pains when thereafter his newborn children kept dying. The puzzling deaths of eleven children born immediately following the episode was attributed by Okogun and many of his relatives to the dark activities of the native doctors and associated witchcraft who made taking the lives of his children their coven revenge. However, malaria could have played a part in the deaths of the infants for a number of reasons.

Okogun's plan was to use corrugated iron sheets to roof the house. At that time, a bundle of twenty sheets of iron sheets cost one pound two shillings. Uhuomonye, his senior sister and head guardian for good reasons, rejected his plan to use iron sheets. She said Okogun would be killed off out of envy because at that time only the Enogie and Chief Odigie used corrugated iron sheets for parts of their palaces. Okogun decided not to use thatch leaves but to use the special Urhobo woven raffia palm leaves called *baboo* locally to roof his new house. This was the material for roofing most houses in Benin City at that time.

By the time he closed his rubber plantation camp, he had completed roofing the building and just needed to install doors and other fixtures. Chief Odigie, the Ologbosere of Ewohimi died about three native years after Okogun completed the building. That puts the completion of the building about 1941/42 since Chief Odigie died in February 1944.

When the building became habitable, Omolafe and Arhetuemen moved in. He first took Maria home. Shortly after he took Joseph who was sickly to Maria at home under the supervision of his sisters. One of his cats went with Joseph. Not long after Angelina returned from Umunede after she recovered from a serious illness. Lucy, Okogun's second daughter was brought from Umunede to live with Omolafe. Okogun remained at Umunede with Enimaluole while continuing his usual cloth trade that took him round on his bicycle to the markets earlier mentioned. Later Okogun's residence at different times accommodated his cousin Osagie Aki and family after he had returned home from Benin and Madam Uhuomonye Ogieyan when she returned from Uzebu years after Pa Ogieyan's death. Some of Okogun's cousins and wives lived in the building when they were at home from abroad on visits. Eventually Okogun and Enimaluole returned from Umunede to take up timber business at home as will be related.

Some teachers at various times also lived in the house. Among these were Messrs A. A. Orukpe from Irrua/Ewu, Sunday Udo from Ohordua and Miss Isidahomen of Ohordua. Mr Okanu, the Awka/Nkwere trader and blacksmith also lived in part of the house. Two of Okanu's sons were *Robert* and *Michael* whose mothers respectively were *Ugbor and Masidi.* The women traded in the processed tobacco for smoked pipes., Oji, an Awka blacksmith had his shed and residence across the road in the premises of Mr. Akhigbe Wilson Odigie. Akhigbe Wilson Odigie got Oji to train Isaiah Akhigbe Odigie, Akhigbe's son to become a blacksmith.

A prohibition attached to living in Okogun's house by Ofuri Market based on some advice from seers was that nobody must take anything whatsoever belonging to someone else from the market into the house.

CHAPTER FOURTEEN

TIMBER BUSINESS AS CAMP OVERSEER UNDER CHIEF PAUL E. ODIGIE

Timber business with Chief Paul Ebhohon Odigie

Chief Odigie's first son *Paul Ebhohon Odigie* inherited his chieftaincy as the second Ologbosere of Ewohimi. Chief Paul Ebhohon Odigie decided to embark on timber business. His late father Chief Odigie had earlier sent him for training to learn the timber trade.

On one of Okogun's visit home from Umunede, Chief Paul Odigie pleaded with Okogun to join him in the business because Chief Paul wished that Okogun brought his earlier experience in the timber logging industry into their cooperation. Chief Paul Odigie promised to help Okogun to raise capital to the tune of one hundred and fifty to two hundred pounds as assistance to Okogun in his cloth and tailor business at the end of the cooperation.

At the beginning, Okogun continued doing his business at Umunede but decided to be spending extra days at home to give the assistance requested by Chief Paul Odigie whenever he visited Ewohimi.

Okogun went into the forest with some men and compiled a list of mature timber that could be felled for logs. He gave the list to Chief Paul Odigie. The list was sent to the UAC who responded and gave approval for Chief Paul Odigie to exploit timber for the UAC in the allocated forest *Area B28*. Area B28 was part of *Ewohimi Forest Reserve* which was established and demarcated in negotiations[42] between the Ewohimi Community and the Colonial

Government between 1930 and 1939.The Chief then formally invited Okogun to join him on a fulltime basis. Okogun agreed but had to convince his wives who did not at first support his decision to leave Umunede for the timber business. He explained that they should give the business a chance as he could always return to his usual business if things did not go well as envisaged.

Okogun had unsold stock of cloths. His colleagues in the business agreed to help him sell the stock so he could go home to participate in the timber business with the Chief. Mr Ebhohimen accepted twentyfive pounds sterling worth of cloth from Okogun. Mr. Okonobo accepted to help him with selling fifteen pounds sterling worth of unsold stock.

With these arrangements completed, Okogun returned to Ewohimi to join Chief Paul Odigie in the timber business.

A week before Okogun got fully involved in the timber business, Chief Paul Odigie went with Odalo of Idumunguokha, Ewohimi to Okotie's timber camp in Igueben and convinced the Ibos there to leave Okotie's job and come over to his own business. At the month end following Chief Paul Odigie's visit, the overseers in Okotie[43] and Ugbodu timber camps left their camps with some of their men to join Chief Paul Odigie's camp.

Shortly after, *Mr Norman* who was a United Africa Company, UAC Manager toured the camps and met confused and demoralizing situations at the camps at Ugbodu and Igueben. He was told that Chief Paul Odigie's activities were the cause of the problems. Mr. Norman returned to Sapele and got his recommendation that Chief Paul Odigie must never work for the UAC. The recommendation was adopted by the Company. Mr. Norman armed with the Company decision about business with Chief Paul Odigie, returned to report to the Enogie about what Chief Paul Odigie had done to destabilize the camps at Igueben and Ugbodu and the decision by his Company. Chief Paul Odigie was summoned to the Enogie, His Royal Highness, HRH Enosegbe I's Palace to be informed of the consequences of his actions.

Chief Paul Odigie was shocked at the developments. Chief Paul Odigie then lost the business. Okogun raised issues with the Chief for not waiting for him and for not taking him into confidence before embarking on his recruitment drive. Meanwhile Okogun had left his thriving business at Umunede for the failed timber business.

Timber logging in the free Area B27

After the loss of the opportunity to work with the UAC, Chief Paul Odigie and Okogun learnt that a new European interested in the timber business had set up office at Agbor. They then went to discuss with the European at Agbor. The European's clerk or secretary was *Chief Anuku of Agbor.* They got a positive interest from the new European. This time, their project was to exploit timber logging in the free area, Area B27.

They went as usual to get the Enogie HRH Enosegbe I's consent to allow them carry out the project. Enogie Enosegbe I refused to grant permission because he had some grouse against Chief Paul Odigie. The Enogie's grievance concerned Chief Paul Odigie's failure to pay a fine of a cow and other minor items arising from a case in the Palace against one of Chief Paul's junior brothers. Enogie then asked Okogun to team up with *Chief Okogie Imanyelea* to do the business in the free area. Okogun had ethical and moral difficulties with the Enogie's directives. Chief Paul Odigie and he were from the same Aigbiya lineage.

Secondly Chief Okogie was Okogun's inlaw and he did not wish that Okogie and himself should come between the Enogie and Chief Paul Odigie. Chief Okogie gave his first daughter, Christiana to Okogun's nephew Joe Esezobor Ilegbodu partly because of Joe E. Ilegbodu's connection with Okogun. Okogun was the one who at the start took Christiana from Ewohimi to Joe Esezobor in Kaduna. Secondly, Okogun knew the details of the Enogie's grievances against Chief Paul. He therefore respectfully refused to go along with His Royal Highness's directives and explained to the Enogie his reasons for not obeying the Enogie's suggestion or directives. Okogun then advised Chief Paul Odigie to pay the fines and regain the Enogie's friendship. Chief Paul Odigie agreed to pay the fines[44] of a cow and other minor items and delivered them to the Enogie's Palace. The breed of the cows then was indigenous to Southern rain forest parts of Nigeria as distinct from the llama breed of the Fulanis. The Enogie then gave his written consent to Chief Paul Odigie to exploit timber in the free area. He and Okogun proceeded to work.

Chief Paul Odigie set up the camp for the workers near Odu River along the Ewohimi to Asaba via Idumuje Ugboko-Onicha Ugbo road which was motorable at that time. The camp was at the border with Area B28 where the UAC had set up a timber logging camp. Okogun was the Overseer in charge of Chief Paul E. Odigie camp while Mr. Joseph Imansuangbon was the Chief Clerk and Head of the Secretariat at the camp. As Overseer, Okogun's monthly salary was three pounds eighteen shillings. The Overseer in the UAC camp was a man whose build was stocky, *Mr. Omonramen from Ubierunmun, Uromi.*

Trespass into Area B28.

Area B28 was part of the *Ewohimi Forest Reserve.* Chief Paul Odigie authorized the felling of a timber around the Iyaho source of River Odu which was outside the free area but part of Area B28. When the UAC Manager came around and learnt of the trespass, he became violent to Mr Omonramen for not taking appropriate steps to act on the trespass. The matter did not go beyond the camps but meant caution for Okogun and Chief Odigie.

After the UAC incident on the Iyaho timber, Chief Paul Odigie started planning to get Mr. Omonramen sacked from his post as Overseer in the Area B28 UAC camp. The plan was to set up a rival Ewohimi candidate for the man's position. Chief P. Odigie considered that Chief Okogie Imanyelea should be the right person to use for his purpose. Chief P. E. Odigie for certain reasons could not approach Chief Okogie directly but kept nursing the idea. It should be recalled that his disruption of the timber camps at Igueben and Ugbodu cost him the loss of being the UAC contractor in charge of Area B28. Mr. Omonramen would not, at the risk of losing his job, cooperate with his taking timber from parts of Area B28.

Chief P. E. Odigie felt that the situation would be different if an Ewohimi man was planted as Overseer in Area B28 through his own influence to replace Mr. Omonramen.

Attempt to expel Okogun from camp

The timber business under Chief Paul Odigie with Okogun as Overseer was moving on well. Some jealousy and envy and rumours came into play all apparently unknown to Okogun. Chief Paul Odigie decided to set a trap for Okogun to get a case against him. His plan was for *Mr. Josiah Eloiyeghuain Awa* to take over the camp as Overseer. Mr. Josiah Elo. Awa convinced Okogun to use some of the labourers to work for Okogun in Okogun's farm. He had powers as Overseer to do so. Okogun was convinced and selected three of the workers to go to his farm rather than do their official duties the next day. Convinced that the deal was made, Mr. Awa went home to report the successful execution of the plot to remove Okogun to Chief Paul Odigie. Night came. *At midnight, Okogun took ill from a fever.* Morning came. Okogun then sent his wife Angelina to tell the three labourers not to go to his farm but return to their normal assignments for the day. He handed over the management of the camp for that day and until he recovered from the fever to *Mr. Josiah*, an Ibo and *Mr. Napoleon Odigie* and stayed back in his camp residence. Later, that morning *Mr. Enosolease* brought a letter which Chief Paul Odigie got *Mr. Samson Osagie* to write for him, expelling Okogun from the camp and the timber business he was helping to run.

The letter was handed over to Mr. Joseph Imansuangbon, the Chief Clerk for deliverance to Okogun. Joseph Imansuangbon was curious. He opened and read the letter.

The sack letter: contents and outcome

The content of the letter was summarized into three parts:

Chief Paul Odigie had heard all about Okogun's activities in the camp. He was serving his own interests using the workers in his farm and so on.

The Chief in the name of Idinrio and God begged Okogun to leave the Chief Paul Odigie's camp and timber business to the Chief who is the owner of the business. Chief Paul Odigie knew how much Okogun contributed to the business. Refunding Okogun's contribution would not be a problem. On investigation, the other camp officials discovered that Okogun was in his camp residence and was indisposed. No labourers were sent to work in Okogun's farm. The people who heard what happened in the camp were annoyed at Chief Paul Odigie and Mr. Josiah Elo Awa's actions. Mr. Josiah Awa fled from the camp. Chief Paul Odigie was embarrassed and lost face. Okogun did not allow Mr. Joseph Imansuangbon to tear the letter. He kept the letter and got someone to help him to write a reply to Chief Paul Odigie.

In his reply, Okogun agreed that Chief Paul Odigie knew how much Okogun contributed to start the business but asked the Chief about his estimate of the loss he had sustained abandoning his thriving business at Umunede after Chief Paul Odigie appealed to him to bring his timber experience into the timber business to help the Chief. The letter caused great pain to Okogun and he showed his pain in the family.

His wives and children felt the effect on their father. The feeling of frustration and loss was so palpable that Okogun related that one of his sons[45] who stayed in the village with the mother while he was in the timber camp near Odu River wrote a letter to him.

The child suggested in the letter that Okogun could keep all the children away from school for one year so they could join to make a large farm whose harvest could yield money to return them to school. At that time school fees were paid in all schools and at all levels.

After exchange of harsh words between Okogun and Chief Paul Odigie, they were both reconciled but the damage had been done though temporarily to their cordial and brotherly relations. The hurt and damage gradually faded away and no one in their later life and interaction could believe that they ever had any serious disagreements or quarrels.

Chief Idiagbonya,litigation over Omovuon's cow and Area B28

The opportunity to be trained as Overseer in Area B28 came to Okogun without his planning it. *Pa Omovuon Okuoebho*, Okogun's father had given a cow to *Chief Idiagbonya* of Idumuogo to be looked after by Chief Idiagbonya as an indication of their mutual friendship. The practice then was that the offspring of the cow would be shared according to established practice between Pa Omovuon and Chief Idiagbonya. The cultural practice between relatives and friends could be with chicken, goats, sheep, and cows. The practice was also referred to as being inlaws (oruan). After Omovuon's death, Chief Idiagbonya refused to engage with Okogun on the cow in his care and therefore virtually assumed full ownership of the cow. Okogun was forced to take the matter to the Customary Court at Ewohimi to claim his right. On the day that his case with Chief Idiagbonya came up for hearing, there was judgement delivery on future timber exploitation in Area B28. The court ruled that in the future from then on, only indigenes of Ewohimi should be contractors to exploit timber from Area B28. An agreement was then signed between the Enogie and the Colonial Government. According to Okogun, he had forgotten about the judgement on Area B28. He kept having sleepless nights over the fact that he abandoned his lucrative business at Umunede because Chief Paul Odigie had convinced him to bring in his timber logging experience and join the timber business at Ewohimi.

The Chief no longer wished that Okogun remained in the business. Okogun felt betrayed and wondered what he could do to get out of the unhappy situation.

One night, *his mother appeared to him in a dream* asking him if he had forgotten an agreement that was signed in the Enogie's Palace concerning the Area B28 Forest Reserve. On waking up, he kept thinking about what his mother had told him in the dream. Eventually he recalled what his mother's question was all about. He then remembered the judgement given on timber exploitation in Area B28 on the same date that his litigation over his father's cow was called for hearing. While he was still visiting the Enogie's Palace as a youth, the Enogie signed the agreement on behalf of Ewohimi indigenes. The agreement specified that in future, only Ewohimi indigenes can be contractor whenever Area B28 was freed for timber prospecting and logging. Okogun decided to use his knowledge of this technical court decision, which appeared to have been forgotten by all to his own advantage.

The Enogie of Ewohimi HRH Usifo Enosegbe II threatens litigation over Area B28 trespass

Okogun went to HRH Usifo Enosegbe II to tell him of the court decision which made the Company exploiting timber at that time in Area B28 a trespasser. The Enogie Usifo Enosegbe II asked for time to check his old files. The Enogie was unable to find such agreement in his files. Okogun thought hard and suspected that late Chief Odigie who was a close confidant of the Enogie Enosegbe I and the Okaigben spokesperson at the time of the litigation agreement might have received and kept a copy of the agreement. Area B28 was entirely on the Okaigben side of Ewohimi.

Hon Joseph O. Odigie, one of the sons of Chief Odigie was known to be in custody of file of documents kept by his late father. Okogun then approached the Honourable to help search for such an agreement in Chief Odigie, his father's files. Honourable J. O. Odigie found the document after a thorough search. For security and political reasons, he did not wish to part with the document or file as parting with the document could lead to its being lost or seized.

Okogun had to plead hard with the Honourable to assist him as the document was a masterstroke card in his efforts to get appointed to the UAC as contractor or get some compensation in his then situation for reminding Ewohimi people of their legally recorded rights over Area B28.. Eventually, Honourable J. O. Odigie graciously agreed to carry the file with the document and accompany Okogun to the Palace. At the Palace, Honourable J.O. Odigie did not part with the file but opened the file to let Enogie Usifo Enosegbe II read the document. The Enogie, looking at the document as Honourable Odigie opened the document page, drafted his letter accusing the Company then logging in Area B28 of trespass with a threat of litigation. The same Company was then exploiting timber in nearby *Area B24 covering Ebelle and Oghu forests in Ewohimi.* The Enogie got his protest letter delivered.

Immediately after receiving the Enogie's letter, the Manager of the trespassing timber Company hurried to Ewohimi to plead with His Royal Highness and stop any threatened litigation. He appeased the Enogie and agreed to comply with the agreement as soon as possible when Ewohimi provided an indigene to be contractor for the timber logging business in Area B28. The first agreed step apparently was to send an Ewohimi indigene knowledgeable in timber business as camp overseer.

Naturally the Enogie, to reward Okogun who had the necessary experience, nominated Okogun to Council at Ewohimi for appointment as Overseer/ Contractor for Area B28. The Council approved.

CHAPTER FIFTEEN

OKOGUN IS APPOINTED TRAINEE OVERSEER IN AREA B28 CAMP UNDER MR. OMONRAMEN

Once Chief Paul Odigie learnt of the approved nomination of Okogun for appointment into Area B28 Camp, Chief Paul Odigie revived what had become a rivalry between Chief Paul Odigie and Okogun. Chief Paul Odigie got *Mr. Ashworth Onakhinor* on his side. Chief Paul Odigie and Mr. Ashworth Onakhinor put forward some other name to substitute and replace Okogun as Overseer/Contractor in Area B28. Chief Paul Odigie openly declared that he would use all in his powers to dislodge Okogun from getting appointed. The Chief was not happy that Okogun was leaving his camp for better prospects. Chief P. Odigie and Mr. Onakhinor went to the Enogie to present their arguments against Okogun's appointment.

The issues they raised included the fact that Okogun was not a member of the Ogboni fraternity. Apart from themselves, *Chief A.D. John* was another notable and prestigious member of the Ogboni Fraternity in Ewohimi. It must be mentioned that Chief Paul E. Odigie courageously resigned his membership of the Fraternity years before he died though at some costs as was told. The Enogie considered asking someone else to be appointed while Okogun's name remained in the books but later dropped the idea and insisted on his original nomination of Okogun that had gone through Council. Okogun's struggle to get the employment he had been nominated for and approved by the Council was long and marked with courage, dedication to the course of justice and a struggle against oppression and persecution even from relatives. Chief Paul

Odigie and Mr. A. Onakhinor belonged to the same Ibhiaigbiya larger family of Idinrio who by tradition are cousins.

The struggle took Okogun on his bicycle rides to several of the Managers of the UAC at *Ekpon, Agbor, Amahor and elsewhere* armed with petitions and documents. The Enogie, HRH Usifo Enosegbe II did not oppose his efforts but gave tacit approval to them. Among the Managers who were all Europeans to whom he delivered documents, were *Messrs. D. D. Smith, Convoy or Connolly, Parrot and Hew*[46].

At the end, Okogun triumphed. He was appointed and was sent to the UAC Area B28 Camp as Trainee Overseer under Mr. Omonramen. The good news of his appointment enhanced the joy on the safe delivery[47], a few days earlier, by Ailegbesuan of a bouncing beautiful baby girl. Ailegbesuan Angelina had labour pains and was trying to get to town possibly to the Maternity when the baby arrived as she reached Idumu-agho. Okogun with part of his family including Angelina was still in Chief Paul Odigie's timber camp near River Odu along Idumu-agho farm road at the time.

The baby was delivered at Okogun's sister Mrs. Owobu Ikekhide's house at Idumu-agho. Okogun resumed duty as trainee overseer on APRIL 1, 1950. April fool's day turned April blessings day for Okogun.

Experience under Mr Omonramen

The appointment under Mr. Omonramen as trainee overseer was quite interesting in many ways for Okogun. Mr Omonramen assigned duties to Okogun as he felt he should and treated Okogun with due regard. Omonramen gave Okogun appropriate residence in the camp. Okogun moved into the Camp with two of his wives: Ailegbesuan and Maria leaving Enimaluole to look after his residence by Ofuri Market in the village. Mr Omonramen also felt unsafe or uncomfortable with Okogun's presence. Omonramen had been told that Okogun had some extraordinary powers and was from a strong family.

Mr. Omonramen was so worried that he invited his brother a self-acclaimed wizard to come to him in the camp at Ewohimi. Omonramen's senior brother came to Ewohimi to carry out an investigation about Okogun. He had spent days with Omonramen in the Camp when on one afternoon, Okogun suddenly got invited to Mr. Omonramen's residence in the camp by Mr. Omonramen.

Okogun was very worried and he was scared. He felt unsafe. He told his wives who encouraged him to summon up courage and go. He acted exactly as encouraged by his wives and did what he had to do to protect himself and be on guard.

On reaching Mr. Omonramen's house, he met Mr Omonramen and his senior brother visitor in the sitting room. They offered him a sit. They welcomed the visitor by performing the usual Esan ritual of breaking kola nuts, also widely practised in other Nigerian cultures.

Mr. Omonramen's senior brother as the eldest man[22] among them, broke the kola nuts and led the prayer. He offered Okogun a lobe of the kola nut in the usual way. Okogun was reluctant and they noticed his feeling of insecurity and assured him that all was well.

Okogun took the kola nut offered to him. That done, senior Omonramen went on to discuss his mission of coming to Ewohimi and his findings. He, Omonramen senior had been in Ewohimi for several days then. As a wizard, he claimed, he had been out during all the nights he had spent in Ewohimi looking for and interacting with the local witches and wizards. He checked all the covens and did not find Okogun in any of them. His brother's fears therefore had been groundless, and his investigations revealed that Okogun was a good man. Okogun should therefore feel free to eat the prayer kola given to him. Okogun's fears were thus dispelled and he gave a sigh of relief.

Mr Omonramen, the Overseer thereafter felt at ease in Okogun's company. Later Overseer Omonramen related a strange story about their father's declaration on witchcraft. Mr. Omonramen as a young child had accompanied their father on a visit to a neighbouring quarter. The journey to the neighbouring quarters took him and his father through a footpath across a bush. On the homeward journey their father asked him, as is usually the case when parents walk with their young children, to walk in front. He walked on without looking backwards until he emerged from the bush on their own side of the village. He then noticed that their father was not following and was not in sight. It was dusk and he was afraid but had to wait till their father emerged.

Their father, on arrival, confessed and explained the cause of his delay in the bush path. Their father started by saying that the life of a wizard was not a good one. That he had come across on the ground along the footpath, a sacrifice (*izobo)* meant for witches and wizards (*emhankhain, ebo-ason*). He divulged the fact that as a wizard, he could not pass without eating from the sacrifice. He therefore declared to his son that witchcraft should not be given to one's children. He had therefore initiated only Omonramen's senior brother into witchcraft (given to eat). He further stated that if there were benefits that witchcraft could achieve for the family, the senior son would take charge. Thereafter the Overseer Omonramen and the trainee-overseer Okogun became close friends.

A giant python/boar constrictor is killed and the Enogie demands his traditional rights

There was another incident during Okogun's stint as trainee overseer. One of the brave workers at the camp fought and killed a boar constrictor or python which he spied standing parallel with and leaning on a tall tree waiting for a prey. With assistance from colleagues, he dragged the dead snake which was over nine feet long to the camp and presented it to Mr Omonramen. Mr. Omonramen being an Esan instructed that the reptile be taken to the Odionwele or the Enogie[48]. The Enogie got the report and after waiting for days without hearing from Idumu-agho's Odionwele then *Pa Ikhile*, he summoned Pa Ikhile to the Palace to resolve the matter in accordance with the traditional guidelines. The carcass of the reptile was delivered to the Enogie who decided on its disposal according to the customary rites. The killing of dangerous beasts by anyone was one of the heroic acts usually rewarded by the Enogie with chieftaincy titles. Parents of such brave men or women also rewarded the persons.

In 1952 after one and half years of Okogun's appointment as trainee overseer, the camp and timber business by the UAC in Area B28 was dissolved. It was not clear to Okogun why the UAC left the business in Area B28. All the workers including Omonramen and Okogun all packed their belongings and left the camp for their various homes. The Camp was evacuated. Okogun then needed to work out the next business plan.

CHAPTER SIXTEEN

OKOGUN IS FORCED TO PULL DOWN HIS OLD RESIDENCE TO REPLACE IT W ITH A NEW ONE TO FACE THE MARKET

In 1951, the Enogie of Ewohimi decided that the *Ewohimi Ewatto Ohordua road,* which passed from *Idumigie* through part of *Idumuguokha-noriuwa* through bushes and a steep hill, called *Ozoguor or Aitanu's hill* should be closed and replaced with a less lonely road to go from Ofuri Market through Uwi-Idinrio to Ewatto and Ohordua. The new proposed road was then surveyed. The surveyed road passed through the back of Okogun's house with a few feet from the walls of his house. The toilets of his house located a distance from the house were cut off from the house and located across on the other side of the new road. Okogun had no alternative but to pull down his house and rebuild. The old house faced the *Idumu-agho-Idumobo-Uzebu* road with Ofuri Market to the right of the house.

The Uwi-Idinrio Community as was the practice mashed a portion of the mud that would be used to erect the walls of the new house. As the mud for the proposed building was being mashed at the old building area, a point was struck. To the surprise of all onlookers, unadulterated palm oil, from its appearance, gushed out from the ground at that point. When asked, Okogun calmly replied that the palm oil was associated with some protective charm made on the grounds before the former building was erected. The palm oil was mixed with the new mash. Special Yoruba-speaking wall setters probably from *Akoko Edo* and *Ekiti* areas were brought in to erect the wall of the new house. Okogun then in 1953/54 felt that it was safe to roof the new building with corrugated iron sheets to fulfill his dream of the early 1940s when he erected his first residence on the same site. He gave the new building a corrugated iron sheet roof.

The preparation of the mashed mud for the new building started late in 1953. The building was completed in 1954. In 1954, there was public confession of witchcraft activities by some men and women. The episode was triggered by the alarm raised by one Mr. *Azali* of Uzebu who said after eating in a man's house, he found himself at night in a gathering on the street when he tried to sleep. The confessions were supervised by the charmed masquerades led by *Obomhenzoya* from Uzebu. Obomhenzoya was famous as a masquerade that exercised extra ordinary magical and spiritual powers. The witchcraft confessions of evil perpetrated by them, as they believed and said, included the death of one of Okogun's daughters that Okogun named *Aimuagbonrie.* The name literally means one does not die carrying the world home: interpreted to mean one dies and leaves everything of the world behind. Aimuagbonrie was living then with her grandmother, *Iloalo* at Oghu when she died. The confession was that by agreement with Oghu witches and wizards, the life of Aimuagbonrie was taken. People drew various conclusions from the sad loss of Aimuagbonrie at the time the new building was being erected.

The decision to destroy the old building for a new one might also have been encouraged by the fact that in March 1953, Enimaluole, Okogun's eldest wife died. Her children Mary, Lucy, Joseph, Robert and Aiterebhe survived her.

OKOGUN'S RESIDENCE COMPLETED 1954

Okogun's first three wives and their business

Okogun always showed appreciation for Enimaluole for giving him strong support in the building of his family and fulfilling the role that Esekhor proclaimed as Esekhor was about to die. He regarded Enimaluole as his partner in progress. He mourned her in a special traditional way.

Okogun was married to three wives up to the mid-1950s. They were *Enimaluole Iyawo, Ailegbesuan Angelina and Imanrhokanbhor Maria.* They lived as sisters, respected one another, had much regard for hierarchy especially with respect to morning and other formal greetings.

Enimaluole was very industrious and traded mostly on salt. She mounded wet salt using various sizes of gourd fruit ends as her mold. The open end of each mold with the salt slurry was sealed with a leaf of *Jatropha curcas* (*oluluebo)* cut to size and placed on a metal sheet mounted over a fire to dry. The dried and firm salt sizes sold for one penny, two pennies and three pence, respectively. Enimaluole and Angelina were good loom weavers of the native cotton cloth.

The other wives Angelina and Maria also engaged in this mini salt industry and market. They all had their allotted plots in the farm in which they planted pepper, garden eggs and cassava. In some years, they also planted melon and pigeon peas (*olele*). The planting and harvesting of pigeon peas were communally done in the family under Okogun's supervision.

Enimaluole sometimes helped *Madam Isemuan, Mr. Michael Obomense's mother and Ugbadegu of Pa Aigbe of Ueren Ogbe's family of Uwi-Idinrio* to sell dried bush meat on her own market booth. The dried bush meat served as side attraction for her salt wares. She also wove cloth for men and women and sold harvests of pepper and cassava tubers from the farm plots allotted to her as was the case with her other colleagues. Ugbadegu also allotted plots of farmland to her in his farm. Ugbadegu was an interesting character who was dumb but could mutter some words. He was very observant and wise. Because he could not engage in the usual conversations, he would listen, observe, and contributed to discussions by nodding and mutter *omagbe e* meaning "it is very good". He made this statement even when there is bereavement to show his sympathy.

Lucy stops schooling

In 1951, when things got somehow uncertain with the timber business, Okogun decided that he would no more be able to pay school fees for *Lucy Ebatele Atupele* but that he would do his best to keep the boys in School. Lucy is Okogun's second daughter. Enimaluole, Lucy's mother decided to take over the paying of the school fees as Lucy was doing quite well in School. In 1952, Enimaluole fell ill after an accident with Okogun. She could no longer trade and so Lucy had to stop school in 1952. Lucy was to be in Standard Five, semifinal primary school year. It should be stated here that Lucy, from about 1948 till then, led the Okogun farm weeding gang made up of his junior brothers.

Enimaluole, her death and mourning by Okogun

Enimaluole died[49, 50] at a very early age on March 5, 1953 indirectly from injuries sustained in the accident. Five children, three females and two males survived her. She had instructed Okogun before her death to send her most junior child, Aiterebhe[51] to her junior sister *Oshioaye Telefi* who was married to a Muslim from Kano that at that time settled at Ubiaja. Okogun did just that. Enimaluole made prophetic statements that came true about the future life of her children while ill on her death bed.

She did the extraordinary by giving plates to *Mrs. Christiana Ebemamhen Ilegbodu nee Okogie*, one of *Pa Joe Esezobor Ilegbodu's* wives with the instruction to give the plates to the wife[52] of her second son, *Joseph* as if she was sure that Joseph who was then fourteen years old would live to the age of marriage and consummate a marriage.

Okogun was very sad over her death. Custom and tradition prescribed that a husband mourned the first wife in a special way involving some rituals. If the husband was polygamous, he was required to ritually mourn only the first wife. Okogun mourned Enimaluole accordingly wearing rags, having a bow and arrow by his side, and staying and sleeping on the floor for four nights and without having a bath. The children were surprised and felt uneasy to see their strong father performing the mourning rites.

gods in Okogun's house and compound

Okogun had gods and charms, which he said were all protective and harmless to people. There were some, which were just medium sized stones like the one called *ihiezi rock* in the compound near the hedge at the entrance into the compound. The ihiezi stone was probably taken from a part of the Odu River called Ihiezi. There was the tall tree, called *iyantor* (literal translation meaning ownership of land) *Newbouldia laevis (Ikhinmin)* located strategically at a corner of the compound. The spirits of ancestors in general are venerated at the iyantor shrine. *Idigun* was the blacksmith's god. A small hut was made for *Idigun* and the structure served the dual purpose of Idigun worship and blacksmith workshop because it had the anvil, hammer, bellows and furnace place and iron tongs or pliers, etc. that were typical blacksmiths' implements.

Veneration of ancestors and Ukhure

At a corner of the sitting room inside the house, the inside house shrine for the veneration of the family male ancestors' spirits *(alu-arinmin)* had several short sticks between one foot(30cm) and one and a half feet(50cm) long. The sticks about two inches (5cm) in diameter were made from branches cut from the *N. laevis (*Ikhinmin) tree. Each of these sticks *(ukhure)* was dressed at the base with several rings of laced cowries. Each ukhure represented a member of the dead family fathers. The one for Omovuon looked newest and most prominent of the collections. Okogun had one for Esekhor, his mother along the passage leading to his bedroom and not in the public view. All reparations for the violations of family relationships including malice, grudges, evil thoughts, words and actions always included using prescribed pounded yam and meat sacrifice at the ukhure shrine. It was always a communion service in the issues of malice and grudges. An additional symbolic ritual was to place charcoal on a broken gourd that was used to motion the malice and grudge out of the head and chest of the guilty family member. Trans-family violations went to the *Ogbe bhi Ohen* shrine or the community *iyantor shrine* located at the beginning of the community farm road.

Often, violations of family relationships were supposedly detected when someone had health and other challenges that forced the relatives to go to diviners to find out the cause of the challenges. Reparations may include other benefits for the diviner and the people know that the diviner's findings often may have nothing to do with the spirits of the ancestors. The practice was abused by some diviners for personal gains apart from what their clients needed to present as consultation gifts and gifts of gratitude. To ensure that the diviners do not unnecessarily invoke his spirit against his children when he died, Chief Odigie Osaguona Ilegbedion, the Ologbosere constructed what would be the Ukhure to represent him when he died. He was reported to have cast his own ukhure in bronze with his pubic hair sealed in it and then presented it to the people to say that his ukhure would never go against his children after his death and no diviner can prescribe sacrifice to him from any of his children.

There was *osun* consisting of a small pot holding some liquid, stones, cowries, special objects, sticks and long canes of a special plant (*aghenren otan*) in his bedroom.

There were one or two charms *(aban)* pinned to the wall or on top of the door with inverted u-shaped strong iron pin. Aban was used to pin down problems, death, persons' spiritual attacks, etc.

A shade was made in the women's quadrangle for Esekhor's gods (*ake and olokun*). The Esekhor gods were held and served by Uhuomonye the most senior sister of Okogun and daughter of Esekhor as the chief priestess. The gods came with her when she left Uzebu to be initially housed by Okogun before her son Willie Ehikhamen Osalumense Ojieyan (Ogieyan as pronounced in Ewohimi dialect) also left Uzebu to build his house near Ofuri Market. The gods then were relocated when Uhomonye moved them to her sector of Ehikhamen's house.

Ehi (Guardian Angel) symbolism and recognition of the Creator

In the lintel of the main door entrance into the house at the sitting room was an equilateral triangular hole in the wall. A cylindrical white chalk was placed in the hole and it was the God's angel or guardian Angel *(ehi)* shrine. By the ehi hole were some specially shaped small leather pouches that enclosed charms which had nothing to do with ehi but served as extra protective measures. The various gods except *ehi* were worshiped in various ways and seasons. *Ehi* which represented the dedication of the residence and the occupants to God's protection through the guardian angels was not worshipped. People knelt there to pray to God through their respective guardian angels.

Okogun related an incident which appeared to him to support the defensive powers of *ehi* and the protective charms with it at the main door entrance into the house. It concerned a very important man from the family of one of the chiefs in the village who was senior to Okogun. The man decided surprisingly to bring, all by himself, a keg of palm wine to Okogun. Okogun liked his palm-wine. As the man stepped across the main door to enter the house holding the palm wine, the keg without touching any object detached itself from its neck downwards. The palm wine from the shattered keg flooded the ground at the entrance. The man was shocked and without saying a word looked at Okogun with awe and turned back. Okogun in his wisdom and trust in God did not pursue the matter further with the man.

The ancestors were worshiped during the annual festivals and when there was need for a member of the family to appease the ancestors for violating some injunctions or commandments or for bearing malice, etc.

Esekhor's ake was also worshipped annually during ukpeze Eguae feast and when there was a sin against the god or a covenant taking ritual for a female. Items like relics taken from the ake or Idigun could be placed under a fruit tree to scare off people from harvesting the fruits. Iyantor was worshiped for protection or if there was a violation of commandments.

The worships most of the time involved two or three molded pounded yam placed one on top of the other and a bowl of soup with wildlife or sacrificial goat meat. The most popular wildlife meat was antelope meat. Other meats were from the local rabbit or wild giant rat, porcupine, cutting grass and wild pig. When sacrifice was because of violating community and family commandments on harmonious and peaceful life, a live goat procured by the guilty may be prescribed for atonement sacrifice at the community shrine.

Idigun was worshiped with special spice sauce made with tortoise meat that is well spiced with alligator pepper *(asin-edo), Aframomum melegueta* K. Schum.*;* Benin/Guinea pepper (*ighele/ighere), Piper guineense* Schumach and the roots of an aromatic plant called *osunmadan (Pentadiplandra brazzeana* Baill.). The historical significane of Idigun, the god of iron shrine dates to Ehimin, Okogun's great great grandfather who failed the initiation ritual into the native doctor's profession as already described.

Osun was worshipped annually with a fowl and pounded yam made from special white yams *Dioscorea spp. (akpe) which must be harvested* from Okogun's farm. Okogun usually planted this species first in the new farm to ensure early harvest for the osun worship. The osun worship must be carried out before new yam is eaten in his house. *The worship ushered in the new yam season.*

It was notable and significant that it was only *ehi* that was used only for prayers kneeling by the door and not worshipped with sacrifices. *Mr. Johnson Iyamah Imhanredon*[53] explained the role and significance of ehi and why it was not worshipped.

There was a wide-mouth large earthenware bowl of water containing sticks, cowries, stones, kernels, special water-impermeable round objects made of baked clay that was used for having protective baths, and this was never worshipped. Located on either side of the main entrance or gate into the premises was a tall plant from a *Ficus spp (obadan)* or from *Newbouldia laevis growing* on either side of the gate to which were tied across the path the young buds of palm trees(*igiomen)* during the annual ancestral festivals. Mr. Iyamah[54] explained that the *igiomen* were used to usher in good spirits into the premises during the festival.

The gradual removal of the gods

When Okogun built the new house, the ihiezi was left out. The others that were brought into the new premises gradually all faded away with time. At the end, those that remained were unceremoniously removed from the house as shall be described.

Okogun was able to gradually remove the gods from his residence and larger family life for three reasons.

First, as already explained he was the living head of the most senior house or family in Aigbiya of Idinrio line. Even though his Ehimin – Eze line could not retain the divination traditional doctor title, the seniority of his house was not contested. His family line ownership of the head blacksmith workshop and god of iron shrine, *Idigun* was recognized. As the then current head of the head-house who had Christian sympathy, he had some authority to decide on the fate of the gods.

He knew that there could be consequences and attacks for his action, but he acted with conscience and faith in the supremacy of God.

The second reason was that at a point Okogun became the most senior living male and hence father of the Eze family line as well as the second or third oldest man in Idinrio. The older cousins and his older sisters who insisted on worshipping their ancestors through the gods in Okogun's premises had all passed on. At his ripe old age, he was expected to take responsibility for the worship of family gods and to be the voice of the living in speaking with the spirits of ancestors, praying, and interceding for the living larger family members.

As time passed, if anyone came to report that he or she wished to make sacrifice to the *Idigun* because a diviner had prescribed that as the solution to the children's problems, Okogun would reject the sacrifice and declare that his *Idigun* was not the type that created problems but brought blessings and protection for people. To satisfy the anxious and superstitious relative, he would take the person to the *Idigun* and pray for the person and for healing and blessings using a white piece of chalk or powdered mixture of white chalk and common salt: there was a saying that white chalk and common salt do not quarrel, and the mixture symbolized peaceful coexistence, protection and blessings.

Thirdly, Okogun supported and encouraged many of the younger members of his family when they decided to be Christians. He prayed for such members of family, requested them to be genuine Christians and practise their faith. He assured them that if they practiced their Christian faith, no harm could get to them.

As a result, the sacrifice usually consisting of food and meat had fewer and fewer consumers as the years came and passed until Okogun was being left with the wives to share the pounded yam and meat sacrifice. They ate the sacrifice with most of the children keeping their distance. Most of the children had with his encouragement become Christians.

Okogun's herbal practice and ethnobotany

Okogun's ancestors and sisters were hunters, blacksmiths, and traditional doctors in their various rights. He therefore practiced herbal medicine as a side business only for special illnesses. He knew the use of many herbs and plants and knew their native names as well. His stint in the timber industry widened his knowledge of ethnobotany. He knew and passed on to his children and wives the use of such plants[55] like *Cleome orientalis or* C*leome ciliata* Schumach. & Thonn. *(umomo otor), Calliandra portoricencis* (Jacq.) Benth *(ivu), Schumanniophyton magnificum* Harms. *(aide), Newbouldia laevis* (P. Beauv.) Seem. ex Bureau *(ikhinmin), Abrus precatoris* L. *(ikpenlo afinamen), Bryophyllum pinnatum* (Lam.) Oken *(alumekue, ebe gbidigbidi), Myrianthus arboreus* P. Beauv. *(ihieghe), Anthocleista vogelli* Afzel. Ex R. Br. *(orinmoghu), Erythreophleum suaveolens* (Guill. & Perr.) Brenan *(*sashwood, ordeal plant, *ohankin), Ocimum gratissimum* L. *(aranmokhor), Musanga smithii* R.Br. (*ohoghe), etc.* He was a specialist in the treatment of swollen spleen in mostly children. He used chalk and *Cleome orientalis, Aframomum melegueta* with antelope part. Okogun passed this herbal treatment to his most junior wife Madam Julie Agbonizebeta.

C. portoricencis with a pinch of faeces he said was used to get masqueraders into excited moods. The potion was called *ohenre.* The practice parallels the use of skatole, a chemical that is found naturally in human faeces, to give aroma[56a] to ice cream.

M. arborea roots he said were used with ordeal plant, sashwood to potentiate the extract when prejudicially given to those regarded as extremely wicked persons or witches or wizards. Such persons were regarded as undesirable elements in the community. The roots of *M. arborea* have triterpene acids[56b] which explains its role in the ordeal concoction.

S. magnificum was used to arrest vomiting following snakebite so that other anti-venom recipes could be applied. *M. smithii* was also tapped for drinking water during dry season.

A potion containing rat's eyes for seeing charms at night

Okogun was interested in wooing a girl possibly to become his wife before he met Enimaluole. The family of the girl was probably in *Idumuogo* area in Eguae, Ewohimi.

He would normally visit the girl at night to spend time. The mother of the girl gave tacit support to his association with the daughter. But the case was different with the girl's father who had strong objections to his mission. He kept making his night visits to the girl in the women's apartment. Okogun had to go through the parlour or living room in the men's apartment to have access to the women's apartment.

He realized that the father in desperation was aiming harmful charms at him. He reported to a native doctor who prepared a potion for him. The potion was made from substances that included the eyes of rats. He would rub the potion over his eyes. He was told that with the potion rubbed over his eyes, he would see the location of any harmful charm placed on his path to harm him. He successfully used the potion once to avoid such a trap made by the girl's father to harm him on a visit to his girlfriend at night. The man realizing that he had avoided stepping over the trap by clambering on the mud seats by the wall in the parlour, called him a wizard. After the incident he terminated his relations with the girl and mother.

Charm to possess extraordinary out of person vision: death of a daughter and reprisal

Okogun was liked by many people for various reasons which included his regard for elders and his generousity and kind-heartedness especially towards the aged and oppressed persons. His admirers included diviners wrongly referred to by the West as *African witch doctors*. One such admirer offered to give Okogun, probably while still at Uzebu, a charm which empowered him to have vision of night activities especially witchcraft in the village when he slept. He accepted the charm which was an object that he was instructed to place under his pillow at night while he slept. One night at Uzebu, as he slept with his head on the pillow and charm, he had a vision involving his third daughter, *Oyugbo.* In the vision he saw Oyugbo being carried away by a woman whose face he knew. Suddenly, the child became a goat and was slaughtered. Shortly after the episode or the next day, Oyugbo suddenly took ill and died. He related the vision experience to Uhuomonye, his most senior sister and guardian. Uhuomonye got the description of the woman Okogun saw in the vision and Uhuomonye knew the woman. Uhuomonye decided to arrange a trap that would prove the alleged woman's guilt or innocence. Early in morning Uhuomonye scrubbed her sitting room at Uzebu mixing materials taken from Esekhor's gods (*ake and olokun)* with the scrubbing emulsion at the entrance from outside to the sitting room. She ordered that no one should pass through the door and invited the suspected woman to visit her for some gift and discussion. Uhuomonye was in the habit of giving gifts to the woman. The woman came in through the front door to Uhuomonye's sitting room. Uhuomonye had discussions and paid the usual courtesies to her and she left to return to her residence. The woman after the visit was attacked by acute diarrhoea and died not long after without recovering from the disease.

Okogun decided to throw the extra-body vision charm away into the bush because according to him, he was able to have visions of evil but was powerless at preventing the evil seen in the visions. Such powers he decided were useless.

CHAPTER SEVENTEEN

OKOGUN AS A TIMBER CONTRACTOR: HIS LORRY, AGBOR PROPERTY DEVELOPMENT AND OTHER BUSINESS ENTERPRISES

Okogun to join the Ogboni Fraternity or lose participation in the timber business

After two years of closure of the United Africa Company, UAC Area B28 camp, the issue of indigenous contractor to exploit timber in the forest was revisited at the instance of Okogun through the Enogie of Ewohimi, HRH Usifo Enosegbe II. Okogun was used to the races to be run in negotiating with the various timber interests. The Management of the UAC, now under Mr. Matthew/Martin also knew him. The Enogie had no problem proposing that Okogun should be the indigenous contractor to exploit timber in that forest. When the proposal was known, a lot of strong influences rose to oppose Okogun as the sole contractor for the business. Okogun belonged to no cult in a place where the Ogboni influence was strong among some highly placed persons in the society. Eventually, the Enogie agreed to a compromise whereby it was agreed that *HRH the Enogie himself, chief Paul Odigie, chief A D John, and Mr. Okogun Omovuon* should be joint contractors for the timber business. A condition was set that Okogun should join the *Ogboni Fraternity* to which the other three belonged[57]. Okogun reluctantly but provisionally agreed to abide by the conditions set for his acceptance as one of the contractors. Date after date were set for Okogun to join the cult but Okogun kept postponing his initiation into the cult. He kept pleading for time to enable him to put together all that was required for the initiation.

The other members had lost their patience with him. They then decided to give him an ultimatum by setting a final date for the initiation. A decision would be taken against him and leave him out of the timber business if he failed to submit to the initiation event. On the night before the morning when he was supposed, without fail, to travel with the persons taking him for the initiation, he was attacked by a serious feverish illness and he could not leave his house. On investigation, HRH the Enogie Enosegbe II found out that he genuinely fell ill. After this, he was left in peace reluctantly by the Ogboni members.

They probably got convinced that Okogun's spirit did not accept the Ogboni spirit. They retained him as one of the four contractors but would often leave him out of many discussions.

Okogun's investment of his timber business returns from the timber business

News came that a UAC-affiliated Expatriate Mr. Matthew or Martin had applied to reopen timber business in Area B28. Okogun led the way to run the race leading to the reopening of the Area B28 timber camp. He used his knowledge of the UAC and the timber logging terrain to advantage. The Area B28 timber workers' camp reopened in 1954 under the four personalities as contractors. Okogun in addition to being one of the contractors supervised the timber logging business. After the first year of business, Okogun's share of profits from the business was one thousand two hundred pounds sterling. That was big money then. The business lasted for about four years. Okogun prided himself on the way he used the money he got from the business.

Agbor property development and Lorry business

Okogun bought a plot of land at *Ireguae* Street near the market at *Boji Boji*, Agbor. Mr. Josiah Ajieh of Omen Eguae who had helped him almost twenty years earlier at Agbor, identified the property and directed him to it. *Mr. Ehikhamen of Ikemenzelomon*, Okaigben and *Mr. Gabriel Iyoriobhe of Idumobo* who was like his godson, all Ewohimi indigenes who were successful traders at Agbor helped in the feasibility study and negotiations leading to the buying of the plot of land. They also helped to ensure that no one trespassed on the land.

Okogun spoke the Ika language fluently having lived at Agbor and Umunede and had made other friends at Agbor. One of such family friends we later came to know was *Mr. Ebeye* of Boji Boji Agbor. His fluency in the Ika dialect and in other Ibo dialects helped.

By 1959, he had built[58] on the plot of land. This was a major achievement at that time. Chief Ekwunife followed by his son Joseph served as caretaker of the property until their respective deaths and no reliable replacement was available.

Okogun sent his children to Secondary Schools and laid out plans to educate some of them to the highest level so that those so educated would later help in the education of his junior children. In pursuance of this objective, when one of his sons, Joseph unexpectedly passed the entrance examination and was admitted as a student to read chemistry degree at the University College Ibadan, Okogun decided to sell the Agbor property to pay the fees. Joseph objected and *the Catholic Mission* under *Bishop Patrick J. Kelly* of Benin graciously came to the rescue. Joseph was offered a Catholic Mission sponsorship and made to sign a bond to teach for the Catholic Mission for eight years after the four-year course. The Bishop released Joseph to return for his Ph.D. studies after eighteen months service at St. Anthony's College, Ubulu Uku.

Agbor Property built 1959 sold 2014

Honourable Joseph O. Odigie graciously took Okogun and Joseph to *Ibusa* to meet the Reverend Father *Catholic Education Secretary* and the bond was signed. Hon. Joseph O. Odigie was witness.

The Transportation business

Okogun later bought a Bedford lorry in a cooperation with the then Manager of the UAC Produce and General Merchandise Company Shop at Eguae, Ewohimi which they used for the transportation of palm produce to the ports in the Delta and for the transportation of passengers and traders to and from Onitsha and the Delta. They wrote the adage "Evidence of Labour" on the face of the lorry whose licence plate Benin registration number was *B2010.* The UAC Shop Manager was an Ijaw man named *Mr. Toba.* On the 28th August 1956, an agreement was signed between Okogun and Mr. Toba handing over full ownership of the vehicle to Okogun. Okogun paid three hundred pounds (£300:00) to Mr. Toba for this purpose. Okogun ran the business until 4th October 1957 when he sold the lorry for two hundred and fifty pounds (£250:00) to Mr. *Andrew I.O. Isimanreonkhai* of Iselu, Ewohimi who paid two hundred pounds cash. He was to pay the remaining fifty pounds over sixteen months.

Some of those who worked as lorry Conductors for Okogun were *Mr. Benson Imontu of Uwi-Idinrio/Idumuguokha-ugbolobhede*, Mr. *Felix A. Odigie* then residing at Idumobo and Mr. *Dickson Asoa* from Idumigie, his mother's village.

It must be mentioned that about the same time, *Chief Paul E. Odigie and Mr. S. Okagbue, the then John Holts Manager* combined to buy a lorry for similar transport business carried out by Mr. Toba and Okogun. Paul and Okagbue had the word *"Patience"* on the front hood of their own lorry. Patience took palm produce from the John Holts to the Delta Ports.

Margaret Edelokun and Julie Agbonizebeta married as young wives

Okogun was able to buy and enjoy the luxury of a pleasure car but he did not, and he used his wealth in the way described. All he did for movement was to keep changing his bicycles when they aged. He enjoyed riding his bicycles. Probably one of the last bicycles that he bought was a Raleigh bicycle with licence plate registration number *MW061605* for which he paid ten shillings as registration fees to the Ishan Central District Council, Ubiaja on 11th December 1969.

Okogun often referred to the discipline he enforced on himself to avoid luxury and influence by investing his wealth on the education of his children and in business. It is appropriate to discuss at this point of relative prosperity, Okogun's fresh marriages to expand the size of his family and a sort of provision for his old age. Between 1955 and 1957 Okogun married two young wives *Margaret Edelokun nee Otoagwa* of Okogun's mother's quarters Idumigie who also belonged to *Chief Ihaza of Idumigie* family and *Julie Agbonizebeta nee Ighainghain* from *Idumebo/Ikhekhe*, Ewatto. These young girls then as he said later were additionally to look after him in his old age because the other two surviving wives were beginning to show signs of age. Margaret had the Primary School leaving Certificate and hence was to help Okogun with secretarial issues. Julie did really help with the farm and other duties and survived Okogun to help look after the family compound and lands after Okogun's death, but Margaret did not survive him.

OKOGUN IN THE 1970s

The death of Margaret Edelokun

Margaret was literate and that was one of the other attractions Okogun had in her. Unfortunately, Margaret died very young on Christmas Day, 1967 at *the St Camillus Catholic Hospital, Uromi* during childbirth. It was a very sad and shocking tragedy for all. Okogun registered Margaret at the Catholic Hospital. It was not clear why he did so because his wives delivered their babies at home or at one of the Maternity Homes at Ewohimi or Ewatto or Ewossa. The records kept by Okogun showed receipts of payment[59] of hospital fees beginning from August 1967. His last payment to the Hospital for surgery was twelve pounds on Christmas Day 1967. Margaret Edelokun did not survive the surgery and the baby was still born. Obviously, a good midwife at Ewohimi who diagnosed complications well ahead of time must have recommended the hospital care.

Sorrow enveloped Okogun, his inlaw Otoagwa and their families. The Christmas celebrations could not be for the two families.

There was the problem of taking the body back to Ewohimi from Uromi. All transport owners had gone to their homes for the Christmas and New Year celebrations. No transporter could be found. Okogun found the situation embarrassing. It also aggravated his sorrow. Joseph was home from Ibadan for the celebrations and he had a Peugeot 403 saloon car. There was a strong and popular superstition that a driver who carried a dead person in his vehicle ran the risk of having unpleasant incidents including seeing the spirit of the dead person if he looked through his rear mirror. To save the embarrassing situation, Joseph prayerfully decided to drive to Uromi to bring the corpse to Ewohimi despite all the superstitions associated with such a duty.

Okogun felt some relief and prayerfully supported Joseph's decision to undertake the adventure as it appeared. Mr. Otoagwa, the bereaved father kindly decided to accompany Joseph to accomplish the unpleasant task even for Mr. Otoagwa. Mr. Otoagwa's and another man's presence was reassuring to all. There were no incidents in the execution of the task and the corpse was safely brought for burial at home. Mrs. Margaret E. Okogun left behind three surviving children, Victoria, *Thomas, and Solomon.*

Other businesses embarked upon

Okogun made other investment efforts that had varying degrees of success or failure. He built a complex having several stores and a residential part by Ofuri Market. The building was at the junction *of Iselu and Idinrio – Ewatto – Ohordua* roads.

The miniplaza was completed and opened for use on July 31, 2017

One of the stores was used to store palm kernel sacks. Palm kernel traders operating at Ewohimi and from Igueben bought the palm kernel at the market and kept the sacks of palm kernel in the store till they were ready for evacuation. In those days Chief Esangbedo's lorry vehicles brought his palm kernel traders to buy palm kernel from the market. Another important group of occupants at the complex were Igbos who were tinkers. The stores business was a success story but by 1993, the building had virtually fallen apart and was eventually abandoned. The development was partly due to the situation that had befallen Ofuri Market as earlier related. As a memorial for Okogun a miniplaza has been built on the plot of land where Okogun built his stores.

Mr. Okanu was a blacksmith from Awka. He and *Mr. Oji* another blacksmith who resided in the Akhigbe W. Odigie premises by the market from the 1940 s had by this time returned to their homes due to old age.

Messrs Bosah Chukwura and Chike were at a time staff of *the John Holts Stores* and palm produce depot opposite the market by *Idumu-odu* Street during the time of *Mr. Okagbue* who was the last Manager of the Stores before it was closed. Mr. Okagbue took over from Mr. *Ononye* as Manager of the John Holts at Okaigben, Ewohimi and they were all Onitsha indigenes. Okogun saw the Igbos as brothers and friends to the extent that he sent one of his sons, *Felix Osatohanmhen Okogun* to live and serve Mr. Bosah Chukwurah.

In those days, an itinerant medical doctor came in his car monthly on a day visit to attend to patients at the John Holts premises. Mand B injections and tablets were popular with the people in the village who had much faith in the efficacy of the prescriptions. One of the pieces of advice given those days was that one should not use onions in meals when on M and B injections or tablets. The other Igbos were mainly tinkers who mended leaking metal containers like kerosene lamps and the four-gallon tins used initially to import kerosene into Nigeria and afterwards turned into use for palm oil and water. The tins also served the people as vessels for fetching water from the Odu River and the tins of water, about 18 litres, were carried back home on the head over the five-mile journey.

The Ugbodu forest venture

Okogun wanted to expand and further exploit his knowledge of the timber logging industry. Apparently, *Mr. Ugbukpon of Ohordua* had informed him about a forest in *Ugbodu* in the Delta State which the Ugbodu people were willing to lease to any timber prospector. Okogun went to Ugbodu and successfully negotiated with the people who granted him access to the forest. The people demanded that he paid the relatively large sum of two hundred pounds cash before entering the bush to start his business. Two hundred pounds was considered a large sum of money at the time and few could afford to pay out such a sum. He paid the money after sighting the bush from the road and seeing some timber trees. He brought in his reliable timber-tree finders to go into the bush and take a census of harvestable timbers. The total number of timber trees counted was considered not enough to make the business profitable. Okogun declined to engage in the business and demanded a refund of his money. The people promised to refund his money but after several futile trips to Ugbodu to get the refund of his two hundred pounds, Okogun gave up. The investment was a failure.

Western Nigeria Development Corporation Palm Oil Plantation and Mill, Ewohimi

In the mid-1950s, the Western Nigeria Government decided to establish a Cooperative between it and the Ewohimi Community for the purpose of establishing an oil palm plantation with an oil mill at Ewohimi. The community participants in the Cooperative were required to pay about two pounds as members of the cooperative. In return, the members were to nominate able-bodied men to work mainly as labourers in the Plantation. Okogun joined as one of the members of the Cooperative. The Cooperative was dissolved in early 1960s, when the Western Nigeria Government decided to take full ownership of the Plantation and Mill. The Government takeover of the full ownership of the business happened just before the creation of the Midwest State of Nigeria. The Plantation eventually passed into the control of the Delta State Government as part of the assets sharing agreement between Edo and Delta States created out of the existing Midwest State (renamed Bendel State by the Military Government of General Gowon). It was an odd asset for Delta State because Ewohimi is in Edo and not in Delta State. Eventually Delta State sold the plantation to Chief *Anthony Anenih* of Uromi who thankfully bought it back into Edo State.

A money-doubler deceives Okogun

The other attempt to invest should be mentioned for its oddity in the life of the widely traveled Okogun who always referred to himself as a *"traveler man".* A con man had tracked him down to Ewohimi from Agbor with the business to double money. The man was recommended to Okogun by some Agbor associates whose word Okogun trusted. The man came on the fateful day in a vehicle that he claimed to be his own as part of his business success story. Okogun had been told success stories about the man. He was sceptical about the business but produced some cash for a trial. The man carried out what looked to be a *"successful operation" that* encouraged Okogun to bring out much more cash of his own and from other persons hoping for bigger returns on the investment with instant returns.

The man's vehicle driver had positioned their vehicle for easy take off. The experiment now failed, and the man and his assistant having collected the genuine cash jumped into his car to speed off. Okogun was still agile and fit as a former acrobat. He jumped on to the side bumper of the car and held on to the vehicle as it sped away with him holding on and standing on a railing by the side of the car while calling attention to people to stop the vehicle. His efforts yielded no success and he had to jump off the moving vehicle at *Ikemenzelomon*, about half a kilometer from his house. The money doubler escaped with his loot.

The kerosene business

Between 1966 and 1967 Okogun engaged in kerosene retail trade. The first available receipt was dated 20th October 1966. He deposited funds with a major distributor at Agbor and was made a sub-depot retailer at Ewohimi. He acquired and used a large metal tank[60] which was filled from time to time by a kerosene tanker from Agbor. The amount of kerosene supplied varied. One of the supplies was 283 imperial gallons (1,286 liters) for which Okogun paid forty-eight pounds ten shillings (£48:10/).

Taxation

Okogun kept receipts of his tax and water bills. The records show how diligent the Government was in the collection of taxes and the people's cooperation in the payment of taxes. For 1957, Okogun's tax Assessment came from Ibadan, the Capital of Western Region of Nigeria. This was during the period of the timber Contractor business. He was assessed on the past year's earning of four hundred pounds (£400:00). He was given personal allowance of one hundred pounds; wife allowance of one hundred pounds and children allowance of one hundred and sixty pounds. He paid one pound ten shillings as tax on the remaining forty pounds on 30th December 1957.

For 1959, his tax assessment came from the Ewohimi, Ewatto and Ewossa District Council whose Headquarters was at Ewohimi. He was assessed on the past year earning of two hundred and fourteen pounds (£214:00) because the timber business was no more.

He paid a total of nine pounds eighteen shillings and four pence (£9: 18: 4d) as tax on 25th November 1959. This included one pound towards the *Establishment of the Joint Education Board.* The rest was for the Services of the Council.

Okogun held a public office

Okogun was appointed a Member of the Eastern Ishan District Council Tax Assessment Committee by a letter[61] from the Council dated 12th August 1970. The letter came from Ubiaja the Headquarters of the Council.

CHAPTER EIGHTEEN

OKOGUN AS A FAMILY AND COMMUNITY MAN

Okogun was a great lover of his wives and children and a great disciplinarian.

His positions as the only surviving son of the head family in the Aigbiya group of families and the grandson of Chief Ebalogbhen of Ewohimi were always at the back of his mind. That consciousness of who he was and what was expected of him had great influence on his life and attitudes. He needed tact, courage, hard work and above all reliance on God to fulfill his naturally imposed position and status in society. He was also expected to grow the Eze family[62] by having a large family as well as be able to attract back home members of the larger family who had fled from Ewohimi to escape from perceived persecution.

That Okogun worked hard was clear to all. That he was courageous and bold was known from his youth. That he relied on God and a clear conscience could be deduced from his decision to be the first person to build his family residence at lonely Ofuri Market area as well as his fatherly interest in the progress, development and success of other persons' children. That he was tactful in his dealings was clear from his respect for elders, diabolical persons and constituted authority. He married relatively early, and eventually lived with a total of five wives apart from few reports of his dealings with other women, as was the practice in his time. He was very strict with his wives on issues of respect and recognition of the rule of precedence and hierarchy. Morning greetings, after food greetings, exchange of greetings on leaving and returning to the house and other courtesies were taught and practiced by the wives and children. He taught all and expected everybody to be courteous, polite, tough, courageous, hardworking, and honest.

He descended heavily often with violence on anyone who violated the ground rules. The earlier children tried to behave well at school to avoid any punishment. If Okogun heard that any of his children was punished in the school, he would ask the child for an explanation of what led to the school punishment. The child would receive further beating from Okogun if Okogun felt that the child genuinely was guilty of misdemeanor. He never went to the School to ask teachers about the punishment their children received for misdemeanor. The children therefore learnt to hide their experience of school punishments from their father. Many wrongly misinterpreted his harshness with violators for dislike or hate rather than his love for their success in life. The author, later in adult life said to Okogun: *"A a Baba, you were too harsh on us"*. He replied succinctly, *"What has that turned you into?"* I had no answer but to change the discussion. I had every reason to thank him for the discipline, I received from him, his God-fearing lifestyle and his support of our mother when she took us as children to God after she became a convert to the *Assemblies of God Mission Church*.

Okogun used to remind the children that in Idinrio, the first son used to be sold off as slave if the community felt that such a son would be incapable of heading the family due to laziness, lack of integrity or roguery. As a fact, *Mr. Alenbaluye(Alen) Ighedosa,* second grandson of Pa Ighedosa Omovuon related a family story on this practice. Alenbaluye was very close to his grandfather whose special bag he carried while accompanying his grandfather to meetings and visitations. *Alenbaluye currently lives in the United States of America.*

Regrouping the remnants of the Eze family

After Okogun had settled at home, he and his sisters decided to regroup the dispersed Eze family. Osagie Aki had settled in Benin *City as* a native doctor. *Abielekpen Osimen* was in some remote village in the Ika area beyond Agbor. *Igue's family* was at Idumobo, Ewohimi. *Igue Okede* had become quite aristocratic and recognized by the colonial government officers who made him a "Course" with responsibility for tax collection before he died. Quite aware of the envy around him and possible danger for him and family, he sent his first son *Iyamabhor* to Chief Odigie for mentorship and protection. Igue died young and so Iyamabhor and his junior brother *James Igue* settled near Chief Odigie at Idumobo but kept in touch with Okogun and his sisters. Okogun and his widowed sisters lived together in Okogun's premises. Plots of land were acquired near Ofuri Market for their sons' future buildings. Okun returned from Ohordua after her husband Itama's death. Owobu until her death continued to be at Idumu-agho with the husband Ikekhide.

The next task was to bring the rest of Eze family together at Idinrio from where they left.

Okogun traveled to Agbor to search for Abielekpen in Ika villages where he also traded. On one fortunate day, he got on to a trail from a village market which led him to his cousin Abielekpen. He convinced him to return home. Eventually Abielekpen returned to Ewohimi and set up camp and his residence by the Idinrio Odu River with Urhobos as his neighbours. Other Ibhi-Eze men *Amandin and Ebehigie* also set up their abode with Abielekpen in the camps.

Madam Uhuomonye decided to visit Osagie in Benin City. She was well received by Osagie and family. She requested that Osagie who had been receiving messages from home to return to Ewohimi made good his promise to return home. Osagie's main support in Benin City was his *wife Aminetu* who hailed from *Atuagbo, Irrua.* Later Osagie got a second wife *Ebhodaghe from Ohordua.* At the end of Uhuomonye's visit to Osagie, she felt that Osagie was finding it difficult to take the decision to return to Ewohimi. She tricked Osagie and got Aminetu to travel back with her to Ewohimi. When Osagie waited in vain to have Aminetu back to Benin from Ewohimi, Osagie packed his possessions and returned to Ewohimi. *Iribhor*, a man belonging to Osagie's Aki lineage also returned from the Benin area. Okogun encouraged and supported James Igue, *Abu Iyamabhor and Okpoko Iyamabhor* to secure plots of land to develop as their residential premises close to his own premises by the market. Iyamabhor himself remained until death at Idumobo leaving his other children, *Oriabor, and others to settle at Idumobo. Ebehigie* built his residence in Idinrio near *Ikekhua of Ogbeide's* family. And so, all living Eze family members regrouped. They strengthened their family relations with their cousin *Erinho and her son Ifiobhor* of Okede, Ewohimi. There was also *Mr. Akasi and family* who lived until death at Ikpoba Hill in Benin. He was buried by Okogun when he died. His daughter Mary was for a time an active member of the Ibhi-Eze family.

Some other Eze family descendants were *Omonakhin* who at a time lived at Okede after losing her husband at Idumu-agho, *Oriunuebho,* son of *Ugbotiti* and father of *Otobo* at IdumuguokhaUgbolobhede and *Arinminigbe, son of Ailekhoenowu* at Idumebo Ewatto. And so, the remnants of Eze's family became reunited. Arhinminigbe's senior brother, *Pius* was reported to have served in the British Colonial army during World War II.

Links with the Ebalogbhen of Idumigie lineage

Okogun and his sisters were very keen to maintain strong links with their mother Esekhor's family at Idumigie and beyond. *Chief Omole of* Idumu-agho's *children Ade/Mary, Ozuogie, Pius B. Owobu, Enoho and Otiti whose mother Omoze* was Esekhor's junior sister were Okoguns's first cousins. There were several Chief Ebalogbhen's children and grandchildren in Okaigben and all over Ewohimi. Chief Ikhahon was the reigning Ebalogbhen during Okogun's lifetime.

Among these were *Mrs. Oboh* at *Izumen* Oghu *who was the mother of Dominic, Julius and siblings, Mrs. Ukpebor, Sir Stephen Ukpebor's* mother all natives of Izumen Oghu and Mrs. Imansuangbon, the mother of *Joseph Imansuangbon of Ikeken.*

Okogun's Ewatto roots: Chief Idogun, Odigue and Chief Agbontaen of Benin

Okogun's maternal grandmother was *Aitolo* whose mother was *Airhegbeogun. Aitolo was a daughter of Chief Idogun of Idumebo,* Ewatto while Airhegbeogun was from *Idumu-arhu,* Ewatto. Others *were Mr. Odigue and his brother Momoh* (Momoh lived at *Sapele)* of Idumebo, Ewatto. It was the Ewatto lineage that linked him and *Chief Agbontaen of Benin* as cousins. Chief Agbontaen and Okogun looked alike. Agbontaen took so much to Okogun that he pleaded with Okogun to change his surname to his Agbontaen's surname and be seen by the Bini people as Agbontaen's sibling. Okogun as expected turned down the offer from Agbontaen who was very rich and influential in Benin City. Okogun decided to ensure that the name Agbontaen remained in his family.

He first gave the name Agbontaen to Erabor, Joseph's second son but when he observed that Erabor was not using the name, he gave the name to his last son Francis and that is the name we all call Francis. Okogun was a great family man and maintained his relationship with all his larger family members and let his older children know about these family links.

Teaching the children to read, swim, kill snake, wear native cloth, etc.

Okogun was keen to teach his children at home, on the way to the farms, in the farm and in the stream at Odu River. Okogun could count to hundreds in Esan, Ika and Igbo but had limited ability in counting in English and in reading the alphabets. He taught in both languages as much as he knew in each language. Later in life when he was told how well any of his earliest children were doing in the upper classes in the primary school, he would ask if the child was not the one, he taught the English count one two three just a few years before.

He taught the children to show courtesy and politeness wherever they went. The children on waking up in the morning greeted all the mothers in the wives' apartment and then went to knock on their father's door to greet their father if he was still in his bedroom. He instructed the children to greet when they walked on the streets and on the way to the stream or farms and when they came across elders.

He taught his children to swim in the Odu River. When returning from the Ugbodu farms, the Okaigben people stopped to have a bath at Odu River, which they cross to those farms. They also stopped to fetch drinking water on their way to their farms in the morning. Okogun would throw his children one by one into the water and watch them protectively as they tried out his advice to them and they learned to swim. This way the children learnt to swim.

He lectured the children on how to kill snakes, especially the spitting cobra which at a time infested his compound. One of such cobras went into an unoccupied room in the women's apartment where hens were kept when hatching their eggs. The hen raised its cry of alarm and Okogun sensed that it was a snake attacking the hen. He went back to his apartment, put on his rain boots reaching nearly up to the knees, took his sharp cutlass and went into the room where the hen was, with the door shut behind him. He attacked and killed the snake after a fight with the snake. The snake had a reddish comb on its head and had red marks on its under- side. Such spitting cobras are said to be able to crow like cocks.

In attacking the spitting cobra, one must avoid the spray of the cobra's venom that it releases from its mouth aiming at the attacker's eyes. One tried to spit at the cobra first and hit the head and as fast as possible, hit it towards its tail to incapacitate its ability to lift itself up.

He taught the children how to put on native dress whether it was the Esan toga *(igbu)* or the flowing Nigerian national dress - the *agbada* dress.

Healthcare for family

Okogun practised ethnomedicine as he was from a family that had a long tradition of ethnomedicine. He combined available orthodox medicine with his knowledge of ethnomedicine. The first treatment given to an indisposed family member was herbal remedies prepared by Okogun himself and if it concerned female health issues, he would consult his senior sister Uhuomonye who was versed in herbalism treatment in general but especially female problems. There was effectively no hospital at Ewohimi until the late 1970s when the Community Hospital built from the late 1960s by Okaigben people was taken over, staffed, and equipped by Government. Before then, the Dispensary at Eguae served as outpatient hospital which for a long time had Mr. *Okhuebor of Idumigie*, Ewohimi as a very devoted, diligent, and effective Dispensary Head. The first Maternity Home at Eguae, Ewohimi was established about 1950. The Maternity was of the highest standard and was first headed by the then Agnes Odigie

Usually, for what was considered serious illness cases, the diviners had to be consulted. The diviners would say if the sick adult had violated ancestral commandments or prescribed norms. If the patient were a child, the diviner would check if any of the parents sinned against the spirits or the child as a reincarnation of a known dead person was suffering for evil done in the previous life. The diviner would prescribe the sacrifice of atonement to be made to pave the way for success with the herbal treatment. In serious illness, the patient was usually taken to a healing home that could be the home of a relation where the treatment was carried out by the host or another herbal doctor. The Dispensary was used mostly but not only by the staff and pupils of the schools.

When Enimaluole, the first wife was ill, she was first taken to Pa Abielekpen who was still in his camp near the Odu River and later brought nearer home to *Pa Adoghe,* one of Okogun's larger family members and elder in Idinrio. When Maria, the third wife fell ill, she was taken to Chief Idogun's house at Idumebo, Ewatto. This was the earlier practice which gradually changed over time to downplay the resort to the diviners. The change happened rapidly after the death of Uhuomonye.

For stomach problems which were usually attributed to worms, if not poisons, herbal worm expellers were very effective. The common orthodox drugs used *then were castor oil and Epsom salt as purgatives and M & B injections and tablet for infections and stubborn pains.* Medical doctors, as they were called then, visited Ewohimi monthly to treat the sick. As already mentioned, they were said to be visiting from Onitsha and used the John Holts premises by Ofuri Market as the consultation centre. It should be recalled that the John Holt Managers of the John Holts Company at Ewohimi were Onitsha indigenes.

For fevers the patient was treated and laid near a fireplace. The treatment by Okogun sometimes involved rubbing some hot ointment all over the child's body and then covering the child with blanket. Quite often the child sweated profusely and recovered after such treatment.

The morning ritual to treat worms and other ailments was to drink or lick herbal medicines even before leaving for School. The unpleasant tastes of these herbal remedies did not recommend them to children.

Later in life, when access to Hospital treatment became available and especially after Uhomonye had died, Okogun's wives delivered their babies mostly in Government Maternity Homes and seriously ill persons were treated in dispensaries and hospitals. The consultation of diviners became rare and far between for stubborn illnesses. The diviners consulted had to be famous and known to have effective practice and there were not many of them that Okogun believed in. Some of them were *the Eboaide family* of Uzebu, *Ibhiosanoman family* of Idumuguokha-Ugbolobhede, a few in other parts of Ewohimi, Ohordua, Ekpon, Ebele, Ewatto and *Otakpor* in the Ika area of Delta State.

Okogun's health and temporary marriage to Aminetu

After the death of Pa Osagie and the completion of the burial ceremonies performed by Okogun who was appointed in accordance with tradition as the Administrator (akheoa) of Pa Osagie's estate and family, the larger family empowered Okogun to take care of Aminetu as his wife. Aminetu was still relatively young and had three children, a daughter *Ofuri* and two sons *Johnson Ekemenomhen* and *Monday* for Pa Osagie before Osagie's death. Okogun had relations with Aminetu and got a daughter, *Egbeke later Mrs. David Aguele* through Aminetu.

Okogun enjoyed a robust health and he had fevers and minor ill-health episodes which were easily successfully treated. Not long into his marriage to Aminetu about 1954, Okogun fell seriously ill. The illness was unusual and everyone in the family was concerned. As was the practice then, Okogun's sisters went to consult diviners possibly the Ibhiosanomhan group of native doctors at Idumuguokha- Ugbolobhede. They were told by the diviners that the ancestral spirits were responsible for his illness. The spirits had taken the side of one of Okogun's cousins Mr. Iribhor who was bearing grudges that he, Iribhor ought to be the one to whom Madam Aminetu should be customarily betrothed. Okogun's marriage to Aminetu was instantly dissolved and Aminetu was asked to get married to Iribhor.

Apparently Aminetu did not accept her union with Iribhor but remained in the family until her death when her body was taken with pomp and pageantry to her parents' family at Irrua. She survived Iribhor by many years.

Farming life and activities

Okogun loved farming. He had farms about a mile from his residence on his ancestors' lands. He was born when his parents had their residence in those lands. The other farm was quite far from the village. The farm was in forests that were up to six or more miles from the village and across the Odu River in the Ewohimi farming area referred to as Ugbodu. Odu was a goddess worshipped by Okaigben people. Ugbodu translates literally as Odu farm though there is a village called Ugbodu in Delta State beyond the boundary between it and Ewohimi. There is the story among the Ugbodu indigenes that their ancestors migrated[61a] from the Yoruba *Owo* area and that they settled temporarily at Ewohimi before moving through the forests to their present location . The Ugbodu farms for Ewohimi people were important because the forests were older and more fertile. The harvests from those farms were on the average much better than in the small farms near the village. Okogun also had rubber plantations and inherited kolanuts trees in the ancestral lands near the village and near the Odu River on the way to Ugbodu farm. The main farms had maize, yams mainly, cassava and other soup ingredients like pepper, garden egg, melon, pumpkin, and others planted by the wives. When he farmed at the derived Savannah part of Ugbodu, he also planted pigeon peas, *Cajanus cajan* (L) Millsp. *(olele)* and another variety of beans (*ihin-orhor).*

Major seasonal works on the farm were done sometimes on communal labour basis, by inlaws, and friends who brought along their friends or relatives to assist. *Messrs Joseph and Michael Odia and Agbonkpolor* of Uhie/ Ikemenzelomon, Ikekhua of Uwi-Idinio already mentioned, *Inlaws Palmer, Iyere and Ogiekpon/Francis, Pius Omotese* who were brothers and cousin of Maria, Okogun's third wife, inlaw Akpolo, husband of Okogun's first daughter, Mary were among those that occasionally helped Okogun in his farms. These persons worked without being paid. They were just fed while on the farm.

The weeding was done mostly by children in their teens and adolescents. Between about 1947 and 1953, Okogun's second daughter Lucy led the other children to weed in the farms. The eldest daughter Mary lived with Uhuomonye at Uzebu and was not available to work in Okogun's farms. Along with Mary, *Obeto*, Owobu's daughter and Egiamanyo Blackie later popularised also as Magdalene also lived with Madam Uhuomonye at Uzebu.

Okogun performed a small ritual before planting the seed yams in the heaps. He would sprinkle some watery liquid on the yams while saying some incantations or prayers and followed up with scattering sand he took from the soil on the yams. He said the ritual was to prevent damage to the tubers from soil nematodes and other organisms. During planting he would send the children to go count the remaining heaps to be given seed yams to enable him to decide on the number of seed yams or pieces to make and the children knew the unpleasant consequences of making a mistake and miscounting. Thus, the children learnt to be accurate and to work with figures. He taught the children how to thread yam tendrils on stakes and together: always clockwise. He taught his children how to plant, harvest and process farm products: maize, beans, and yams for storage. He had a special identification mark on the head of his harvested yam tubers. The mark resembled the letter K.

He made yam barns. The yams were tied in columns on stakes made from the main ribs of palm fronds or other durable sticks. The main support pillars of the barn were stems of live plants like *Newbouldia and Spondias mombin* L. *(ogheghe).* Iron traps were set at strategic points in the barn to control the giant rats and other animals that ate the yams. At the entrance of the barns, fetish objects were placed to discourage thieves from stealing from the yam barns.

Iwenakhamen (Iwe) Jacob Itama: faithful service to Okogun and family

Iwe, short for Iwenakhamen also later called Jacob and his brother *Abumere* were brought along with their *mother Aluge* to Ewohimi from *Uokhuen,* Ohordua by Madam Okun, one of Okogun's sisters after the death Okun's husband Itama. Since Okun had no surviving children of her own, Aluge was probably in Itama's family through Okun who married her to have children in Itama's name. Iwe was under ten years old when Okun returned to Ewohimi about1947/48. He was not in school and apparently there was no plan for him to go to school. After Okun's death, Iwe remained with Okogun at Ewohimi. Okogun planned that when he grew up, he should learn some profession of his choice. Iwe was given to Maria, one of Okogun's wives, to assist her and be looked after by her because Maria at the time did not have grown up children of her own. Her earlier children died as babies or infants.

Iwe gave very faithful service in the family especially in Okogun's farms. Iwe was naturally never pleased that he was not sent to school. He was taught, to a little extent, to read and write by Okogun's children, and was able to write his own name. Iwe, in fairness to him, could not wait for the plans that Okogun had for him. He therefore ran away from home without giving a hint about where he was. Years after he left home, it was discovered that he was at Sapele. At Sapele, he learnt to become a motor mechanic and visited Okogun at Ewohimi. Okogun promised to link him with his children who would help him set up his workshop. The plan did not again materialize as Iwe died not long after. Iwe's death was painful to Okogun and many of his children who did not have the opportunity to reward Iwe for his service to the family.

Okogun's involvement in the marriages of his children

Pa Okogun showed deep interest in the marriage choices of his children. He wished that his children married from good homes though he would not stop his child's interest in a future spouse if the child made up his or her own mind provided that he would make his opinion known. As much as possible he maintained good relations with his inlaws. The marriages before his death are mentioned here. His inlaws through his daughters were Mr. Akpolo of Uhie, Okaigben, Ewohimi who married Mary, Pa Okogun's eldest daughter and who long before Mary was of age, gave Okogun two pounds as deposit to enable Okogun pay a sum to Osobor for his marriage to Mary's mother Enimaluole; *Prince Odigie Enosegbe* of Eguae who married Lucy, *Pastor Christopher Ailende* from Oghu who married Felicia Ekeagboniyokpa Efua, *Mr G. Agboli* from Ogwashiuku who married Celestina Uwamusi Tobore (the name Tobore was given because of what Okun said after she had an encounter before her death with Maria Imhanrhokanbhor), *Engineer E. O. Inegbedion* of Ekpoma who married Aiterebhe Anthonia, *Mr.Imontu Aguele* from Idumuguokha nonriuwa who married Egbeke, *Mr. G. Omole* of Idumu-agho who married *Khairhiala Omisi Irene, Mr. Roland Imarenezor* of Iselu who married *Tessy Odion, Mr. Godwin Ighodalo* of Uzebu who married *Linda Obhokhan and Mr. Clifford E. Afeyodion* of Idumu-agho who married *Mammy Mary.*

He insisted, as a typical Esan father, that he was not selling his daughters and therefore took token sums as dowry. It was a surprise to the children that Okogun and *Pa Osebor* of Ekpoma knew themselves as friends when the later accompanied *Pa Inegbedion* to Ewohimi to conclude the marital rites between Engineer Inegbedion and Anthonia Aiterebhe.

Okogun got involved in the provision of service to his inlaws through his sons. When possible, he accompanied his sons to finalise the traditional rites of marriage when the issue of dowry had to be settled. His inlaws through his sons *were Pa Peter O. Odigie* through Joseph who married *Justina, Pa Ero* of Benin City through Felix who married *Esther, Pa Enabor* of Ewu through Felix who married *Victoria, Pa Ailuese-edo* Ikhahon of Idumu-Oleghe through Amuda who married *Ifiobhor and Pa Vincent A. Iguanre* of Iselu through Robert who married *Beatrice Ese.* Okogun had become very old when Felix initiated his marriage to Agatha nee Pa Omonzokpea of Oghu, Ewohimi and the marital rites were concluded after his death. The occasion of concluding the marital rites often brought happy memories on all sides. This was particularly so with Pa Peter Odigie, Mr. Iguanre and Pa Ailuese-edo. Such memories usually brought in experiences in the farms. Okogun recalled with relish the acrobatic dance prowess of Pa Iguanre's brother or cousin and their exploits together as dancers.

Okogun gave names to his grandchildren that reflected events in his life and the lives of his married children. A few of his grandchildren were fortunate to spend some years of their primary school years at home with him. In the Conclusion chapter below one of them Ogbeide Franklin Okogun speaks about his experience with his grandfather.

Okogun cared about the welfare and affairs of his nephews and nieces. He first took Patrick Egialegbele Ilegbodu to Onitsha. Patrick later in life joined Pa Johnson Ogbebor in Onitsha and became an artisan with the Government Public Works Department (PWD). Chief Okogie Imanyelea reportedly handed over his daughter, as Joe Esezobor Ilegbodu's bride, and it was Okogun who took Christiana Ebemamhen Ilegbodu nee Okogie to Esezobor when he was still in Northern Nigeria. He helped to arrange building sites for some of them.

Okogun had to travel to Lagos to arrange a settlement when Anna *Enogialeguan* and Rose Imhanrenrio had a disagreement. Benson Ilegbodu was sent to Okogun at Umunede to enable Benson attend the senior primary school classes that were not available at Ewohimi. Cousins Wilson A. Enaiho and Pius Omiunu of Idumobo also had their senior primary schooling staying with Okogun at Umunede.

CHAPTER NINETEEN

OKOGUN'S INTEREST IN THE EDUCATION, MENTORING AND TRAINING OF YOUNG PEOPLE AND CHRISTIANITY

Okogun as has been discussed wanted very much to acquire Western education. His sisters supported by their parents, for good reasons, did not consider Western education for Okogun at that time to be in the interest of their family. Okogun therefore could not go to school. Okogun was one of the strong enthusiasts in the efforts made by Okaigben people, initiated before his death by Chief Odigie to establish a primary school at Okaigben. Odigie had planned to establish Odigie Memorial School. He died in February 1944 before he could do so. Okaigben people guided by Honourable Joseph O. Odigie decided to go ahead with the project under the more embracing name of *Okaigben Memorial School*[63] located near Ofuri Market behind Okogun's premises. The School opened for pupils in January 1945. Okaigben built the classrooms through communal efforts by the various Okaigben quarters from Iselu to Idumuguokha – Ugbolobhede. The first teachers *Messrs Isaiah C. John (from Eastern Nigeria), James Igue and Miss Agnes U. Odigie (later Mrs Okojie) who were Okaigben indigenes* were employed and paid salaries by Okaigben community through donations and community contributions. Honourable J. O. Odigie often recalled that Okogun was the first person to donate at the first meeting of the village to raise funds for the school. This was in the years 1944/45 while Okogun was still operating his businesses from Umunede with his bicycle.

In those days, respective families chose one out of many male children to be given Western education which was fee paying. The others had to be in the farms to feed their families and support their brother who was in school. The fortunate school child joined the rest in the farms at weekends. Some of the farm harvests were sold and part of the money was used to pay school fees for their brother. At the beginning, raids were carried out by Government to forcibly recruit children for school just as were done for recruitment into the Colonial army and for tax defaulters. Until late 1930s, Ewohimi people resented and rejected religious missionary activities and Western education institutions.

Parents wanted to have their children for their farm labour. Many parents got their children to hide in the ceilings of their homes at the approach of the children-for-school raiders.

Okogun transferred his unfulfilled desire for literacy into getting his children and other peoples' children to go to school. He decided to give at least basic primary education to all his children and costly secondary education to those who could make it and with the assistance of the senior children. At the beginning and for various family reasons, it was only his first daughter Mary[64] who lived with his senior sister Uhomonye that was not sent to school.

Okogun's 1970s family meetings and important decisions

Until Chief Obafemi Awolowo, the first Premier of Western Region introduced free primary education in 1955, school fees were paid in primary schools. When primary education became free, Okogun decided that he would send one person from each wife's branch of his family to secondary school. Such children he expected to help him later to train the junior children beyond the primary school level. For example, in 1971 and 1978, after the Nigerian civil war, Okogun held family meetings[65] with all his children (Appendix II). At the meetings, the junior children were assigned for the purpose of their secondary education to the leaders among his children. The professions into which the children would train were also planned. His decision to abide with his agreement with Madam Aiyobase and her Ohordua family to the effect that Amuda should use Enato as surname and not Okogun was discussed and reaffirmed though Amuda was sent to school and was completely raised, with short interludes, by Okogun. Aiyobase and her people had instituted court[66] actions against Okogun over Amuda's paternity and the fact that Aiyobase performed all the marital rites including the payment of dowry to have Angelina as her "woman wife". Okogun eventually won the case in the Court. Okogun revisited this matter on his hospital bed. The first meeting was summoned during the period of the Nigerian Civil war.

Encounter with Biafran soldiers

Okogun was friendly with the Nigerian Civil War Biafran soldiers stationed to mount roadblock at Ofuri Market because he spoke the Ibo language and its Ika dialect and had lived in Agbor and Umunede, regularly visited Onitsha market in his Umunede years and had Igbos living in his house at various times. He would sit in his house at the veranda and was able to observe the happenings at the roadblock mounted by the Biafran soldiers at the Ofuri Market. Okogun always was his brothers' keeper. During the Biafran war, many people fled from their usual abode to return to their respective places of origin. Many such refugees who hailed from Ewohimi, Ewatto, Ohordua and Emu had to pass through Ofuri Market.

On one of those days, Okogun observed that the soldiers were questioning one of such refugees and the soldiers made as if they wanted to shoot the refugee. He walked towards the soldiers to save the person. He did save the person but one of the soldiers was not happy that Pa Okogun interrupted them in the process and threatened to shoot Okogun's legs to maim and render him unable to walk and interfere with their operations at the market. Okogun spoke to them in Igbo and told them about his friendship and that of some of his children with persons of Igbo origin. At that, the leader of the soldiers warned Okogun not to interrupt them on duty again and spared him.

In sending his children to school, Okogun got mocked by some men because the size of his farms had to be small and he had to depend on assistance from inlaws, communal labour, friends and later paid labour to work in his farms. Okogun campaigned in the community on the importance of sending their children to school. He went into open confrontation with many. A notable case was his open quarrel with one of his neighbours, *Mr. Ikhuiriona Ogienor* who refused to send his first and only son *Mr. Okonobo Ikhuirion*[67] to school until Hon. J.O. Odigie intervened. To immortalize Okogun's zeal for children to be sent to school to acquire Western education without losing their own culture, the annual Pa John Okogun Omovuon Academic Prizes Award for top performing students in all classes at Okaigben Primary School was instituted in 2002/2003 (Appendix IV). Arrangements to organize the best somersault acrobat prize for the cultural aspect have had some logistic problems.

Okogun used his own life experiences to guide other people's children. Okogun decided to make himself a public mentor and guide for adolescents who had passed school age. He did so in his own way. He advised adolescents who had missed or dropped out of school to go and learn some form of trade or professions. The easier professions for such young men were motor mechanic, bricklaying, trading, and tailoring. On Ofuri Market days he would sit in the veranda in front of his house and observe the people and events at the market. When he noticed any young man that he had advised on developing himself lazing about in the market, he would get close to the young man presenting a friendly disposition until he got sufficiently close to the young man who then received slaps from Okogun for not taking steps to develop himself. This earned Okogun the name *"The dispenser of slaps by Ofuri Market" (ogbolubi non ribhe egb-Ofuri)*

He meted similar treatment to those who had received primary education and remained jobless at home. He advised such persons to leave home to seek other employment if they failed to secure teaching jobs or learn some trade away from home.

Many men later in their lives came back to show their gratitude in cash and kind to him for his earlier advice to them. The slaps were no more part of the interaction with the young when he became old and as times had changed. His friendship and public mentorship of the young continued till he died. He was even reported to have prophesied to a young man about the young man's business which he suspected was not a clean one at that time. He congratulated the young man for his successful business thus far and advised him to be satisfied with the gains the young man had made up to that time, to change business and take up other business. The young man did not heed the advice and was confronted by law enforcement agents shortly after.

Okogun continued to receive gifts of gratitude till the end of his earthly life from both men and women for the counsel and blessings he gave to them earlier in life.

Okogun's advice on taking alcohol and on polygamy

There were two things he did that he did not encourage his children to engage in. Okogun loved his palmwine, though he was not a drunkard. He did not encourage his children to drink alcohol. His reason was that he once, as a sign of love, allowed one of his infant sons to have a sip from the palmwine he was drinking. The son[68] immediately got sick and had a severe episode of vomiting. He told his children that taking alcohol would have to be decided upon by the children themselves. He decided from the early experience in his life never to offer alcoholic drinks to his children but to allow the decision to take alcohol to the discretion of the individual child.

The second was based on his experience of polygamy and the changing structure of society. He felt that polygamy was manageable and necessary in his own time but that it was much of a task to be polygamous in the generation of his children. He did not wish that his sons saddled themselves with the task though he said there were some benefits to be derived from polygamy. He said that it was advantageous to have half brothers and sisters.

Some other young children and adolescent that lived with Okogun

It was the practice in those days to send one's children to live with successful men and their families for mentorship. Many people admired Okogun's interest in the growth and development of the youths and his ability to counsel and discipline young persons. They therefore sent their children to live at various times with him and his wives. There were many but some are mentioned here. *Alice,* Ailegbesuan's niece and daughter of Ailuhi came from Ohordua. *Queen and Charles, Palmer Anyangbe's* daughter and *Ebahi, Peter Anyangbe's* daughter. Queen, Charles and Ebahi were Maria's nieces and nephew from Oghu, Ewohimi. *Victor Cole,* Agnes Odigie's son came from Idumobo, Ewohimi under a special cultural arrangement with distant cousins. *Philip Odigie* was sent by his father Hon Joseph O Odigie to live with Okogun. Others were Okogun's cousin *Sylvester Ogieyan,* Ehikhamen Ogieyan's son, *Rose Isidahomen* from Ohordua while she taught at Okaigben Memorial School, *Josiah I Okodu* of Idumodu, Ewohimi. There were those who lived with him at Umunede. *Patrick Ilegbodu* lived briefly with him at Umunede until he decided to go to Onitsha to meet Pa *Johnson Ogbebor*, the father of Chief Sunday Ogbebor, Ifeanyi and their siblings; *Pa Chief Aguele Airiagbonaye,* the father of Henry, Chief (Engineer) Emmanuel Aguele, Prince Solomon Aguele (a onetime Edo State Chairman of the Peoples Democratic Party, PDP), Attorney Wilberforce Aguele and their siblings and other Ewohimi people then living at Onitsha.

Those sent to live and school from his house at Umunede were Benson Ilegbodu, Omolafe's son, *Wilson Enaiho* and *Pius Omiunu* who were cousins from Idumobo, Ewohimi.

Okogun as a good man and Christian at heart

While at Agbor and Umunede, Okogun had come across a Christian preacher, whom he referred to as *Lamipo (Olamipo*). Apparently, Lamipo's group or some other Christian group had converted Okogun. He was also found to be versed in learning the evangelical message spread by the group and preaching it effectively to people. The group at Umunede therefore found him worthy of being made an Elder in their organization. The Christian group arrived at his residence at Umunede ready to perform the ceremony needed to make him an Elder of their Christian organisation. One of the conditions they informed him was that he had to be monogamous. Meanwhile he had fully married Enimaluole whom the group thought was his only wife. Ailegbesuan Angelina had come away with him from Ohordua. Esekhor had sent the log of firewood to Maria's parents when she was born as a symbol that her son, Okogun would marry her when she came of age. Esekhor also paid two pounds as part deposit to her father Pa Anyangbe before Esekhor died. In effect, Okogun had three wives even though Maria was still underage. Angelina had the same fair complexion as Okogun and could have been taken by the group for his junior sister. Okogun could not in good conscience send Ailegbesuan away or stop his marriage to Maria. He informed the group of his dilemma and that he could not be monogamous. The plan to make him an elder in the Church was then dropped.

Okogun's pedigree, upbringing and his interaction with Christians had made him into a man with a pure heart. He would not participate in evil and was not known to collude in doing or hiding evil. If there was a problem getting at the truth on issues, Okogun was relied upon to deliver the solution if he knew it and if he felt it was appropriate and of good purpose to do so.

Three special pieces of advice from Okogun to people

One of Okogun's favourite pieces of advice to his children and others was that they should never revenge and that if anyone was planning evil against them and they knew it, they should never try to plan evil against such a person. Rather he advised that if issues or matters concerning the evil planner arose, the person should treat such issues concerning that evil planner as if there were no problems between them and the evil planner.

He then added that such an approach served to neutralize the evil intentions and plans against them by that person.

Another advice was on choosing a profession and doing one's duties on a chosen job. He would start by saying that he was not conscious of any evil that he had deliberately done that would, as spiritual atonement, obstruct the lives of his children. Therefore, he advised that one should carry out the duties of the chosen profession the way one's colleagues carried out their duties as required by the organization. He added that whatever happened while carrying out such duties even if dangerous should be accepted by his children as God's will.

Generally, he advised young persons, especially on the importance of living a good life, God-fearing, and not planning evil against others to be successful in life and after earthly life. These points were clearly part of his audio recording.

Mr. *Gabriel O. Imoinsi* related an incident concerning a young man who for some reasons brought palmwine gift to Okogun. The person was shocked when Okogun told him that he was of the mind to send him away with his palmwine because of the bad reports he was having about the young man. Others present made comments and eventually, Okogun told all present that it would look uncharitable if he rejected the gift. He made it known that he was accepting to pray over the palmwine for the man so that the wine sharing ritual could be performed on condition that the young man from then on would live a better life.

Several events happened to show how, as an elder in the village, Okogun approached issues in a manner sympathetic to the Christian way. There used to be village gatherings at Idinrio to make every adult in the village to take an oath to commit to the good of the people and not to harming people in the village. Such public oaths were usually administered when many incidents of sudden deaths, deaths of infants, unusual diseases with livestock were occurring in the village. Okogun had become one of the elders. The people requested the Christians to take the same oath using fetish symbols and the Christians protested. Okogun then recommended that the Christians be allowed to use the Bible. He was then accused[69] of being a secret churchgoer.

On another occasion, Idinrio young men living in Lagos, came home to report that they had been told by some diviner that witches and wizards at home were responsible for the failures of their business ventures in Lagos and elsewhere. They then hired a native doctor who claimed that he would be at Idinrio to reveal those who were engaging in the alleged destructive witchcraft. When the native doctor[70] came, Okogun supported those in the village who opposed permitting the supposed process of revealing the identities of witches and wizards in the village by the diviner or seer. When asked for his reasons, Okogun said that if the native doctor carried out his mission, many in the same families or living in the same houses would become enemies and would no more be on speaking terms. He wanted peace and harmony in the village and in families. Several incidents reveal Okogun's private sympathy for Christianity.

Once, one of his sons on visit home with his family informed him on a Sunday about the time for Mass at the Ewohimi Eguae Catholic Church. When he looked at his watch and the time for the Mass to start had passed, Okogun took the son to task and asked why the son and family were still not gone for the Mass. The son explained and as a joke asked him why he was not accompanying them to Mass if he was so interested in his children going to Church. His reply was that if he stepped into a Church as member, he was not sure that he and his family would be able to withstand the opposing spiritual and physical battles that would arise as reaction from the larger family and the village. Also, he was always very pleased to receive Men of God in his house as visitors.

Whenever Reverend Father *Anthony MacDonagh* who was Principal at Saint Anthony's College, Ubuluku, Delta State where Joseph taught from 1963 to 1964 visited his residence, Okogun already beginning to grey, always knelt, and asked for Reverend Father MacDonagh's blessing. Father MacDonagh was younger than Okogun.

A scapegoat analogy: scape-cock

Finally, there were several distressful tragedies of deaths, illness and other evil things happening in the Idinrio federation. The village people as was the usual practice sent emissaries to famous diviners to investigate the matter, diagnose the cause of such evils and prescribe the solution. The diviner told the emissaries that they needed to pray publicly to God and for the intercession of their ancestors to end the evils happening in the village. The public prayers had to involve taking a sacrificial cock in a procession saying prayers through the streets. The cock must be held in the procession by a "holy" man for their wishes to be granted. The emissaries suggested names of the usual persons in the village that carried out the roles like that of parading the sacrificial animals on such occasions recommended for the appeasement of God and their ancestors. All their nominations did not meet the spirits' approval as the diviner could see. When Okogun's name was given to the diviner, the diviner returned a verdict of approval by the spirits. The emissaries conveyed their reports to the elders in the village who then approached Okogun to play the role of being in front of the praying procession to parade the sacrificial cock[71]. Okogun got furious and accused the people of indirectly declaring him to be a wizard and strongly objected to their demand. They pleaded with Okogun that on the contrary they knew him to be a God-fearing person.

They explained to him how the spirits prescribed the criteria for selecting the proper person to play the role, how his name was chosen and the need to help the village. Okogun agreed to play the role in the public interest as they saw it.

Okogun did not routinely attend any Church and did not get formally admitted to a Church until the very end of his life as shall be related. However, he prayed as a matter of routine to the Almighty God in his house and often prayed for the intercession of his ancestors, who had led good lives when on Earth, as required by the traditions and customs of his people.

CHAPTER TWENTY

OTHER COMMUNITY ACTIVITIES: OKOGUN THE OGIE-ESE

Okogun readily made his widely traveled experience and wisdom available to community affairs and development efforts. In those days, communities held regular meetings to discuss community welfare and challenges. In Okaigben, the full Okaigben general meetings to openly discuss community issues were usually held at Ofuri Market before Chief Joseph O. Ighodalo built and donated the Okaigben Community Hall. Most of the leading elders would call at Okogun's house if they arrived early for the meetings. Okogun's policy was to keep his doors open to visitors partly because his residence was by the market and because of his nature and general love of people. He had to make sure that he always had the traditional kola nuts in his house to use in the entertainment of visitors. The elders had the long pipe-smoking device prepared with appropriate tobacco for them before the practice gradually died. Palmwine or some hot drinks like brandy and gin, if available, was also served without ice. In Okogun's time, the men and women were very active in community efforts and governance under the leadership of the elders and leading chiefs headed by Chief *Esongban* of Okaigben. The Esongban was installed an Elder (Odion) if he were not already one before his coronation as Esongban so he could preside along with the head elders at the Okaigben Council meeting. *Chief Omoigiade Osoh* headed the senior chiefs from the Idinrio arm of Okaigben. Okogun participated in community discussions and duties and played his roles at the various age-grades that he passed through. Like his contemporaries, he participated in the community efforts that led to the adoption and inauguration of

Okaigben Development Association, OKDA in 1965. OKDA under guidance from the elders established the Ewohimi General Hospital now named Clara Oshiomhole General Hospital in memory of the late wife of a former Edo State Governor Adams Oshiomhole, carried out the construction of access roads, scholarship awards, market sanitation and other development efforts.

When Okogun got old at above 80, the Idinrio community wished that he became one of the spiritual elders (*Odion-egbe*). He took the first steps. Pa Aghughu made him his traditional godson(*oror)* and he concluded the tradition by carrying out the ceremony whereby he got

Pa *Erieminlamen Ighodalo*, the elder brother, of *Chiefs Jeremiah and Joseph Ighodalo* as his own godson (*oror)*. When the Idinrio community threatened to sprinkle white chalk on him to make him an Odion - egbe because he did not voluntarily complete the process, he decided to be installed as an *Oka-igbama* deputy to the Odion-egbe grade.

Pa Okogun was not interested in chieftaincy titles: afterall, the people already referred to him as king of the crowd (ogie-ese). When His Royal Highness Usifo Enosegbe II suggested making him a chief, Pa Okogun declined. One of his reasons was that he already had three chieftaincy titles assigned to families in his lineage. The titles were the *Eholor* in the Ihon family, the Ologbosere, Chief Odigie and the Osoh, all Idinrio of the Aigbiya lineage to which Pa Okogun belonged. He also gave some reason to prove that he belonged to the group who do not take the oath of allegiance to the Enogie as the chiefs must do during their installation. Pa Okogun also did not wish to leave any complexities behind for his children.

Some close associates and contemporaries of Okogun

Okogun's social network was wide and was spread throughout Esanland, Agbor, Umunede, Issele-Uku, Benin, Sapele and Warri where he met the man, he called Mr. Collins, Professor Frank M. A. Ukoli's father.

I have already mentioned several persons who were associates of Okogun. It is impossible to mention all his close associates. As children, we could not know all. Some names that should feature are certainly missing in this account. It is necessary to go into detail about some of the interactions that went on and to mention other persons that have not been referred to.

A striking aspect of the interactions Okogun had with people was the fact that he never let disagreements lead to severance of relationships especially with relatives. He usually tried to make up quarrels from a position of strength. Okogun had serious disagreements with Chief Paul Odigie. Until his death Chief Paul Odigie and Okogun maintained a cordial and brotherly relationship which seemed to have put all that happened between them in the timber business behind them. The Chief was very good at taking walks around the village. Chief Paul Odigie would often walk early in the morning from Idumobo to be with Okogun to hold discussions on various family and community issues. The Chief consulted Okogun on issues bothering his mind. He also took Okogun's advice seriously. An example was when Okogun confronted and urged Chief Paul Odigie on sending Odigie's junior children in his care to secondary educational institutions.

The exchange of early morning visits was also very important in the interactions between Hon. Joseph O. A. Odigie and Okogun. They also discussed and took advice from each other on their family, community, and other issues. Whenever Mr. *Johnson Okokhue Odigie* and his junior brother Mr. Peter Okunbor Odigie were in town, similar interactions took place.

Peter Odigie was much younger than Okogun but according to Peter, he had related with Okogun from their childhood days. He had consulted Okogun on issues over the years. Okogun had admiration for Peter and was always pleased to seek advice from Peter and to counsel Peter. It was thus apparent that they were both pleased when in 1968 Joseph and Justina decided to be life partners and wedded in the Catholic Church. Later in life, Peter and Okogun were often seen together as brotherly inlaws even on market days sitting in Okogun's veranda discussing and keeping each other's company with or without their beloved palm wine. The palmwine tapper most of the time was *Mr. Okie Aghughu* aka *ematon* (iron), son of Pa Aghughu of Uwi-Idinrio. There were some other good palmwine tappers.

Perhaps the man who spent the most time with Okogun among Chief Odigie's children was *Pa. Wilson Akhigbe Odigie.* The children of Okogun and Akhigbe only knew that the two men were not siblings when they grew older to be teens. At first the children thought that Pa Akhigbe was Baba Okogun's junior brother.

Chief Odigie had decided to give a plot of his land by Ofuri Market to Akhigbe for his residence long before he died with the wish that Akhigbe be close to Okogun. Chief Odigie considered that both had something in common. Each was an only son from their respective mothers. Akhigbe had become a very successful and good tailor operating at Onitsha. He also rebuilt his house by the market in 1953/54 using the same special wall setters that Okogun used for his own house the same year. Okogun and Akhigbe were always seen together. They both always attended a periodical meeting at Eguae on their respective bicycles together. The meeting appeared to be at that time to have many of Ewohimi home-based elites as members.

The members discussed issues of mutual personal, family and community interests. They also saved money collectively so that the collected funds were given out in turns to members. It was for the members, a savings account as there was no bank in Ewohimi. The meeting was always hosted with drinks, as both men often returned from the meeting with evidence of having been entertained with some palm wine.

Other men who were close to Okogun as friends and contemporaries were *Mr. Osemende Odiana* of Iliki in Uwi-Idinrio, *Mr. Amhandin* of Idumu-Igun in Uwi-Idinrio who was *Oboh's* father, *Mr. Oko-Oza* who had his house near the Post Office at Eguae, *Mr.* Momodu of Idumu-Okhuen, Idumagho, Chief Francis Aguele Airiagbonaye of Idumu-Agho whose residence was next to Akhigbe's house. Amhandin prefered to call Okogun Johnny coined from his English name John.

Okogun had a brotherly relationship with *Mr. Ukekemuke Abhulimen* of Ozogwor, Ewatto who was the father of Pharmacist Benjy Ukekemuke, his senior brother Odile, and their siblings. Okogun convinced his friend Ukekemuke to send Odile to the Okaigben Primary School which was doing very well at the time. There was also Mr. *Airhekholo* at Ozogwor who was a good palmwine tapper was.

Okogun gave a goat of very good breed to Mr. Ukekemuke Abhulimen to keep and take care of. This made both men inlaws of a kind. Almost on an annual basis, the goat produced offsprings. The offsprings were usually carried to Ewohimi by Pa Ukekemuke's children including Mr. Benjy Ukekemuke Abhulimen. The goat offsprings were shared happily between Okogun and Ukekemuke along cultural lines. Okogun and Ukekemuke and the other close associates had their special words as greetings whenever they met, and no one knew how they came about such words for their greetings.

Okogun also had special greetings with Oko-oza which was *gbeminrhu* (could translate to "cover up the thing"), with Mr. Momodu it was a sound HMMMMM... MMM.

Okogun regarded *Mr. Lawson A. Ilegbodu* as a junior brother. He admired Lawson a great deal and Lawson also took him as a senior brother. Okogun used to tell stories of how good an asologun dancer Lawson was as a young man. When Lawson was an Assistant Registrar at the University of Ibadan, Lawson accepted Okogun's son Joseph into his family at Ibadan for some time. Lawson and the mutual friend of Okogun and Lawson *Chief Michael A. Borha* of Ubiaja, got Joseph to study successfully for admission to the then University College Ibadan. Chief Michael A. Borha of Ubiaja was a very close friend of Okogun. When Chief M. A. Bohra was the Federal Permanent Secretary in the Nigerian Civil Service in 1959, Okogun sent his son Joseph to him. Mr. Bohra was to help secure a job for Joseph who had just completed his secondary education at Saint Patrick's College, Asaba. Between Mr. Bohra and Mr. Lawson Ilegbodu, they decided that Joseph should study for the entrance to the University even after Okogun informed Bohra that he expected Joseph to develop himself further in education and that he had completed his education plan for Joseph.

Okogun explained that he had many branches in his nuclear family and needed to develop one person from each branch to spread development and load in the family. Okogun had consulted me in 1957 when we agreed, using the same principle, that his son Robert of the same mother as I should not attend Annunciation College, Irrua after passing the examination for admission to the College so as to give Felix who was a few months Robert's junior the opportunity to go to Secondary School. Okogun was not in the position at that time to pay fees for Robert and Felix together in Secondary Schools.

The Ighodalo's – Chiefs Jeremiah Ighodalo, Chief Joseph Ighodalo and their senior brother had fraternal relations with Okogun. The most senior of the Ighodalo's, Mr. Erieminlamhen Ighodalo was the traditional godson (*Oror)* of Okogun.

Okogun at Ibadan on the occasion of the conferment by now Pope Saint John Paul II of Papal Knighthood of Saint Sylvester on Joseph and Justina Okogun, April 1985.
L. to R. Standing: Igotie Ogieyan, Clifford E. Afeyodion, Uncle Joseph O Omole, Charles E Ighalo, David Afemhenikhu, Augustine Eseraegbo, Navy Commander Alphonsus Odigie and Benson U. Ikhile. Sitting L. to R. Mrs. Maria Ighalo, Uncle Chief Jeremiah A Ighodalo, Joseph, Justina, J Okogun Omovuon, John S Eduwo. Squatting Left, Edwin Odigie and Right, Solomon A Okogun

Mr. Akhator of Uzebu was one of Okogun's distant cousins and contemporary. There was also *Pa Ailenbuade* of Uzebu, Ewohimi.

Eigbike Gabriel Ukpebor of Eguae-Oliha, Ewatto

Mr. Eigbike Gabriel Ukpebor of Eguae-Oliha, Ewatto was a friend of Okogun whose background and reported[72] interaction with Okogun says much about the two men.

Eigbike was first an employee of the local Council and later joined the Public Works

Department (PWD) as a road mender. Eigbike was also a devoted Catholic Christian. It is not known how they became friends. Eigbike played the role of a drummer in Igbabonanrimin which may have brought them together and they both had parental links with *Abhurhu* quarters in Ewatto. Okogun was senior to Eigbike and hence Eigbike took to Okogun as his mentor. Eigbike related some of the things they talked about when they met. The first was on the need to send children to school. Okogun encouraged Eigbike to give Western education to his children and warned that if he did so, he would court jealousy and subdued hatred from some people for doing so. Okogun encouraged him to do good works. The second was on the purpose of life. When Eigbike visited Okogun one Ofuri Market day, Okogun called Eigbike's attention to the Market in session which would become clear when the buyers and sellers returned to their abodes. Okogun would then declare that life on Earth was like visiting the Market for business only to return home at the end. Home was either Heaven (*Eguae-Osenobua)* or House of Fire (*uwa-erhain)*. Hell was also referred to as the next world where the beds and ground were covered with sharp-edged broken kernel shells (*arinmin ni ihian ivin*) and Heaven was referred to also as *Ughe-orhor (*harvest time street).

Okogun as an Elder had many followers and admirers. His popularity and cordial fatherly relationships with so many people earned him the title *ogie – ese* meaning king of the crowd or king at the center or crowd-puller.

Okogun in accordance with the contemporary practice had women lovers. Such lovers or concubines were very few and the children did know about such women until long after his death. He kept his association with other women very private and as far away as he could from his wives and children.

Two courageous night encounters

There were several courageous deeds in Okogun's life. The solitary walk from Benin to Ewohimi and the experience taking timber logs to the Niger have already been described. Two other events of rare courage need to be mentioned.

In the 1940s and 1950s, there was a booming John Holts Company Branch already mentioned which occupied Chief Odigie's property facing Ofuri Market. The Company had a general merchandise store that sold building materials and household goods. The Company also retained palm kernel and palm oil buyers who bought these commodities at Ewohimi and neighbouring markets for the John Holts Company.

The produce was processed, graded, and periodically taken for export by lorries to the ports at *Koko, Sapele and Warri.* Most of the palm kernel buyers were from Ikemen-Ezolomon or their relations from other quarters. Among these buyers were *Messrs Jeremiah Agberhankhe, Ikhile* (aka *Obhiodede), Johnson Akuetae and Sunday Imhansuonmon.* Others were Messrs *Idoghor* of Idumobo *and Imhenrion* of Idumu-Agho. There was also *Mr. Akpata,* an obese Igbo man who resided at Chief Okogie Imanyelea's house.

The night guard of the John Holts stores *was Pa Osobor* of Aigbanloghor-Ologhe, Okaigben. One night, men of the underworld drove in to rob the John Holts Company. Apparently, their cutlass failed to work on Osobor. They therefore resorted to tying him up. Osobor being a strong man struggled with the thieves and as they tried to gag him, he managed in groans to call Okogun's name with a drawl that woke up Okogun in his house. Okogun with his very loud and sonorous voice shouted in *Esan, ola orin khin n n!?* (Who is tha-a-a-t?!). He rushed out of his house and without putting up a fight the robbers fled in their waiting vehicle. Some years later, a known robber from Ekpoma *Mr. Idene-Ekpoma* came to confess and pay respects to Okogun who he said had something awe=inspiring in his voice which frightened them when they attempted to rob the John Holts years earlier. This incident is fully described in the concluding chapter of this book in the contribution from Mr. Amuda E. R. Enato as an eyewitness.

The second encounter at night happened on his way from Ohordua late at night. He could not leave Ohordua until very late at night. He was advised to spend the night at Ohordua, but he insisted on returning to Ewohimi. He had his bicycle fitted with a carbide lamp as his means of travel. He had just surmounted the crest of the hill called *okhun-irie* (the sky is not far so described because of its height) on his way from Ohordua in the Ewatto direction, when with the bicycle fitted with a carbide lamp, he noticed weird figures moving in opposite direction towards Ohordua. Just then the carbide lamp went off or dimmed on its own. It was unusual for the carbide lamp which he had fully charged to last his journey to Ewohimi to go off or dim and he was deeply disturbed and afraid. He cautiously watched, in the twilight, the human figures partially covered in rags. One of them was carrying a shallow calabash basin (*ugba*) with contents which it tried with great effort, to overturn on Okogun.

The basin appeared to be too heavy for the figure and so it could not have the contents poured over Okogun.

After several unsuccessful attempts to spill the contents of the basin over Okogun, the figures decided to continue their journey. They moved on past Okogun and the bicycle carbide lamp suddenly came on again. Okogun with great relief, and summoning up courage, hurriedly arrived back on his bicycle in Ewohimi. The next day he related his experience to his sisters. He was told that the witches carried some disease affliction in the basin that they were trying to overturn on Okogun. The affliction was being taken by the witches to Ohordua. He was asked by his sister Uhuomonye and others if he had recognized any of the faces. Being a man about town as a trader, Okogun did recognize one of the faces that looked like that of a woman he had seen living in Eguae – Oliha, Ewatto. He was advised on what he could do to meet and consult the woman in broad daylight to confirm if he suspected correctly. He took off and located the woman in her residence. The woman was with her cotton wool spindle and was spinning the cotton wool into thread on a spool.

Okogun very respectfully greeted her and presented some kola nuts to her. Okogun then told her that he Okogun always moved around and often at night and sometimes in dangerous terrains. Okogun wanted her to assist him with some protective charms. The woman became first livid and then furious. She declared that Okogun had come to accuse her of being a witch. Okogun pleaded with her that his mission was on the contrary and with the rebuff, Okogun respectfully left to return and reported back to his sisters. The opinion he and those he told the story formed was that the woman was involved in the Okhunirie hill episode.

CHAPTER TWENTYONE

THE BEGINNING OF THE END

In Okogun's last days on Earth, some of the children got directly involved in his life and hence gave eyewitness accounts. The events described in the following pages are mostly eyewitness accounts of Okogun's life just before his death.

Mama Angelina Ailegbesuan's death

For the past few years Mama Angelina now the most senior of Okogun's wives, had been living with her son Felix Okogun in Benin City. She developed some health issues and could not return home. Eventually, she died in Benin on January 18, 1993. Her death at about 80 brought sadness so early in the New Year. Mama Angelina was a very peaceful and broad-minded mother with good-will for all. She took all Okogun's children as her own. Her attitude contributed to the fact that most people thought that she was my mother. Mama Angelina returned to the Assemblies of God Mission Church, into which Enimaluole had led her before they had a ban to stop going to Church from Okogun's family, and became a devout Christian. She sanitized her apartment by getting a Pastor to help remove and bury in the backyard all fetish objects that she had in the apartment. When she died the first sympathizing persons came to my house to express their condolence. We celebrated her burial ceremonies in a glorious and impressive manner both at Ewohimi and at Ohordua on the 12th and 13th of March 1993. During the burial celebrations to honour Mama Angelina's memory at Ewohimi with dances, feasting and booming of guns, Felix and I were with Pa Okogun. He said to us in Esan that we should also celebrate him the same way when he dies.

We could not react perhaps because his wish came as a surprise to us. He looked hale and hearty and we did not think that his death was near. On hindsight, was Mama's death a signal to him? Okogun had a very robust health as already discussed. He was hardly seriously ill. There were three hospitalisations. The first was at Agbor at the time he was living in that area. He had surgery, which was probably for hernia. That condition may have arisen from his being on his bicycle most of the time doing business as cloth, tailor and rubber merchant in Delta and Edo States of Nigeria. Okogun thought that he saw what he took to be God's face during the treatment process at the Agbor Hospital. He said he noticed someone with a very broad and extensive face looking down over him as he lay on the Hospital bed after the surgery. The seer that he related the experience to, told him that it was God appearing to reassure him and heal him.

He had a very serious illness already discussed that made him bed ridden for weeks and apparently, it was a life-threatening one. He was not taken to the hospital. A native doctor or doctors treated him. That illness was when he briefly married Madam Aminetu widowed by Pa Osagie Aki's death as already discussed. The second hospitalization occurred at a very old age and it was again a surgery. This time it was to remove cataract from his eyes. The surgery was carried out at a Hospital in Warri when Felix Okogun, then a Water Board Manager at Warri, hosted him. Joseph and Felix agreed that Felix should host Okogun at Warri to get the surgery done and Joseph took Baba Okogun and Agbontaen Francis from Ewohimi in his car to Felix in Warri. He left from Warri to Ibadan taking little Agbontaen with him to start schooling at Ibadan. After the surgery Okogun passed through a phase of what the doctors called delirium. Okogun still on the hospital bed would be conversing with dead people that those around him did not see. Prominent among those he mentioned as being around him was Chief Paul Odigie who had died earlier. Much of the discussions featured the dead asking for his opinion on cases in the village that needed to be adjudged. He would request the dead to leave him in peace and go away to decide on issues without bothering him. During those episodes, some concluded that Okogun was about to die and prematurely gave the people in the village and others that impression.

Okogun recovered fully from the successful surgery though his sight did not fully return as he ended having a blurred vision.

Okogun received a sign that his death was near

The third hospitalisation was at the very end of his life and certain events preceded the hospitalisation. In September 1993, Joseph returned from Germany. *Isi Ikhola Joan Okogun*[73], one of Okogun's granddaughters was visiting the country from the USA. There was petrol crisis in the country. Long queues of vehicles wishing to buy fuel featured in all petrol stations in Ibadan. There were political problems in the Country and demonstrations associated with *General Babangida's* annulment of an election that gave *Chief M.K.O. Abiola* of Abeokuta victory in the Nigerian Presidential election.

On September 8, 1993, my indefatigable cousin Mr. *Jasper Ojieyan (Ogieyan)* graciously brought from Lagos my imported Mercedes car after he renovated the Port-vandalised vehicle by buying the missing parts and refitting the vehicle for the road. He also got the car licenced LA 7252 in Lagos. I had returned from Study Leave from Germany on August 21 but brought in the vehicle by Sea to Lagos. I then decided to make a quick preliminary visit home to check on Pa Okogun, my fatherinlaw Pa Peter Okunbor Odigie and other families and friends in Edo and Delta States. It was a risk traveling but all were anxious also to see me.Our second daughter Isi Ikhola Joan who was visiting from the USA wished to see her grandparents, other relatives, and their places. Isi was not on her best health state. Her body appeared to be reacting adversely to the change from the United States of America to the water and food in Nigeria. She insisted on travelling.

There was also the problem of putting gasoline to fuel the vehicle. After spending two days on the queue between us, Osahon and I got fuel into the old Toyota car. We syphoned fuel from the old car to the Mercedes Benz car. On 10 September, I took off for Edo accompanied by my motherinlaw *Mrs. Grace A. Odigie*, Isi, *Ikeafe Luke Enosegbe* my nephew and our last child *Aigue Ehiomen Anne*. At Benin, I provided the simple customary items and my fatherinlaw blessed the new vehicle. We left for Warri and spent the night with *Engineer and Mrs. Inegbedion* and family. We were pleased to find that *Emmanuel*, my brother who was indisposed was then better and living with the Inegbedions.

Next morning just after 10am, we took off for Ewohimi and arrived at about noon. We met Pa Okogun sitting as usual in the front veranda and *Mr. Pius Usifo, Mr. Iseria's* senior brother was by him.

Okogun got up immediately on sighting us and went into the house. He returned shortly after with kola nuts. He prayed over the kola nuts broke the kola nuts and shared to us following the tradition.

His prayer over the kola nuts was:

> *Facing me he said "I thank God for three things now that you are back.*
>
> *You traveled and have come back safely, and you have met me alive.*
>
> *I thought that I would not see any of my children in the diaspora before I die: Now, I have one of them Ikhola*[73] *(Isi) here with me.* Ikhola was Okogun's name for Isi Joan.
>
> *People have been mocking you over your old car*[74] *that you could not change, now you have bought a new car"*

We explained that our mission was just to see them at home and let them know I was back and that I needed to take formal leave from the University of Ibadan to be at home with them for about two weeks while Isi needed to return to her studies in the United States. I promised to be back to Ewohimi as soon as the University approved a short leave for me.

We then left Ewohimi about 2:00PM and found our way back to Ibadan via *Ewatto-Ubiaja-Uromi-Irrua-Ekpoma-Iruekpen-Sabongida Ora-Ifon-Owo-Akure-Ilesha-Ife-Ibadan roads.* Thank God as we miraculously found fuel for the vehicle at Ubiaja and arrived safely back in Ibadan at dusk.

An SOS from Pa Okogun through our cousin Mrs. Beatrice Griffin

On Sunday September 26, 1993 at 2:30PM, our cousin Pa Joe Esezobor Ilegbodu's first daughter, *Mrs. Beatrice Griffin* suddenly showed up at our 14 Saunders Road University of Ibadan residence. She had never visited us at Ibadan. After the usual courtesies and expression of her sudden and unannounced intention to visit us, she proceeded to tell the purpose of her mission.

She had visited home to see her father Pa Joe Ilegbodu who was ill and had returned with him to Lagos for medical attention. Pa Okogun had instructed her to first take her father to hospital and immediately thereafter, to come to Ibadan to order me to come home without delay because he needed to discuss with me. Beatrice kindly carried out the charge and met that I had coincidentally loaded my car ready to take off that afternoon for Ewohimi. The spirits were certainly working together. She probably would have met that I had left for Ewohimi, if I was not waiting to receive *Professor Donald E. U. Ekong* my Ph.D. degree academic mentor who was visiting *Professor and Mrs. Kendrick Udoh (Mrs Dora Udoh* was one of Professor Ekong's junior siblings) on the campus. The Udohs' residence was directly opposite 14 Saunders Road on the other side of the street. Immediately after receiving Professor Ekong at the Udohs, I left for Ewohimi. *Erabor*, our fourth child and second son in our family traveled with me. We departed at 3:30PM and got to Benin after dark. This was not the time to take any risks traveling beyond Benin at night as we had done in the past with grave consequences when we had divine assistance. We checked into Room 121 at the University Palace Hotel, Benin City.

Early in the morning we went into town to brief my brothers before leaving for Ewohimi.

Brother Robert was not in his office at Palm House nor at his residence. Brother Amuda's Nigerian Observer Office was sealed due to ongoing industrial action but I met brother Amuda and family at his residence and briefed him so he could brief others. We left Benin for Ewohimi via Agbor. At Agbor we visited *Mr. Willie Usiraido* at his shop and met his wife. We visited the late *Mr. Gabriel Iyoriobhe's* family. *Obhokhan Iyoriobhe* helped me locate an electrician on Doharty Street to repair my car radio and then a block industry where I deposited money for 400 blocks and seven bags of cement to be delivered to me at Ewohimi for the demarcation wall around our compound. A staff of the block industry *Mr. Kingsley Oriahi* accompanied us to Ewohimi to know where to deliver the blocks to.

The situation at Ewohimi

We got to Ewohimi and met that by coincidence, *brother Robert and sister Aiterebhe* were already by Baba Okogun at home. They had arrived unsummoned without knowing that their father Okogun was seriously ill. Okogun was on the floor in his room with his legs virtually paralysed. Brother Robert spoke quite harshly to me urging that I must this time take full responsibility by taking our father Okogun to hospital at Ibadan.

Baba related how the impossible by his standard had happened: "*Okogun fell!" (Okogun de)* he said with alarm on his face. Okogun was known from his acrobatic days never to fall and now he had experienced a fall. Okogun immediately passed on to me important documents[75] which he had jealously kept hidden for me. He then directed me to one of his boxes. In the box were copies of photographs of some of his children and grandchildren and envelopes. In one of the envelopes, was a letter from Tessy Odion Imanrenezor nee Okogun in which Tessy reassured him not to entertain any fears about her life in the United States of America as well as her resolve to play vital roles in the family. He was finding it difficult to move. Dr. Jamgbadi had a hospital in town and had been looking after him. He was not in town on the day I arrived Ewohimi.

The next day 27th September, Dr. Jamgbadi, returned from Benin and was summoned to give medical attention to Pa Okogun. It was agonizing for us to see a man who to us was so strong and agile in a state in which he could not stand up to do anything for himself. He had to be carried even to have a bath. He had to have his bath in the unroofed enclosure (*egun)* behind his apartment. I had to carry him on my back to and from the enclosure. Going down into the enclosure and climbing up back from it into the house was not so easy for me but I had to show Pa that I was strong enough to carry out the task without both of us falling. A fall would have been disastrous, and we never had one for the days that I had to undertake the task all alone. When *brother Felix* arrived, he supported him on my back to take him for his bath.

After some days during discussions, Okogun then told the story of his getting very ill while I was in Germany. He was taken to Benin and lodged with *Robert*. One night he said, God gave him the sign that his time to die had come. He got up knelt and pleaded with God telling Him that unless his sins were too heavy or serious, God should please allow me to return from Germany before taking him to fall asleep dead. He was then taken to see a doctor, probably *Dr. Sunday E. Okojie* who gave him a simple treatment that led to his recovery. I then informed him of my dream on 25th May 1993 while I was in Germany. The only details I gave were that in the dream, he died and then got up to instruct me on how to get things done without my naming the things he wanted me to do in the dream. And we left it at that but thanked God that I met him still alive. He looked strong enough on the outside, but he could no more walk.

His legs were paralysed. We brought in Dr. Jamgbadi, a medical practitioner who was having a successful practice at Ewohimi. Dr. Jamgbadi's handling led to inconsistent results. The doctor did not divulge to us what his diagnosis was. Eventually, Dr. J Jamgbadi advised that we took the old man to a more advanced and better equipped hospital. Robert insisted that the old man must be taken to the best hospital this time around and that could only be the University Hospital at Ibadan. That meant that I should take Pa to Ibadan and not take him to Robert in Benin or to Felix in Warri as on previous occasions. We all agreed that Pa had to be taken to the University College Hospital at Ibadan. We then told Pa of our decision and he expressed no opinion; but it was obvious that he expected me to take him to Ibadan. Bear in mind that his nephew Pa Joe Ilegbodu had just been taken to Lagos for treatment in a Hospital in Lagos. We kept the decision to ourselves and did not announce it to others until the evening preceding the morning of our departure for Ibadan.

Even in Pa Okogun's state, he was still quite humorous and cheerful. He showed me the scar on his genitals where he had had surgery at Agbor as earlier mentioned and wondered prophetically whether his health problem had something to do with the genitals.

He showed me the money that *Mr. Victor Cole* had kindly sent to him from the USA.

CHAPTER TWENTYTWO

PA OKOGUN'S ORDERS THE SANCTIFICATION OF HIS PREMISES: JOURNEY TO IBADAN

The next day in the evening, we told Pa Okogun that we had to move early the next morning. He immediately requested us to go and bring in the Catholic Church Parish Priest at Ewatto. That evening he had *Pa Aghughu* with him. Pa Aghughu, an Odion-egbe was his customary and traditional godfather and longtime colleague from their early days. They were also famous acrobats and danced together as earlier stated. He came to visit and console him on his illness. Pa Okogun excused himself and signalled Pa Aghughu to leave as the Reverend Father arrived.

At that time October 4, 1993. Ewohimi was under Ewatto Parish. The Parish Priest was *Reverend Father Ambrose Alumiasunya*. We went to him and happily he graciously agreed to the old man's request. On arrival at our residence, Pa Okogun told him to help lead us to get rid of all the fetish objects and shrines in the premises starting from the main building and through the women's apartments. Before this day, Pa Okogun had asked me to take down a charm pinned with a staple to the lintel of one of the doors in his room saying, "they are tired" (egbe lo ale). I hesitated but prayerfully emboldened myself and pulled it down. We started from Pa's room to collect and assemble the charms and shrines. Okogun said pointing to the osun: "Take it, Joseph will not have time for these".

We took the Reverend Father through rooms and places in the main house that had the fetish objects. Father Ambrose would sprinkle Holy Water on each object before we took them away. We did the same through all the women apartments[76]. We assembled all the objects at the back of the premises. Under supervision of Reverend Father Ambrose, we dug a shallow grave into which we threw the objects. The Reverend Father once again sprinkled Holy Water on them, followed by kerosene and set them ablaze to burn out completely.

We went back to report to Pa Okogun that his will had been done concerning the shrines, charms, and fetish objects and how the objects were disposed of. He then asked *"if the said water will no longer be fetched"(a mhan khi se ene amen?)* referring to his being baptized into the Catholic Church. We informed the Reverend Father of Pa's request.

Father Ambrose said that Pa still had two wives namely Madam Maria Imanrhokanbhor and Madam Julie Agbonizeta and so he could not baptize Pa unless he wedded one of them.

We did not deem it appropriate to explain to Pa Okogun why the baptism could not be given. We thought he was going through much already, and the Church had the Baptism of Desire provision in its provisions. We then left that aspect of his request for Ibadan.

The Reverend Father left, and we continued the preparation to leave early the next morning. We got prepared to leave before daylight at about 5.00AM.

A wet stormy morning and car pedal lock key problem

We were all ready just before 5.00AM to get into the car and take off. *Mr Silvester Eraze*[77] who was then a medical student at the University College Hospital came to join us from Idumuguokha-Ugbolobhede to help us manage Pa during the impending journey to Ibadan. Just as we started dressing up, the sky became heavily overcast and it became windy. Then a heavy downpour of rain began. Pa insisted that come rain and thunder, we should take off while the rain poured down even if he was going to get wet in the process of boarding the vehicle. It appeared the gods were up in arms against us and Pa Okogun appeared to have felt that a spiritual battle was on that must be faced and fought back.

Then I took the car key to open the car for loading. *The bunch of keys fell to the ground and the unbelievable happened*: the key to the car pedal lock broke in two, but the two segments were held together by a tiny thread. That meant we would be unable to free the vehicles's clutch and brake pedals and hence unable to drive the car. The implication was frightening because I was at a loss how to get the lock cut by a welder. No welder was easily available, and the position of the lock was difficult to access. The journey would have to be postponed and Pa would be quite unhappy if we had to do so.

Felix came looking for me wondering what was delaying me from opening the car. I related to him what we were being confronted with. At first, he stood and panicked. Then he asked for the key. I gave the key to him ensuring that the tiny thread holding the segments together was intact. He went to the car held the two segments of the key together and carefully pressed it to the position for opening the lock. The lock snapped and opened and then the two halves went completely apart.

It was a heavy relief to all that Felix opened the lock and we thanked God for His help in getting that done. I drove the car as close to the veranda steps as possible.

We loaded the vehicle and when all was ready, we went to inform Pa that all was set, and he had to be taken into the car. By this time, the downpour was at its heaviest. We carried Pa. While others spread the available umbrellas over us and Pa Okogun to protect us and Pa Okogun as much as possible from the downpour. We got him into the car slightly drenched by the rain. I sat in front of the car to drive while Silvester Eraze and Erabor sat with Pa at the back seat of the car. It must be said that rains in October were then usually heavy but short lived and was used then to marsh mud for making the walls of buildings. For this reason, Esan people called rains at this season "mud water or water for mashing mud" (*amen-eken* or *amen iho eken*"). The strange thing with this day's rain was its suddenness and the many hours. It lasted unusually for a long time.

To fulfil all righteousness, I needed to inform the elders about taking Pa Okogun, an Oka-igbama in the village away from home. I then instructed the nightwatch, *Mr. Itilah Arhebogie* to help me inform the elders: *Chief Michael Osoh, Pa Egiahumhense Osoh, Pa Isebita Aile and Pa Aghughu* about the developments and Dr. Jamgbadi's referral letter to the University College Hospital (UCH) at Ibadan. The referral letter was addressed to *Dr. Ogunniyi* by Dr. Jambgadi. It was about 6.00AM when we drove off taking the Ofuri Market – Iselu road. The downpour continued and the roads were heavily flooded making it impossible to know where the potholes were to avoid them. We prayed to God for a safe journey.

Ewohimi to Ibadan

I had several cassettes of music artists to play throughout the journey which I thought should put Pa Okogun in at least some good spirits despite the pains which we later learnt he was going through because of his later diagnosed condition. I wanted to start the journey with *Ogenete's* Esan album which was a mix of the music and songs of various Esan dances of asologun and acrobatic dances including igbabonanrimin. Pa Okogun always enjoyed listening to the album. I placed what I thought was Ogenete's album in the slot. It turned out that the cassette was *Handel's Messiah* album. I apologized to Pa and told him that I wanted to play Ogenete's cassette first. As I reached out to change the cassette, he requested that I left the Messiah to play and that he liked the music. I was surprised that he appreciated the album to that extent, but I was pleased that the Holy Spirit had intervened, and we were starting the journey with such a sublime and divinely inspired music. All through the previous night, I was asking God to help us decide whether to go the Agbor - Benin – Ijebu – Ibadan route or the Ubiaja – Uromi – Ekpoma – Sabongida Ora – Ifon – Owo – Akure – Ilesha – Ife – Ibadan route knowing that we were embarking on a journey that could encounter many trying events.

On getting to the T-junction at Iselu, I swerved right to take Ubiaja – Uromi direction. The downpour continued until we were nearly at Ifon and the Messiah cassette music played up to about the same point. I then inserted Ogenete's album. When Ogenete was playing, Pa was reminded of his days as a famous dancer. His eyes, wet with tears as the music played, betrayed his sad emotions which he had hidden from us. We hoped that UCH would play the magic and bring him back on his feet.

The journey proceeded smoothly and though the fuel scarcity was still on, we encountered no problems getting fuel for the vehicle along the way. At Ile Ife, we stopped at a petrol/gas station to refuel the vehicle. An old woman was by the petrol station begging for alms. When she turned to ask me for money, I pointed moodily to Pa who was in bad shape to let her know that I had serious issues in my hands. I realized from what she said that it was foolish of me to have done so. She said in Yoruba: *Ee gbe ehin e* which was a prayer that I outlived the old man. I thanked her inwardly for her prayer which not only changed my mood but encouraged me to do the best I could to get the best medical treatment for the old man.

We got to Ibadan about 3PM and at Pa's request drove straight to the University College Hospital, UCH. With the assistance of the nurses, Dr. Ogunniyi, clinical Consultants including Dr. F. A. Bella and Professors[77], Pa was swiftly attended to and assigned a bed in the South East Ward 3. Coincidentally, he was placed under *Professor Osuntokun's unit.*

Eventually that late afternoon, the pre-eminent Professor B. O. Osuntokun, on learning that I was in his clinic with my father, showed up with his team to examine the old man. He easily arrived at the correct diagnosis which we later learnt to be advanced prostate cancer. Coincidentally, as I write, I am managing my advanced prostate cancer using mainly herbal capsules together with the initial orthodox treatment that was expected to lead to surgery. The herbal capsules seem to work synergistically with the Western medicine and the surgery has been found to be unnecessary.

The doctors[78] at the University College Hospital, Ibadan probably felt that in my state of mind, I should not be told the details of the problem. The Professor made his prescriptions which included warfarin (indocid) and painkillers essentially. The catheter insertion followed later.

CHAPTER TWENTYTHREE

LIFE AT THE UCH

We left the hospital after Pa had settled down on his bed. We were very grateful to Silvester Eraze who went into his Hall of Residence in UCH while we left for the University of Ibadan Campus to our residence at 14 Saunders Road. I reported to *Lady Justina I. Okogun*, my wife and she was satisfied that we had done the right thing by bringing Pa to Ibadan. She immediately plugged in her hospitality activities to make Pa comfortable at the UCH. Meanwhile, while we were away to Ewohimi, she was able to successfully get Agbontaen to be admitted as a first-year student at Abadina College.

Master Erabor Anthony Okogun who travelled with me to bring Pa to Ibadan, one of Sister Lucy's sons, Mr. Luke Ikeafe Enosegbe and Ogbeide Franklin Okogun, first son of Felix O Okogun were assigned the task of taking turns to keep Pa Okogun's company at the Hospital. Three young men are all Okogun's grandsons. Ikeafe and Ogbeide were then undergrduates at the University and so Erabor who was preparing for admission to the University had to spend the most time at the Hospital with their grandfather.

We immediately informed Mrs. Mammy Mary Afeyodion, one of Pa's daughters living at Ibadan with the husband Mr. Clifford E. Afeyodion. Early from the next day, she and her husband came to the Hospital and joined the care team. Other children who did not reside at Ibadan visited Pa Okogun at the Hospital from time to time.

Okogun's time in the hospital gave him the opportunity to look back, consider the contemporary and look in the future. He was able to prepare undistracted for his death which from all indications he knew months ago was at hand. He spent the time advising us and giving valedictory talks. He appreciated the time that he spent in the hospital with his complete mental faculties right to the very end. During one of our private conversations, he reported with disgust that he heard one of his wives coming close to his apartment to express her admiration for one of Pa's colleagues[79] who died suddenly without going through pains or suffering or getting people involved in the care for the sick. I told him to ignore the remarks because the woman obviously spoke out of ignorance.

Reverend Father Murumba Jem Oguogho baptizes Pa Okogun

One of the first steps Justina and I took on 7 October was to go and invite our friend *Reverend Father Murumba Jem Oguogho* who was then the Parish Priest at Saint Michael's Catholic Church, Yemetu, Ibadan to visit and pray for Pa Okogun. Father Oguogho who hailed from *Opoji* in Esan, Edo State had become well known for his healing Masses and practice of exorcism. He was a very busy Priest, but he readily graciously accepted to visit the old man in the Hospital at his earliest opportunity. Father Oguogho eventually was able to visit Pa Okogun at the Hospital. Father Oguogho was at the Hospital when none of us was present. Father Oguogho prayed for him and preached to him. Okogun told us that Father Oguogho however did not wish that he Okogun responded immediately after the Reverend Father spoke. Father Oguogho told him not to be in a hurry to react to what he Okogun had heard from him but to take his time to reflect and send his reply through me when he had thought about all they discussed and made up his mind.

When I showed up afterwards in the Hospital, Pa Okogun instructed me to go tell Reverend Father Oguogho that he was ready to be baptized. He added that if he be given the opportunity to return to Ewohimi and able to manage an awkward posture, he would take one of his remaining wives to the altar for a Catholic Christian wedding. He also prepared a story for those who would be appalled in Ewohimi by his decision to fully accept Christianity as a Catholic. He would tell them that when he took ill and could not move, they at Ewohimi could not help but that the result of his Baptism and conversion helped his return to Ewohimi alive. We then went as instructed and informed Reverend Father Oguogho.

Father Oguogho had earlier given his opinion that Pa should have been baptized when he demanded it before leaving Ewohimi on two grounds: he was ill and no one could say that he would recover from the illness and secondly, he was going on a long journey and safe arrival at the destination was not guaranteed. He also said that by the Church's teaching, if Pa Okogun died before being formally baptised, he had already received *the Baptism of Desire*.

Father Oguogho baptized Pa Okogun at 6:30PM on Friday October 15, 1993 using his own name John. His godfather[80] was Sir A. P. Amao, KSS a Papal Knight who was also ill and in the same Hospital Ward as Pa Okogun. We were all happy to watch the event and gave glory to God who gave Pa John Okogun Eguaereona Omovuon the grace to desire and receive Baptism into the Catholic Church. After Baptism, Pa Okogun would make the sign of the Cross and say his grace before and after meals in the name of Jesus Christ. He prayed as if he had been a practising Catholic for a long time. On the 16th October, I was at morning Mass at the Pastoral Institute. After Mass, I went to *Chief Patrick M.* Ogiogwa's house to receive a call from one of my junior brothers Solomon who called from the United States. I briefed *Solomon* on Baba's illness and Baba's lament that Solomon was not able to visit him. Solomon also had chats with Ikeafe, Ogbe, Erabor and Agbontaen.

On that day Pa Okogun made some profound statements. I noted six of them as follows:

He had charms in his cupboard at home. Witches and wizards were spreading (distributing) diseases at night. He had cautioned brother Amuda against going against the decision on Amuda's heritage at Ohordua. The bigger family, *Egbe's* decision that made him give up large part of his own family ancestral land to Mr. Asuerinmen Abhukhegbe was not fair[81]. That part of his land included the spot where his mother delivered him as a baby. I encouraged him not to be disturbed about the decision of the larger family and reassured him that we would do with whatever was left of the land. Many people were witches and wizards: "They should get lost, Jesus Christ is the greatest power!", he further declared. We could not tell what was going on in his mind that led to these statements.

We could only guess that having been baptized into the Catholic Church, he was reviewing his past life that had prevented him from accepting Baptism and practice Christianity earlier in life. On October 19, as I came to him in the Hospital and greeted him as usual, He exclaimed *"Okpea, osa akpa men da ghe ebhohie no suwe nin: ebo Omusun i rhe le obhe nu ugha nin, filo kua!"* meaning "Man, it is now that I have seen that your dream: whatever Omusun has put in that room, throw them away!" I was taken aback and could not explain how he had come about knowing details of my dream.

The vision or dream at Hanover, Germany

My six-month study leave *Alexander von Humboldt fellowship award* took me in May, 1993 to the *Hanover Veterinary Medical School (Tierarztlichen Universitat, Hanover*) in 1993. I worked with *Professor Gerhard Habermehl and his team* at the University Chemistry Department in one of the research laboratories. For detailed nuclear magnetic resonance spectroscopic work, Professor Habermehl linked me with Professor *Helmut Duddeck* of the Chemistry Department of the nearby University of Hannover. The study leave was to end in September. I rented a flatlet at the students' hostel which was within a walking distance from the University and often spent some of my afternoon breaks to rest in the flatlet. I went into the flat for a rest on 25th May. As I did not wish to sleep off, I rested my trunk and head across the bed with my feet on the floor. I then dozed off. I had a dream or a vision which woke me up. In the dream Pa Okogun died. He was clad in one of his good agbada dresses and as we mourned his death, he rose and led me to one of the room-stores in his house. That was one of the rooms I used before taking up residence in my own building. One of my junior brothers, Omusun had taken over the use of the room. He then indicated in the vision that his grave should be in the room. I was disturbed. I was happy on waking from the nap that I was in a dream and not in real life. I was worried that my research visit to Germany might be truncated if the man died before I returned to Nigeria. I then knelt by the bed and begged God not to let my father die before I returned to Nigeria. He suddenly saw all this. His order about the room indicated clearly that he saw my dream or that my dream was revealed to him: but by whom?

He then declared that his agony on the sickbed was from God because inspite of God's calls in the past to him, he had been running away from God.

He related an incident as an instance of such calls. Sometime probably in the late 1930s or early 1940s, he was lying on bed in Hospital after what he took to be a hernia surgery. He had consulted native doctors/diviners to find out why he was not getting rich. In a dream while still on the Hospital bed, he was ordered by a voice to look up. He did. He then saw, on looking up, a very big face with large eyes looking down over him. The dream frightened him, and he woke up in fear. On leaving Hospital, he recounted the dream experience to a native doctor/diviner. The native doctor interpreted the dream and told him that God had visited him: he had seen God in the dream. October 21st came, and Pa Okogun was in the best mood since his arrival at the Hospital. He agreed to have breakfast. On that day he continued to pray to God the way he had been doing since he received Baptism, asking for forgiveness of his sins. He told God that the sins were committed out of ignorance. It was like he was making a public confession.

On October 21, Professor *Aghadiuno* did a biopsy on Pa Okogun. Late on October 22nd, Professor Lawani visited him apparently after receiving the biopsy results and decided to carry out surgery. The Professor performed the surgery (*orchidectomy*) on October 23rd. The surgery was successful, and Pa had the usual but minor side-effects of the anesthesia which manifested briefly when Pa spoke incoherently. The next day, he himself confessed that he was partially unconscious the previous day. The surgical treatment was eventually followed up with three radiotherapy procedures on November 9, 10 and 12, respectively.

On October 25th, Sister Lucy, Pa Okogun's eldest living daughter arrived from home Ewohimi. She decided to come to Ibadan following reports given to her by brother Robert about Pa's condition.

Izegbua got in touch with Robert after returning to Lagos from her visit to see Pa at the Hospital. *Izegbua*, our eldest child and daughter had visited the Hospital along with cousin Jasper Ojieyan and *wife Juliet* who came to Ibadan on October 9 also in connection with their children's admission to *Army School* at Akpata, Ibadan. Sister Lucy's presence relieved from the duty Pa's grandchildren Ikeafe, Ogbe and Erabor who were taking turns to stay with Pa in the Hospital.. They could then visit at their free times as Ikeafe and Ogbe were undergraduates at the University of Ibadan and Erabor was studying towards qualifying for admission to the University.

On October 26th, *His Lordship Bishop Felix A. Job* of Ibadan visited Pa Okogun at the Hospital. Rev Fr Mulumba also visited as he did from time to time.

On October 31, Pa wanted God to take him from the world and rejected food, drinks, and drugs.

But late that night, one of the sister nurses, *Mrs Olufajo* talked at length with Pa and convinced him to change his mind. Earlier on this same day, *Engineer Robert E. Odigie* visited him in the Hospital on his way from Ilorin on October 31st. Pa had a fatherly discussion with Robert and as Robert left to return to Lagos, Robert predicted that Pa Okogun was aware of his, Okogun's destination when the time came for him to sleep in death and that it was Purgatory. I did not ask him how he came about the knowledge on Pa Okogun's after death destination.

Pa Okogun's sermons from the hospital bed

While on the hospital bed, Pa Okogun continued to teach people. He gave pieces of advice and instructions to his children and visitors that he knew previously. He appeared to be seeing the past and the future as his last days on earth approached. He remembered details about families when members of such families visited him.

General advice to all was that they should not pick-up quarrels with anybody. People should find their way out of situations that could lead to quarrels or violence and should work for peace always. He was interested in people to the extent that he asked people who visited him about their families and their wellbeing.

Mr. Pius Omotese visited often. Mr. Omotese is related to Mama Maria one of Pa Okogun's wives from Oghu. He was Pa Okogun's inlaw and as a young man used to accompany Maria's brothers Messrs. Palmer Anyangbe, Iyere Anyangbe and Ogiekpon Francis Anyangbe to help in Pa Okogun's farm.

When *Mrs. Edwin Odigie*, accompanied by her husband visited, Pa Okogun asked who her dad was. She told him that late *Mr. John Agbonikhinan* was her father. He surprised her by asking if the woman from Ewossa was her own mother. Her mother sure was from Ewossa but no one knew how the almost

90-year-old man figured that out or recollected the family background of the young lady.

When *Dr. (now Professor) and Mrs. John Anetor* visited him, Pa engaged Mrs. Anetor who is from *Ohordua* to discuss her parents, some Ohordua personalities and families that Mrs. Anetor knew and some that she, being so young, did not know about. Pa Okogun's memory and thinking faculties were, to the amazement of all, as sharp as could be and in excellent state.

Mr. and Mrs. Festus Aiya of Ikeken, Ewohimi visited. Pa had a discussion with Mr. Festus Aiya, then of NAFDAC, Ibadan, about his uncle and family of Ikeken, Ewohimi. Mrs. Aiya was so impressed with Pa Okogun's memory and skin complexion that she asked us if we were sure that Pa Okogun was not an *Ikpotokin* (Esan word for Portuguese).

Chief Jeremiah A. Ighodalo visited often to keep Pa Okogun's company. Other visitors to Pa Okogun included most of the other members of Ewohimi Ibadan Community as well as many Ishan people at Ibadan at the time: *Mr. and Mrs. Benjamin Obaita and his brother Augustine Eseraegbo, Felix Abhumen, and others. Mr and Mrs Gabriel Stephen Iregbeyanogie, late Pa Akebhidigun's son* and wife of Ewatto. *Mr. Omonria* of Ubiaja, a UCH staff and some other Esan community members at Ibadan visited him in the Hospital. All Okogun's children and grandchildren who were old enough to travel and who were in Nigeria visited their father at the hospital.

Dr. Christopher Adubor, later in 1995 to wed Izegbua visited Pa Okogun at the Hospital.

Pa Okogun understood his death was imminent. Pa Okogun was quite sad that he might not see his beloved son Solomon before he died. Tears showed in his eyes as he spoke about his not being able to see Solomon again before he left this world. Pa Okogun then requested that we help to get a good wife for Solomon.

He was particularly pleased to see his son *brother Felix* when Felix came to visit from Benin. He told Felix that he was pleased that he had always cooperated with Joseph and that he was leaving his family to Joseph as the head.

He encouraged Felix to maintain the good relationship between him and Joseph and to act as Joseph's deputy to ensure peace and unity in the family. *Ms Lucy Ebeye* from Boji Boji Agbor was a family friend of Professor and Lady Joseph Okogun. Professor Okogun was the Confirmation godfather of Ms Ebeye's junior brother *Mr. Matthias Ebeye* who was a technologist at the Department of Biochemistry of the University of Ibadan from where he later transferred his services to the University of Benin, Nigeria to become a Chief Technologist. When she heard that Pa Okogun was at the Hospital, she decided to visit him with us. When we introduced Ms Ebeye to Pa Okogun, he immediately gave details of a *Pa Ebeye* and Ebeye's house at Boji Boji, Agbor. Ms Ebeye and we were surprised how well Pa Okogun knew Pa Ebeye who happened to be her father. Pa Okogun and Ms Ebeye switched to discussing in the Ika language. Ms Ebeye took Pa Okogun from then on as her own father who had died earlier.

She brought honey to rub on Pa Okogun's body to mitigate the bedsores that were beginning to develop on the man's skin. Pa Okogun was pleased to be reminded of and to discuss his happy days at Agbor and Umunede.

Mr. Joseph Okanima Omole

Uncle Joseph O Omole came and acted as the senior son of Pa Okogun. Pa Okogun was very close to the Omole family.

Pa Okogun was a nephew of *Omoze,* the mother of Pa Omole's first son *Mr Pius B. Owobu Omole* and therefore Okogun was taken by Pa Omole as his stepson. Joseph Omole was then very young and hence looked to Pa Okogun as his father. Mr. Joseph Omole was very pleased to be able to care for Pa Okogun in the hospital. Joseph Omole was constantly at the hospital to be with Pa Okogun. They both relived old memories of the time when Pa Omole was still alive and Okogun visited him in Pa Omole's estate located away from Idumagho main village and on the way to *Oguoguo fountain stream* – one of the sources of Odu River. Joseph Omole took over the role of giving Pa Okogun a haircut and from time-to-time shaved Pa Okogun's beards and mustaches while Okogun was on the hospital bed. He wanted Pa Okogun to maintain his handsome looks even on the hospital bed. Joseph Omole was also a man versed in Ewohimi culture and language. He often talked in parables and wise sayings of the people. He engaged Okogun in discussions about life and the good past.

Some special declarations and pronouncements of Pa Okogun while in Hospital

Pa Okogun made special and significant statements or declarations and predictions while in hospital. Some of these statements, as already noted, were made immediately after Pa Okogun was baptized. Notable among these statements (not in chronological order) were

"What a back-and-forth affair: They are tired" (They are tired, egbe lo ale, was a metaphor meaning he was tired of living),

"Have you stopped sobbing? ... ..

"When the Uzebu people come, tell them about the structure in my house",

"Let the people know that Okogun has gone home",

"Do not accept any decision by Idinrio to banish Madam Agbonizebeta Julie and her children"

"Witches and wizards spreading diseases at home...they should get lost!
"Witches and wizards spreading diseases at home...they should get lost! Jesus Christ is the greatest power"

General Abacha takes over Government from His Excellency Mr. Shonekan

We agreed with Pa on what time in the morning to take provisions and water to him and his daughter Lucy at the Hospital. On November 17, *General Sanni Abacha* led a bloodless coup and declared himself Head of the Federal Republic of Nigeria to oust the then civilian *Head of State, His Excellency Mr. Earnest Shonekan.* Abacha made a broadcast and the radio and television stations kept playing military music and jingles. The streets were initially deserted and no movements on the streets could take place until late in the afternoon. We could therefore not get to the Hospital until late in the afternoon. The old man inquired about why we were so late in coming. We explained the situation to him.

Reacting, he looked to the ceiling and declared "What a ding-dong affair: They are tired". By that he described the political instability in Nigeria and the fact that he was tired of being in the world. We then began privately to expect and pray for his peaceful death and acceptance into Paradise. After that episode, he stopped being interested in the treatment he was getting to keep him alive. He started frowning at me whenever, I made efforts to buy new drug prescriptions for him. I had to tell him that there was no way we could look on without doing all the doctors recommended to help his condition. I reassured him that we were ready for any eventuality so that he would not think that he was impoverishing us. I suspected that he was thinking that we were spending our funds on him instead of saving for our living and his burial ceremonies.

CHAPTER TWENTYFOUR

"DO SUCH PEOPLE DIE?"!

It is customary for children to brief relatives and elders in the village especially about a sick elder if it is suspected that the person might not recover from an illness. The brief was about the care being given to the sick person and the condition of the person. If the pre-death briefings were not done and the person died, the community would frown at the children and accuse them of not taking adequate care of their parent and for not warning the community ahead of time. In those days, the community could take their own initiatives to try and prevent a possible death if the community were properly briefed about a serious condition. Sanctions would be imposed on the head of the dead person's house if he failed to inform the relatives and community elders before the death of anybody, more so if the person was an elder in the community as Pa Okogun was in Idinrio or if the person was a married woman. Being very much aware of this practice, I decided to visit home and report on Pa Okogun's health and the treatment at the then probably the best teaching hospital in Nigeria. I informed the relatives at home and visited some elders to inform them. I went to brief Chief Michael E. Osoh who was an elder and at that time the ruling Chief Osoh of Idinrio.

When Chief Michael E. Osoh saw me looking gloomy and as I culturally greeted him, he asked in a surprised mood: *"Do such persons die?"!*

The Chief had witnessed many of Okogun's exploits bordering on the superhuman in his hey days. The Chief also told me how he helped carry palm-wine and yam bundles to Omen Eguae when Pa Okogun was carrying out the traditional services in the process to marry Enimaluole. He had assumed that I had come to announce Pa Okogun's death. I explained the situation with Pa's health in the hospital at Ibadan to him. I left Ewohimi to return to Ibadan satisfied that I had prepared the minds of the people at home for any eventuality.

"That woman did not plan small against us", "I told Amuda"

One day, looking in the distance Pa made a sound en n n en? "That woman did not plan small against us (*Eno okhuo rin mhan rhe mhan imhan khere!).* Sighing he declared: *"I told Amuda!"*.

The woman was *Madam Aiyobase.* Madam Aiyobase was a powerful woman. She belonged to a relatively important and prosperous family in Ozen, Ohordua by existing standards at that time. She inherited landed properties and plantation of *Irvingia gabonensis (ohele/ ogbono)* and other economic trees. She had no issues and needed to have children of her own to inherit her family estate. She did what was usual in those days to solve her problem. She decided to perform all the marital rites including the payment of dowry to "marry" Madam Ailegbesuan Angelina into her family. Madam Ailegbesuan was beautiful, and she was to have children for Madam Aiyobase's family. Then came the handsome Okogun, and Ailegbesuan fell in love with Okogun. Ailegbesuan as already described, eventually ended up as Okogun's second wife. It was regarded a most dangerous thing to take the "wife" of a woman of substance like Aiyobase. Madam Aiyobase used all means available to her to eliminate the couple. She commissioned native doctors to prepare death and other charms against Okogun especially. One significant alleged death charm, as described by Okogun himself, involved "cooking" Okogun in a pot over 7 or 14 days after which Okogun should suddenly die when the pot was taken down from the fireplace.

A native doctor put the ingredients together and put the pot to cook. Okogun, armed with charms, courage and his conscience were led to where the pot was being cooked and set eyes on the pot with all the charms on the fireplace.

That peculiar charm rule had a strict injunction. The person being cooked must not see the pot while it is being prepared or cooked. If the charmed saw the pot, all the forces of death aimed at the targeted person turned against the native doctor and the client that commissioned him. Okogun reported that the native doctor and Aiyobase had to pay the prize without his doing anything apart from setting his eyes on the charm pot. For Aiyobase, her head got swollen and her upper and lower jaws, threatening to unhinge, could not hold together. She used a headtie to hold her jaws together as she went about as commanded repealing her curses on Okogun to save her own life.

She had seized Amuda the first son arising from the union of Okogun and Ailegbesuan claiming him to be late Aikpaogie's son. They gave Amuda the name *Thomas Oriabor (HRH Oriabor was the Enogie of Ohordua), Matthias,* etc. Aiyobase took Okogun and Ailegbesuan to court at Emu. They, with Amuda then under ten years of age, made five court appearances at Emu in the mid-1940s. Aiyobase lost the battles but Okogun was warned neither to pay the dowry on Ailegbesuan nor to take Amuda and all Ailegbesuan's children from Aiyobase if he wished to preserve and protect his own family and heritage. Amuda became the first son of Aiyobase.

An agreement was reached. Aiyobase repealed her curses and eventually kept visiting Okogun to stay for days with Ailegbesuan and her children from time to time as a way of nursing her interests. Okogun respected if not feared Aiyobase and did his best to honour the agreement to the letter to avoid the consequences that would follow if he did not comply with the terms of the agreement. With the death of Okogun's first son Akhigbe born in 1931, Amuda who is senior to Joseph with some months, would have been next in line to be Okogun's first son. The agreement with Aiyobase and Ohordua community and the fact that Okogun could not formally marry Mama Ailegbesuan according to customary laws and tradition prevented that from happening. Amuda had to inherit Aiyobase's estate at Ohordua and bear the Aiyobase of Enato.

Okogun on his hospital bed was apparently seeing or reviewing all the dangers, he and Ailegbesuan went through and he was led to make the declaration as well as explain to Amuda why he had to use Enato as surname and take up his inheritance of Aiyobase's family estate. Okogun had earlier explained this at two family meetings[64]. (Appendix II).

He also got a note written in the 1960s that he addressed to Joseph Okogun on this issue, unity, and other issues in his family.

The Nigerian Labour Congress trade dispute and the discharge of patients from the Hospital

The Nigerian Labour Congress NLC had declared a trade dispute and were on strike even on November 15th, 1993. The strike action was still on when General Abacha seized power and removed Chief Shonekan as Head of State. The Campaign for Democracy planned public demonstration for November 18th to call for a democratically elected government.

There was panic and anxiety in the air. Hospital authorities feared that it might not be possible to maintain services at the Hospital and decided to discharge all patients in the Hospital. We were immediately confronted with the problem of how to move Pa Okogun to my residence and how to maintain managing his condition. He could not move by himself as the legs were paralysed by the prostate cancer. We were greatly relieved when the Hospital authorities and doctors kindly agreed to include Pa Okogun in the list of special patients to be assembled during the turbulent period in the Hospital Ward E3. Pa Okogun was accordingly moved to the Ward. On November 20, I dreamt that Pa Okogun had died in Ward E3. The dream was not unusual because the patients assembled in the Ward were the very serious hospital cases. By 21 November, two patients had died in the Ward.

"Have you stopped weeping?"

We the children were naturally distressed at the thought of Pa Okogun dying. We could not imagine what life would be without the security provided by such a strong, courageous, and wise father that he was to us. On November 21, our sisters Lucy, Uwamusi and Mammy and myself were by Pa's bed. At about 12 noon, he summoned me to get closer to him. He then asked me in Esan Language "*Have you finished weeping*?" (*We e vie fo?)* I told him that we had decided to leave things in the hands of God. He then continued

"When the Uzebu people join and they start the discussion, you should leave the Idinrio people whom I had discussed with to inform them about the arrangements and my decisions about my household. If they do not say, you should tell the Uzebu larger family members yourself" I was not sure what exactly he was talking about but one of the daughters caught in to say what she thought the old man meant. Pa nodded in agreement and it was about the hierarchy in his household. Pa had held two meetings that discussed the issue in the early 1970s and in 1978. The minutes of one of the meetings was even signed by Pa Okogun himself (Appendix II).

Sister Lucy correctly sensed that Pa Okogun was giving his valedictory discussions. She became emotional and asked if Pa was departing from her. She brought the issue of Pa using the promise of a plot of land in Okaigben to convince her to accept marriage at Eguae, Ewohimi. Pa did not respond. It was obvious that Pa no more found it appropriate to fulfil the promise. I then advised Sister Lucy not to insist on having land at Okaigben because she did not need the land. She accepted and did not press the issue. On the same day, which was a Sunday, the Ibadan Ewohimi indigenes held their monthly meeting at which they sent a delegation to visit Pa Okogun at the Hospital. Mr. Benjamin Obaita, I think led the delegation and Mr. Festus Aiya then of NAFDAC was one of the delegates. Some members of the delegation gave money gifts.

On November 22, the nurses were able to return to duty and Pa was eventually moved back to his South East Ward 3.

Pa gave me a specific order:

"Do not accept any demand from Idinrio quarters to expel Julie Agbonizebeta and children from the village"

I could not imagine what circumstances would lead to the village elders taking such a decision. I no more asked questions and I just accepted his injunction as given. I kept turning many of these instructions over in my mind. I concluded within me that Baba was handing over responsibility to me and that I must be courageous and get ready to be in charge as difficult as things looked to me. He had convinced me to go through the ceremony[82] of graduating from the Egbolughe age status to the mature manhood status of *Igbama.* I had courage from my Faith and the fact that Pa had been telling me that he was leaving a heavy responsibility behind for me. I had the assurance that since he had done everything to put himself right with God, he would be mindful of us and intercede for us members of his family with the Lord in Heaven.

Final day of the Igbama elevation rites, 1987

Sitting from left Oboabhia Osogieahon, Oboh Amhandin, James Igue, Aihiegboria Osagie, John Okogun E. Omovuon, Egiahumense Osoh (Elder representing the Odionwele supervised the rites), Joseph Ibomhen Okogun (the elevated man), Ikhie Adoghe, Ateme (integrated Urhobo man) from Uzebu, Isebita Aile and Ogudo of Uwi-Idinrio. Standing is Andrew Isimhanronkhai representing Iselu. In the background are some Okogun's children Aiterebhe Anthonia and Omusun Wisdom Peace. Photo taken by S Osabhuohien Igue

Meanwhile Pa's bed sores at first showed signs of healing with the handling by Ms *Lucy Ebeye, Dr Ogunremi* and the use of gifts of drums of dressing from *Sister da Silva of Oluyoro Hospital and Mrs. Margaret Ehimika*[83]. But on November 30, the bed sores again started to get worse and treatment with honey was resumed.

CHAPTER TWENTYFIVE

BABA OKOGUN DEPARTS SMILING

On December 2, I arrived at the Hospital and as usual I greeted Pa in Esan: I said

" Baba, Aisan" (good morning greeting by men in Esanland)

He answered*: "Ihon edionmhan n n n n"* dragging the last syllable *(*meaning I have heard old man*).*

I was both shocked and embarrassed and I said in Esan, "Baba do you not want me to get old like you?" and he said no word.

Before now he would normally accept the greeting using endearing words as used for children and young people when they greet elders. The meaning of what he said gradually became clear: he was handing over the affairs to me. I later recalled one of his earlier statements when he said that he had become like my servant. When he made the statement, he was referring to the fact that he could no longer help himself but had to do what we asked him to do. I reminded him then of an adage in Esan which states *that if you give birth to a child, the child will later give birth to you (oria akha bio omon: omon khi bi oria).* At first parents care of their children but in their old age the children take over caring for their parents.

In his last days in hospital, I noticed that he frowned when I would rush away to look for chemists to buy doctor's prescriptions that were not available in the hospital. One day, he was forced to speak out. He asked, "Why do you have to go and spend money buying whatever drugs and materials the doctors prescribed". I told him that he should not be bothered about that and he should not think that he was draining my purse because by God's grace we were ready for any eventuality. I also told him that we could not just look on while he had pains and not do what the doctors recommended to help him.

Not long after that conversation he ordered: *"Let the people know that Okogun has gone home."* I said in response to his charge that I had heard.

Earlier in the day, about mid-day, Mr Edwin Odigie came happily to the Hospital to announce that his wife had delivered a baby boy. We all including Baba rejoiced with him in the usual way.

December 3, 1993, the last night and the next morning: quiet peaceful death.

There was nothing unusual in the morning about December 3, 1993. But little did we know that that day was going to be Baba's last time with us alive on Earth.

We went to the Hospital as usual. On our way, we first called at Zion Hospital to congratulate Mrs. Edwin Odigie on her safe delivery and to see the baby boy in the customary manner.

Later that day at night my wife Justina went to visit him as usual. During our visit on December 3, Sister Lucy reported that earlier that day, Baba had asked her to gather up his things and hers so that they could go home. She was not sure about what he meant. Baba would not speak to me, quite unlike him. He was also sweating.

The big bottle used for storing portable water for him by the Hospital bed floor fell on its side and got broken spilling the water. Baba made no comments.

Suddenly, I said aloud to him in mixed Esan: "*Baba, ade uwe okhi khian, we khai* worry *we mudia imhan bhe egio Osenobua ye: we a ne erhomon imhan.*" Roughly translated says "Baba, if you are now going away, do not worry, go to God and be interceding for us." Justina took me up for saying such words asking why I should make such a statement. She inquired if I observed anything. The expression came off me quite spontaneously without first thinking about what I was going to say. Baba still did not make any comments.

When it was time for us to leave the Hospital, we prepared Baba for sleep. We prayed around him, sprinkled Holy water on him and around the bed. We were three: sister Lucy, Justina, and I. We left and took the lift down from the third floor (fourth floor in the US count). On getting to the ground floor, I decided again spontaneously that we should return to the Ward SE3. We got back to the Ward.

We then said a short prayer together. Lady Justina remembered that she had a small bottle of blessed olive oil in her bag. She brought out the oil and gave it to me. I used the oil to make the sign of the Cross on Baba's forehead and we each did the same on ourselves. We then left saying good night to Baba who did not respond but observed all that we did.

At home at the University, I kept thinking of Baba's condition and went to bed late after midnight. But from about 3:00AM, I suddenly woke up and could find no more sleep. I then decided to pray using *Sant Anthony's Treasury, a book of prayers*. I used several prayers in the book and ended the prayer session with the prayer for the dying. I prayed specifically for Baba Okogun in case he was dying.

At 5:30AM, I fell into a deep sleep. At 6:30AM, I suddenly woke up quite refreshed. I decided to go to Hospital and Sister Lucy came along. Justina could not go with us because we decided that she should stay behind to represent the family at the two different wedding ceremonies of the children *of Professors J. Obemeata and E.M. Essien* who are our friends.

As I hurried down the steps, I stepped on some slippery substance and fell. The substance turned out to be the faeces of our great pet, Enomen's dog *Toro.*

Toro who had been well-trained by Enomen never stooled or urinated in the house. It would always make sounds of discomfort to indicate its desire to go out and defecate or urinate. This was the only occasion it stooled in the house until it died at Abuja on July 6, 2007.

We got to the Hospital and Baba was not on his bed. At first the nurses did not wish to tell us his whereabouts until a senior nurse called us aside to say that he passed on early in the morning at 5:58AM. Later we got Mammy to join us at the Hospital. We were advised to go to the Morgue to identify his corpse and arrange preservation to enable us complete burial arrangements.

The patients in the neighbouring beds were surprised that he died so peacefully saying that they did not know when he passed on. We were sad but on the other hand satisfied that our parting was well executed the previous night as earlier described and that I prayed for him at home as he was dying in the Hospital.

We left the Hospital. I needed to have someone else accompany me to help look for Baba's corpse in the morgue. That was going to be the second time that I would have to go into the morgue to identify a corpse. The first was when Mr. *Matthew A. AYERE,* the first University of Ibadan history graduate from Ewatto, died also at the University College Hospital in 1969.

I went in search of Mr. Joseph O. Omole to inform him of Baba's death. I met him and related the situation to him. He wasted no time in accompanying me to the Hospital to seek out Baba's corpse in the morgue. We easily located the corpse and noticed that Baba died with a smile on his face. I paid the usual fees to the morgue keepers who did a temporary preservation of the corpse. Sunday, the 5th December was our Parish Harvest Thanksgiving at the Our Lady Seat of Wisdom Church, University of Ibadan. We did what we had to do at the Church and left. I went to report Baba's death to *Professor Vincent E. Aimakhu,* one of my mentors and friend, of the University College Hospital Ibadan. He immediately offered to discuss the embalming of the corpse for longer preservation with *Professor Shokunbi,* the then Head of the Department of Anatomy. On Monday December 6, the Jaja Dispensary Health Centre Director, *Dr. Mrs. Balogun* kindly approved for us the use of the ambulance to convey Baba's corpse to the Department of Anatomy. The corpse was transferred the next day December 7 to the Department of Anatomy.

CHAPTER TWENTYSIX

PREPARING FOR THE LAST RESPECTS AND BURIAL

We had informed Reverend Father Murumba Oguogho[84] on the day Baba died. He assured us that from that day until the burial was over, he would say Masses for us so that the burial would happen successfully, peacefully and safely for all of us and for all who would travel to be at the burial. This was a very welcome offer, and we thank him to this day.

On hearing of the death of the old man, several of his children, relatives and friends called in person. The Ewohimi and Esan persons at Ibadan paid condolence visits to us.

Chief Joseph O. Ighodalo called from Lagos. Brothers Robert and Felix came from Benin, sister Felicia and husband Pastor Christopher Ailende and Cousin Mr. Jasper Ojieyan (Ogieyan) came from Lagos. On Friday December 10, I left for Ewohimi via Benin City. Most of Okogun's children were in Nigeria. Omusun went to Warri to Aiterebhe and returned to Ewohimi on the same day with Aiterebhe and her husband *Engineer J. Ehisuoria Inegbedion.*

When evening came on the next day after supper, all the Eze family members (Ibhi-Eze) assembled for a meeting to fix a date for the burial and make necessary arrangements. The meeting was very successful and reassuring on all sides. The spirit of unity and understanding at the meeting was very impressive and commendable. The meeting went on till 1:40AM. They decided to carry out the burial at Ewohimi starting from Friday February 11th, 1994 when the body would arrive at Ewohimi from Ibadan.

In the morning, Sister Lucy led all the available Okogun and other Ibhi-Eze children and wives, other relatives and friends chanting Christian choruses and dancing through Idinrio streets to herald the forthcoming celebration and burial of Pa Okogun. That event had a strong psychological effect to strengthen the family and to send a positive signal to the people. The days were selected so that the laying to rest of the body would be on one of the Angels' days (ede-ehi) as earlier described. In this case, 12 February was Ofuri Market Day.

Several noteworthy things happened on the 12th December. Many relatives and friends began paying condolence visits. Many, including Engineer Emmanuel A. Aguele came promising support.

Mr. Matthew Aguele (from Idumuguokha-non-riu- uwa, related to our inlaw Egbeke's husband) came and handed over to me N3,200.00 (three thousand two hundred Naira) left by our father with him. *Mr. and Mrs. Ezomon* of Idumu-Isaba, Oghu who said he brought the last palmwine that the old man drank came as well. On the 13th, I wrote and took a letter to the Palace to formally inform the Enogie, His Royal Highness Samuel Usifo Enosegbe II about our burial plans. His Royal Highness was not available, and we left the letter with the *Eson,* the Head Queen among the wives. The next day at 12noon, I left Ewohimi for Ibadan via Benin having left some money with brother, Felix to carry out some repairs and works on Pa's building and on my own building. I took brother*, Bartholomew Okogun* as far as Benin while my mother inlaw, Mrs Grace A. Odigie, sisters Lucy and Mammy and brothers Omusun Okogun and Agbontaen F. Okogun accompanied me to Ibadan. We arrived Ibadan at 6:00PM. The condolence visitors at the weekend from Lagos were Pa W. Ehikhamen *Ojieyan (Ogieyan),* his son and family Jasper Ojieyan (Ogieyan) Mr. *Josiah E. Izevbigie* (he had not taken the Chieftaincy title) with his sister Mrs. *Grace Ogaga* and son Vincent, *Mr. Michael O. Obomense, Messrs. Samuel O. Igue, Igotie Ojieyan (Ogieyan), Engineer Ojeaga, sisters Rose Okogun* and *Akhere Okogun.*

Others who visited before the year ended were brother, Mr. Robert Okogun, Pa's grandchildren *from Lagos Mrs. Josephine E. Aijayain, Mrs. Mercy Owoeye nee Enosegbe)* and *Mr. Benjamin Enosegbe.*

Early in January 1994 I returned to Ewohimi to continue preparations for the burial.

It was important that I met the Enogie physically, if allowed, to brief him about the burial. We were at the Palace on the 8th, 9th and 10th January but were not successful in holding audience with His Royal Highness. On the 11th, we were at the Palace again and on this occasion, *Princes Imenrion* and *Aidelogie* held audience with us on behalf of the Enogie. With that we were satisfied that His Royal Highness had received full briefing about the burial. I paid Pa's indebtedness at two social meeting groups to which he belonged. It was necessary to do so in order that the groups played their prescribed roles to honour a dead member and visit the bereaved family. We concluded other arrangements including visiting Warri on January 12th with Felix to see the doctor managing brother Emmanuel Okogun who had problems health. We also had discussions on Emmanuel's behalf with the Warri Refinery Administration and returned to Ewohimi the same day. Our inlaw Engineer Joe E. Inegbedion and sister Aiterebhe and their friends assisted us in getting to the Refinery Officers and the Medical Doctor.

On the 13th, Pa's distant cousin native *Dr. Samson Osagie* visited us to discuss and brief me on the cultural and traditional burial rituals for men of Pa's status in the village.

We went to Ubiaja to arrange the hire of the General Hospital Ambulance which would convey Pa's corpse from Ibadan. We got a very friendly consideration at the Hospital which agreed to rent the ambulance for two days at N2000.00 (two thousand Naira) excluding fuel and other incidentals which we had to take charge of. *Dr. Joseph I. Esezobor* who was my senior at Saint Patrick's College, Asaba, and a longstanding friend was the Medical Director at the Hospital. He was assisted by *Mr. Aigbokhaebho* in the arrangements for the ambulance.

On Friday, 14th I left Ewohimi for Ibadan via Benin. At Benin I discussed the draft invitation card, poster, and order of services at the wake keeps and Masses with brothers *Amuda and Felix*. Brother Amuda, a Printer himself undertook to do the printing of the programmes at minimal costs. I then left Benin and returned to Ibadan the same day.

Meanwhile at Ibadan, Lady Justina Okogun was busy getting our University residence at 14 Saunders Road ready for the wake keep. She had to work with the University Maintenance Department to fix facilities including the septic tank at the premises and issues concerning the children's education. Visits from wellwishers continued. *The Saint Patrick's College* Anniversary[85] Committee delegation which included *Dr. David N. Maduemezia,* my classmate at the College, *Professor Okwobi* and *Mr. J.N. Nwokolo* was visiting Ibadan and it also called on us. Dr. Maduemezia gave me a token purse to assist me with the burial.

On Saturday 22nd January, *Sir A. P. Amao, KSS.*, Pa Okogun's godfather at the Hospital was buried at Ibadan. Sir A. P. Amao had also died in the same Hospital Ward that Pa Okogun was, a few days before Pa Okogun. We attended the burial ceremonies and paid due respects to the dead. *Dr. Idowu Iweibo* of Chemistry Department assisted us to get the invitation cards brought from Benin to Ibadan through Edo Line. The distribution of the cards then commenced on Monday 24th January.

Among the first recipients of the invitation cards were *Rev. Davidson Okunfolue*[86], Manager at First Bank Agodi Branch and another staff *Mrs F.A. Adigun*. On Wednesday January 26th, *Mr. Benson Uwakhonye Ikhile* then a Chief Technologist in the Department of Pharmacognosy accompanied me to the Department of Anatomy to inspect Baba's embalmed body. We gave the usual courtesies to the technicians in charge who took us to the body. The body was in good shape but the smile on his face at death was no more as obvious as it was on December 4, 1993. Aiterebhe arrived from Warri and left for Lagos with some cards. Izegbua also came from Lagos and left the next day taking 100 invitation cards for Lagos. On the same day Saturday 29th, *Mrs. Josephine Enoluesemen Aijayain*, Baba's eldest grandchild and sister Lucy's eldest daughter arrived from Kano bringing a complete set of gorgeous agbada native dress meant for chiefs. The regalia so to say had been bought by *Miss Eunice Enosegbe*, one of Josephine's junior sisters as a gift for Baba while he lived. Eunice could not deliver the clothes before Baba, her grandfather's death. Mercy her senior sister brought the regalia from Kano to Lagos. Mercy had an unusual experience in Kano on the morning of her journey with the cloth to Lagos. Mercy reported how she was kidnapped on her way to their Kano shop and taken to a Cemetery apparently for rituals. She used loud prayers through Jesus Christ and held tight to her Rosary prayer beads which the kidnappers were unable to detatch from her wrist. The ritualist apparently in fear told the kidnappers that she was not acceptable for the ritual and released her. She also said at a time she saw a figure all in white at the Cemetry. Instantly, we decided that the cloth was providentially arranged as a fitting burial dress for Baba. The dress was so used. On Sunday 30th after Mass, I left with Justina and Erabor for Benin. The next day we left for Ewohimi to check on the preparations for the burial. On February 1st Justina returned to Ibadan to continue the supervision of the Ibadan arrangements.

Some of the issues to attend to before the burial took me to visit the Head of the Police at Ewohimi, with the interesting name *Mr. Aimuokhonemounu* (which may be roughly translated as "verbal controversies or fight cannot be stopped by a third party in the manner that physical combats are stopped"). Omusun was detained in Police custody because of his alleged association with the riots that took place at *the Pilgrim Baptist Grammar School, Ewohimi* and he was also involved with the grand daughter of late *Pa Ukate's (aka Okhoaye* roughly translated "our thought/mind is where our real selves reside"*)*. We had to settle these issues along with arranging the last ceremonies to honour Pa Okogun. On the 2nd of February, Pa Joseph Imansuangbon of Ikeken, Ewohimi who was also an Ebalogbhen of Idumigie grandson like Baba Okogun came and spent the day with us. His visit gave us some needed assurance and strength.

Meanwhile some non-Christians in Idinrio, some of whom were distant cousins were telling some of my brothers and sisters that the burials of great and famous men like Baba Okogun usually go with loss of lives. They prescribed that we needed to take some preventive measures by making charms and sacrifices and employing some diviners and charmers to prevent the loss of lives during the burial ceremonies. Some who rightly were scared for their own safety, privately accepted to cooperate with them without informing or consulting me. Brother Robert and sister Aiterebhe reported the matter and their encounter with the non-Christians to me.

Brother Robert approached the matter by advising such non-Christians to go and inform me as the Head of family as he had no power to take decision on their proposals. He knew that the men would not discuss the matter directly with me. No nonsense and pious Aiterebhe confronted the men head on in her capacity as Christian and daughter of the village (*Omadan)*. She told them to forget their proposals because we would not carry out any pagan rituals to protect our lives and others during the burial. She told them that God through Jesus Christ would be with us using words of the Holy Bible to counter what the men were proposing and that there would be no deaths. The playout of all these suggestions will eventually become obvious.

On Thursday 3rd February, I left Ewohimi for Ibadan via Ekpoma and Benin. At Ekpoma, the students at Edo State University now Ambrose Alli University were engaged in a protest demonstration and prevented my going into the University Campus to distribute invitation cards to the Vice Chancellor and other friends. I went to give invitation cards at NIFOR, the Nigerian Institute for Oil Palm Research near Benin City. *Dr. Celestine I. Ikuenobe* and *Mr. Anthony Irusota* and others were staff at the Institute.

The next day, I stopped at the University of Benin, Ugbowo Campus to give cards out to friends and colleagues. *Professor Sam I. Ahonkhai* of Chemistry Department accompanied me to *Professor Felix Okieimen,* who was then a Deputy Vice Chancellor of the University. The University authorities kindly agreed to send one of their big buses to help with transportation of guests from Benin to and from Ewohimi.

I finalized the draft of the funeral Mass programme with brother Amuda and provided funds for transportation arrangements and other matters for those who would attend the burial ceremonies from Benin. We then left and returned to Ibadan.

CHAPTER TWENTYSEVEN

THE BURIAL CEREMONIES AND THE BURIAL

From Monday 7th to the 9th, all hands were on deck to finalise arrangements for the burial ceremonies. On the evening of 10th February, the Service of Songs was held at our residence 14 Saunders Road, University of Ibadan. Baba's children Uwamusi, Aiterebhe and Felicia came from Ubuluku, Warri and Lagos respectively, while Tessy and husband Roland Imanrenezor and Solomon came from the United States for the celebration. It was very well attended. The following individuals and organisations attended:

Reverend *Fathers Professor F. A. Adeigbo*, the Parish Priest, Murumba Oguogho and *Reverend Father Fadeyi* and *Rev. Professor J. Akano* of the Chapel of Resurrection of the University

The Vice Chancellor and his two Deputies

Head and Staff of Chemistry Department

Deputy Registrar Establishment

Many other academic and administrative and technical staff of the University

Members of Ewohimi Union in Ibadan

Members of Esan Progressive Union, EPU Ibadan Branch

The sermon was given by Reverend Father M. Oguogho who baptized Pa Okogun at the Hospital after discussing with him and examining the old man's life. Reverend Father Oguogho therefore had some first-hand information about the man's life. He extolled Baba's life and remarked that the man had lived a very good life. For that reason, he said, God wanted him to die in Ibadan and receive a glorious exit.

We gratefully received token donations in cash and kind to support our burial expenses from many individuals, and from the entire staff of the Department of Chemistry.

At 6:30AM the next morning the Parish Priest Reverend Father F. A. Adeigbo graciously led the officiating Priests at a funeral Mass when Baba's hearse was brought into the Church of Our Lady Seat of Wisdom, University of Ibadan and blessed. After some delay, the body carried in the ambulance left in a motorcade for Ewohimi at 11:30AM through Benin. The University Maintenance Department gave us the big bus additional to the available vehicles to convey family members and friends to Ewohimi.

We arrived Ewohimi at about 6:30PM to meet a tumultuous crowd that lined the road, starting from the *Igwe Hill around Akugbe Farm,* about 5 kilometers from Okogun's residence, singing and dancing. One of the choruses by the young people was *"Papa original"* as they ran alongside the ambulance carrying the coffin as it moved slowly along the road. There were cannon gun booms at various junctions starting from Eguae through to Okaigben, Ewohimi, Baba's final resting place.

There was a pandemonium as we entered Baba's compound. Suddenly, the lights went off and there was darkness all over the place except at the area in Baba's parlour arranged for the lying-in state. The lights were supplied by two giant generators, one brought in by Engineer Joe E. Inegbedion and his wife Aiterebhe and another hired by the family through Mr. Felix Okogun.

In the confusion, one of my fingers was badly wounded through a bite as I motioned and guided the hearse through the enthusiastic crowd into the house. The darkness was both physical and spiritual. Many were frightened at what they noticed among some persons of darkness performing demonic acts. A spiritual battle seemed to be on.

Many resorted to prayers. One group was led by our son inlaw and his wife, Mr. and Mrs. Clifford E. Afeyodion who retreated with some other Christians to the side of one of the big buses that brought in celebrants to pray through our Lord Jesus Christ to counter the dark forces. It did not take long for the effect of the prayers to manifest as power was restored quite quickly by the technical persons around.

Meanwhile, *Dr. M. Ebose Enosolease* now a Professor of Haematology at the University of Benin got materials and applied stitches and dressing to my wounded finger.

A near fatal accident at Eguae, Ewohimi

The non-Christians who predicted loss of lives during the burial ceremonies almost had a cause to smile. Robert Okogun was assigned an ITF vehicle for the purpose of making some errands connected with the burial ceremonies. On arriving at Eguae, Ewohimi, a young teen suddenly rode his bicycle onto the tarred road in an attempt to cross the Ewohimi-Ubiaja road at the Agadaga road junction. He was hit by the vehicle and fell badly on the hard road surface. The boy was miraculously saved as he sustained only surface bruises and recovered fully from the injuries.

The wake keep that included a Requiem Mass commenced at 7:30PM with the Ewatto Parish Priest, Reverend Father Ambrose Alumiasunyan officiating.

The social celebration with dance bands continued till dawn. As usual, the children, grandchildren, other relatives, and friends were assigned dancing times with the usual money spraying by admirers and supporters. The group of Masters of Ceremony was led by *Mr. Gregory O. Onakhinor*[87]. Celebrants and guests came from far and near: Lagos, Ibadan, Benin City, Ubiaja, Ekpoma and other Esan towns, Ilorin, Jos, Kano, Warri, Ubuluku, Enugu and so on.

The ITF, Industrial Training Fund[88] sent a powerful delegation and gave out vehicles to help during the preparation for the ceremonies. There were so many dignitaries that it is impossible to be fair and mention all that should be mentioned. There were the Odigie's in their numbers including *Lt. Commander Alphonsus* led by my Father inlaw Pa Peter Okunbor Odigie, the Ighodalo's including Chiefs Jeremiah A. Ighodalo and other Ewohimi dignitaries from Ibadan, Chief Joseph O. Ighodalo, the Izevbigies, the Ikhiles and other dignitaries from Lagos and Benin City, Professors *Idowu Iweibo*, *Domingo A. Okorie* (Head of Department) and *Akinbo A. Adesomoju* of Chemistry Department,

University of Ibadan, Professors and staff from the University of Benin and many others. Chief Joseph O. Ighodalo kindly provided accommodation for the Professors and other dignitaries that came for the ceremonies.

The funeral Mass was held at *Saint Matthias Catholic Church, Eguae, Ewohimi at 10:00AM, February 12.* The chief celebrant was *Very Reverend Monsignor Usenbor* who was assisted by Reverend Fathers Alumiasunya and Leo. The sermon again centered around Okogun's good life. The Reverend Father recalled how Pa Okogun called him to clear his house of charms and fetish objects before he left for Ibadan. He declared that Pa Okogun was a great acrobat. "That he made his exit like an acrobat who was dancing with non-Christians and suddenly at the right moment, before the people knew what was happening, flipped his dance and arrived happily among the Christians".

Many persons who could not be at the wake keep joined at the funeral Mass. *Professor Charles O. N. Wambebe*, the then Director General of the National Institute of Pharmaceutical Research and Development, NIPRD., Abuja was at the Mass while Dr. Mrs. M. Enwerem and Mr. John G. Audam, Research Fellow and Chief Technologist respectively, of the Department of Medicinal Plant Research and Traditional Medicine, NIPRD came to the house and presented gifts from NIPRD.

The burial rites

After Father Alumiasunyan had blessed the grave, Pa Okogun's larger family elders prevented him from completing the Christian burial rites. Eventually, he had to leave for other engagements after blessing the grave and the coffin. He instructed *the Catechist, Mr. P. Okhonfoh* on what to do. At 6.00PM, the Catechist supported by the Parishioners succeeded in laying the body to rest in the grave. The people were insisting on carrying out some aspects of the local burial customs and traditions. They accepted that Pa Okogun had been baptized and that he died as a Christian. He had while he lived, been accused of secretly being a Christian.

Pa Okogun before dying instructed us to bury him as a Christian but to give to the people all they required to fulfil some aspects of the customs and traditions for his age grade and status in the village. The children namely, the first living son, the first living daughter, the first grandson and the first granddaughter presented yards of while cloth each to the elders in accordance with the custom and tradition of the village. Some of the cloths so presented were cut into pieces and shared to the elders and institutions as demanded by their rites like the Biblical Jewish burial rites. The elders appointed two traditional administrators (*akhe oa/akhe uwa* literally meaning watcher of house) for Baba's estate. The senior administrator was the teenager *Mr. Michael Omovuon* while the elderly Pa Willie Ogieyan was the assistant administrator.

The people also demanded the following:

a. They wanted to lay the body in the grave themselves after performing certain rituals.

b. They wanted the widows to "give home-going cloths" to be buried with the man.

c. They wanted to carry out postmortem examination on the dead body to remove any diseased organ so that according to them, he should not reincarnate with the diseased organ.

d. They wanted the coffin opened in the grave so that the sand could cover the body to ensure decomposition.

e. They wanted to sacrifice a chicken on the feet so that as he returned to the world beyond, he would hold the chicken as he moved on.

I countered all these demands with various arguments since Pa had ensured that I left the environmental age grade (*Egbolughe: street sweepers) to the Igbama age grade* before he died and so I had some authority over what should be done. In some of the arguments, it was necessary for me to remind them that the man's spirit was present as witness to what I was saying and what they were demanding. Statements like that from me made many of them to calm down on their demands because I was calling on the spirits as my witness. They respected God and the spirits. None of their demands was met except that as the Catechist and Parishioners covered the closed coffin with sand, *Mr.* Asuerinmen Abhukhegbe threw in cloths purportedly from the widows. After the burial, we locked the door leading to the grave. Pa Okogun's nephew Pa Willie Ehikhamen Ogieyan, son of his most senior sister, Uhuomonye as one of the administrators together with *Mr. Agbebaku* of the Chief Eholor family and Mr. Asuerinmen Abhukhegbe sacrificed a fowl outside by the door leading to the room where the grave is. The fowl should be sacrificed on the dead man's feet, but I prevented that from happening.

There is a belief among the people that if a first son were wrongly declared or that if the first son did anything wrong, he would not last more than two or three years before dying. On this basis the people would allow the first son to take responsibility for his actions provided they cleared themselves before God and the ancestral spirits by loudly declaring and insisting on what they know should be done according to tradition.

If I were still in the environmental age grade, what I said would carry less weight during the burial ceremony. As an Igbama, I could be heard if I took decisions on several issues.

The Police Band entertained during the day of the burial. The night was allocated to the various Clubs that came to support the children who belonged to them.

Social events

The next day was Sunday and we all returned to Saint Mathias Catholic Church to make a Thanksgiving. Baba Okogun's family made donations and announced pledges to support the Church. One of my mentors and friend *Chief Professor Emmanuel U. Emovon,* the Obayagbonan of Benin visited from Benin too on this day.

The *Okaigben Development Association (OKDA*) came with yams and palm-wine as a group led by the then Chairman, *Mr. Dennis E. Usifo* to celebrate with us. They extolled Baba's positive contribution to the development and to the affairs of the village. In the afternoon, an acrobatic Esan dance group entertained the celebrants and the crowds that came around.

OKDA members led by the Chairman Mr. Dennis Usifo who came with gifts to celebrate and honour Okogun and some family members: February 1994

On Monday, the 14th February, Mr Felix O. Okogun showed a video of Baba Okogun talking to give details of aspects of his life and in answer to the questions he was asked when he was with Felix in Warri for the cataract surgery. I also played the cassette of Baba's audio recording of some aspects of his life made in late 1971 when he visited my family at the University of Ibadan. The 15th was the day assigned according to tradition for the son inlaws to formally present themselves by dancing ceremonially with their respective wives and children to celebrate their father-inlaw's exit. The inlaws married within Ewohimi, Ewatto and Ewossa were required to present 2 bundles each of five yam tubers and a calabash or jug of palmwine as minimum and were free to add other gifts.

Those inlaws coming from outside these towns were required to add a she-goat to their presentations. The following inlaws came Mr. Godwin Agboli of Ogwashiuku married to Celestina Tobore Uwamusi, Engineer Joseph Ehisuoria Inegbedion married to Anthonia Aiterebhe, Pastor Christopher Ailende married to Felicia Ekeagboniyokpa Efua,

Mr. David Imhontu Aguele married to Egbeke P., Engineer Roland Imarenezor married to Tessy Odion and Mr. Clifford Ebhohon Afeyodion married to Mary Mammy. Those outside Ewohimi were allowed under a dispensation to come in the next day 16th.

After these ceremonial visits, the larger family in charge of affairs permitted the departure of those who out of exigencies needed to return to their respective bases before the traditional formal end of the burial ceremony of four to eight days.

The formal installation of the new head of family by the Okai-igbamas

I was informed that there must be a formal handing over of the family affairs to me by the larger family elders on the 16th. Accordingly, at 5:30AM on that day, I went to *Pa Eraze at Idumobo* to receive instructions on what to do. Pa Eraze was then the head of the Oka-igbamas in the family. The Okaigbamas are deputy to the Odion-egbes (the senior elders) and act in certain cases as this on their behalf. Pa Eraze called in Mr. Julius Ebe, a much younger man who was probably his errand man (owaimhin). I also succeeded in negotiating to have the elders agree to compromise on the traditional mourning period for the widows since Baba died and was buried essentially as a baptized Christian. They kindly accepted to reduce the mourning period for the women. Later that day at about 4:00PM, the Okaigbamas came led by Pa Eraze of Idumobo. The language used for them when they were seated was, "The elders are sitting on the log of wood" (*Edion ri bhu uke erhan).*

I was summoned by them and requested to present certain items of kola nuts and token drinks along with all my siblings who were still around. Some of those who were around also presented gifts to the elders (Oka-igbama group). They then blessed us and praised us for the way we united to give our father a very good and fitting burial with enough food, drinks, and entertainment groups. They blessed us and finally made their pronouncements which started with "*Okogun has gone but Okogun is still alive*". They then presented me to the gathering as the living Okogun. They told me that as Okogun and father of the family, I should see all my siblings as my children and the children were to see me as their father from then on. They briefly explained the implications of their pronouncements and then took their leave.

On that day, I handed over to my cousin sister Rose Imhanrenrio the sum of one thousand two hundred Naira (N1,200.00) which she had kept with Baba Okogun and was part of the money handed over to me by Mr. Matthew Aguele as money left with him by our father. Pa left no debts behind. But several days after, *Mr. Okonobo Iden* came up to say that Baba borrowed some cement blocks from him over a decade ago for repairs of the stores on the position now taken up by the miniplaza. It was not like our father not to pay for such services if that was the agreement. We doubted but after his insistence to be paid, I paid him what he requested.

Mrs. Lucy E. Odigie Enosegbe nee Okogun accompanied by Queen Eson of the Enogie jubilate singing and dancing from Eguae to Okaigben

On the 17th, the eighth and final day of the burial ceremonies, the oldest living daughter of Baba Okogun, Madam Lucy Ebatele Odigie Enosegbe ceremoniously danced accompanied by a dance troupe of women from Eguae, Ewohimi to visit us. Her Royal Highness Queen Eson, the Head of the Enogie's wives led the troupe.

A group of young girls organized and led by the most senior daughter of Mr. *Esanigbedo Adogun* entertained us to an acrobatic female dance.

The eight days of the burial was like a village feast. All the family branches especially belonging to Baba's sisters Arhetuemen and Uhomonye cooked and entertained visitors in addition to what Baba Okogun's children who were the main celebrants had to do. Many cows were slaughtered to make meals for visitors and guests who came in their numbers and were fed with food and drinks. Many of the villagers said afterwards that it was like the village was celebrating a feast during the eight days of ceremonies.

Outstanding family issues settled

We then sorted out some family issues. On Saturday 19th, after returning from the 6:30AM Mass at Saint Anthony's Catholic Church, Ewatto, we were confronted by *Madam Oriunuebho Ukate* who came in with her daughter Queen and Queen's baby purportedly fathered by Omusun. She also accused Queen of stealing thousands of Naira from where she kept the money. Omusun did not want to accept the baby but we decided as a family, after consultation, that the baby had to be accepted as Omusun's baby by the family because Omusun admitted to having had affairs with Queen.

We planned and took decision about Baba's farms near the house and beyond the Odu stream. We also discussed and agreed on the education arrangements for the young children, specifically Florence and Omusun.

Thus, the burial ceremonies ended. The burial was like a festival for the villagers as many attested. As I wrote this biography, I wrote to available Baba's children and grandchildren to let me have any information they might have and which I might have omitted in my writeup and to pay their tributes The next chapter has the deliver**ed tributes.**

CHAPTER TWENTYEIGHT

CONCLUSION

John Okogun Eguaereona Omovuon's life, death and burial gives a glimpse into the traditions, customs, and religion of his people in Esanland-Edo much of which has been abandoned. These practices were like many of those then in other parts of present Edo and Delta States of Nigeria, West Africa. The story of his life attempts to capture the various struggles that Okogun confronted and his successes. The reader gets an unusual insight into the organisations of the village administration, acrobatic masquerades, belief systems and age groups as practiced in Ewohimi and generally in Esanland. Okogun's story also describes several unusual spiritual events and experience in his life that qualify to be referred to as *"stranger than fiction"*. The friendship and interaction between people from all Esan, Owan, Afenmai/Esakor, Benin, the Delta, Yoruba ethnic groups, and the Eastern Igbos not so obvious in these days are clearly seen in the life and times of Okogun. By dint of hard work, courage, and faith in God, Okogun grew from being an early orphan with little or no material inheritance to become a member of a prosperous elite in a community that valued integrity. That a man who used and knew about charms declared that Jesus Christ is the supreme power above all other powers is noteworthy and instructive to many. The story throws some light on the early British Colonial rule and commercial interests in Esanland. The support and protection Okogun got from his sisters who prevented him from acquiring Western education and other good people certainly contributed to his success.

Okogun is a hero in his own right. His acrobatic prowess which involved overcoming the natural forces of gravity and space could be said to have been extended into doing things that appeared superhuman in his time. His lonely courageous journeys through jungles, on land and on water are remarkable. By the time he died, he had been given several hail names. He was *Papa Original*, *Ogie-ese* (king of crowds), *Ogun N'Ose* (Ogun the handsome) and *Ogun gbein gbein* (gbein gbein is used to describe the sound of iron when struck and refers to Okogun's courage and strength).

The heroic scale of Okogun's personality is echoed in the remarks made independently at his death about the seemingly immortality of people like Okogun. Okogun's story needs to be told.

The following seven contributions from some of Okogun's children, grandchildren and inlaw independently corroborate and throw more light into aspects of this biography:

1. ABOUT LATE JOHNYY OKOGUN OMOVUON

by Amuda Erhaze Robinson Enato

Baba Johnny Okogun Omovuon was born into the family of late Omovuon and Esekhor of Okaigben, Ewohimi with about five women. God created him into the family to bring together both close and distant relations. He was created with boldness, truth, honesty, wisdom, love, power, smartness, and such voice that made people to respect him. He was known and popular in Ewohimi, Ohordua, Ewatto and Emu. He ventured many areas in business. Baba was a tailor, a mobile tailor too. He was always going to Ohordua Market.

He helped friends to carry their yams in a big canoe paddled by Urhobo people through River Ihiezi to River Niger to Onitsha for sale. He followed timber log through Rivers Utor and Iyagun to a River Niger tributary. He was overseer in Late Paul Odigie's timber work and later became overseer in U.A.C timber work under one short white man called D. D. Smith. He brought his close and distant relations together and gave them portion of his land for them to build their houses. Uhuomonye came from Uzebu, Arhetuemhen, Osagie Oriere, Abielekpen, Iyamabhor from Idumobo his close friend *Obeahon* from Idumobo. He helped Omonlafe to acquire land by Ofuri Market.

God gave him a type of voice. In 1956, Idene-Ekpoma came to John Holt and told Late Osobor, the night guard that they were here to come and take something from the shop. Osobor, the night guard told them not his presence. They gave him several matchet cuts, but it did not enter his body. They tied a rope on his hand with a stick across is mouth. He managed to call Okogun, then Baba answered with his usual voice. Immediately --

Idene-Ekpoma with his men ran away. Three years later, he came to Baba with many people around, Market day and the market has not gone to the other side of Ewohimi. He said who is the owner of this house, Baba answered, he shook his hand and said, you are a man. He said that he has never been frightened by anybody's voice and that when he had Baba's Voice he ran away. He then confessed and introduced himself as Idene-Ekpoma of Ekpoma and that he was the person who came to John Holt sometimes ago, thereafter he bought some drinks for them. He was a transporter, Baba with *Mr. Toba,* the Manager of U.A.C, Eguae Ewohimi, an Ijaw man, bought a lorry that was had the maxim 'Evidence of Labour' written on the front vizor of the lorry. Mr. *Richard Igumah*, UAC Manager from --

Omhen-Idinrio Okaigben Ewohimi also bought a lorry with the maxim 'Eyezor'. Baba built a house at Agbor and he was getting his monthly pension from there. You can see that he was very wise in many ways.

Baba Okogun was very light in complexion and handsome hence he was nick-named Ogunose and Ogunose is being used today by people to greet his children

If not Okogun with God on his side I would not be alive today till this age because of different sickness I had. I still praise my mother who left Ohordua to meet her husband Okogun at Ewohimi or else I, Amuda would not have been the person I am today. My mother lost about three children at Ohordua before coming to Ewohimi.

May God Almighty continue to protect Baba Okogun and my mother wherever their spirits may be now.

2. PA JOHN OKOGUN OMOVUON, Alias OGUN N'Ose

by Sir & Lady Clifford E. and Mary Afeyodion.

PA JOHN OKOGUN OMOVUON, Alias OGUN N'Ose (my father In-law) was a man of many parts - a farmer, tailor, timber merchant, trader etc and was very versed in native wisdom. He was a disciplinarian and well respected by all and sundry in the community. He stood out tall among his peers. Frankly speaking, I am yet to see his type in present day Okaigben Community in Ewohimi. It beats my(our) imagination how, a man with five wives and, at death 23 surviving children was able to manage his home perfectly well without crisis. The love and oneness amongst them were so amazing. He named our first son "Aisagbonhi "based on what transpired just before our marriage and the baby of the family "Enuwamhangbe "based on his personal observation. He had that aura of authority around him, yet he stood for TRUTH, JUSTICE AND FAIRNESS in all his dealings. Truly, he left a legacy which every child of his (including In-laws) should be very proud of. May his gentle soul rest in peace.

3. Memories of my Father, Pa. Okogun John Egualeona Omovuon

by Solomon Okogun

I am grateful and honored to be given the opportunity to write a page of my memories of Baba. But first, a big thank you to my eldest brother/ father, Prof. J.I. Okogun for taking time and energy to write a biography of our great Baba.

Without his foresight and determination, this piece of our family history would have been lost forever!

My earliest recallable memories of Baba are probably from the age of 4 or 5 years. I remember him at least once a month riding his bicycle past my maternal grandparent's home on his way to attend a village social club meeting at the home of Mr. Okhuebor in Idumigie, Eguae. Mr. Okhuebor's house was just a few houses away from my maternal grandparents' home. He would bring gifts for me and give coins always. Always dressed in clean white Agbada attires that were impeccably ironed!

You are my hero and role model

You were an amazing example of a Father who made sure family was always number one.

You love all your Children with unconditional Love. You made sure all your extended Family members were close to you and doing well.

You detested divisions and quarrels among your children and relatives.... you made sure we all saw each other as simply "brothers and sisters"!

I remember all the private conversations we had Baba.

When I see what I have grown-up to be today, I miss not having you around!

All the sweet memories

Your Barry-toned voice that could be heard from miles.

Your Love and Care, secret places you would hide snacks and food for me to find...siting down and listening to you and other elders discuss life lessons and events are few memories I will always cherish!

Your taught me honesty, hard work, love of family and community as enduring values to cherish!

I remember you as a stern disciplinarian that always fought for justice and fairness in the community!

As a young boy, you would always take me with you to the Edion meetings and gathering in Idinrio, Esongban's courtyard, our maternal Chief Ebalogbhen's home, Enogie's palace and other important visits to elders and leaders of Ewohimi to listen and learn from elders.

Your honesty and good deeds were legendary within our Small hometown and beyond!

At your time, there was no Esan town or village in Esan Land and beyond that never heard of you and your prowess!

Who could ever forget "**OGIESE"?**

You were not perfect, and nobody is perfect! But to me, you were a great father!

I will always remember the good times we had, remember my Baba, my wonderful Dad

I will remember you each and every day and if I need to talk to you, all I have to do is just kneel and pray. One day we will be together again, but until that time I will always treasure h**aving you for a Dad was such a great pleasure;** Baba, I thank you for giving me all I needed for survival in this sometimes-cold world.

"The elders are the history and mirror of the living past. Study them to brighten your life and future." – unknown writer

4. AND HE DIED

by Josephine Ese Aijanyain (Nee Enosegbe).

I could not have asked for a better Grandpa than you, late John Omovon Okogun, an asset to his generation. His beauty and cuteness could not be hidden as he was fondly called "Ogun Nose" meaning A handsome man

Being the first grandchild of Pa Okogun popular called "Baba' is a huge privilege. I was lavished with so much love as even the blind could see it.

Anytime I visited Okaigben, I usually must see him first; he will hold me by the hand and take me inside his chambers "Oduwa" to ask how I was doing and several other questions. He also could not hide his Joy when I was getting married. He mentioned and expressed to his friends how happy and proud he was of me.

As I grew older, stronger, and wiser I reciprocated his love to me especially when I visited Ewohimi with gift items like dresses and his regular blood capsules. He wears the outfits with some form of Charismas and style to the extent that those around would not help but notice that there was something different about his looks as they ask, "you are shinning, what is the secret" His response would be "it's my daughter Josephine's hand work".

MY PAINS

My mum repeatedly informed me of his quest to see me on his sickbed, but I could not oblige him that privilege as the responsibilities of a young growing mother held me bound and I could not see him before his death in UCH Ibadan.

And so "He Died", quickly I rushed to Ibadan as soon as I heard of his demise. At this point I suddenly realized that I no longer have a grandpa.

THE BURIAL

Then came the burial arrangements quickly again and I signified my intention to get his burial cloth. I then remembered that very sister, MERCY in blessed memory once told me that she was getting Baba a special 'HAUSA BABARIGA' worn by elderly Hausa men in Kano during special occasion. It was with heavy embroidery in addition I decided to make for him a white guinea brocade "Up and down" to go with the "Babariga". Mercy went to Kano to fetch them from Eunice who had bought the dress.

I made my intention known to my Uncle, Prof J. Okogun, he approved.

It was beautiful and unique: I handed them over to uncle and returned to Lagos.

BABA FINAL RESTING PLACE

On our Journey to Ewohimi from Ibadan to BABA's final resting place, it was a smooth and memorable ride. I rode in the same vehicle with aunty Celestina and she brought out a bible and read from the book of Kings and said "BABA came to the world with Joy and now going back in glory. We are celebrating BABA's death" and since then I knew that death like this should be celebrated.

In Benin we all waited for one another's vehicles. It was a very long convoy to Okaigben EWOHIM. Even though we arrived Ewohimi late, people lined up on the road from ISELU to OKIAGBEN. As our car drew closer to the people, I heard from a distance one of them counting the vehicles and when my vehicle got to their point I heard "NO 76" with more vehicles still behind. It was awesome

AT THE GRAVESIDE

I went into the room to have a last glimpse of my beloved grandpa and the tears that refused to come ever since his demise rushed down my cheeks as the realization that was the last view of baba I would have. I was lost in thought and all I felt were some friends who quickly held me to console me.

BABA!!! You lived a fulfilled life and will always be remembered today and always.

You were a great man and even greater at death, rest on BABA for I know you are with your creator GOD ADEIU! ADEIU!! ADIEU!!! BABA!!!

5. BABA JOHN OKOGUN OMOVUON

by Ogbeide Franklin Okogun

With Baba the truth is paramount... he always encouraged us then to tell the truth at all time no matter what... in my two years in the village I had a close and personal relationship with him which I will forever cherish. I was also privileged to be there during his last days at UCH... these are my memories Baba, and I will forever love you. I hope and God willing, one day I will be able to tell my story of these memories and my two years sojourn in our homeland.

One thing I can never forget about Grandpa is his bodyguard (The Black Goat) Called GBODUMA. Whenever the goat goes to the market to constitute, Grandpa will ask the Goat questions and GBODUMA will answer by shaking his head. Whenever Grandpa comes outside to receive fresh air, GBODUMA is always there to secure the environment.

6. **My Baba Okogun!!!**

By *Patience Iroghama nee Ogbebor*

Death changes everything! Time changes nothing.... I still miss the sound of your voice, the wisdom in your advice, the stories of your life and just being in your presence. So No, time changes nothing, I miss you as much as today as I did the day, I was told you died. I just miss you! Continue to rest in perfect peace my Baba Okogun!

7. by **Engineer John Enomen Osadolor Okogun**[89]

"As an aside, I remember the story you later recounted how Baba had prayed that you return home before he passed. I think there was a conditional to that prayer. And of course, it was answered. As to the burial, I do remember you chartered a bus very similar to the ISI bus for the kids and I think some of your friends took us there. It was a very memorable and fun ride. As to the ceremony, all I remember... is chaos, because half the village was there night and day. And, at random, introductions to cousins and reintroductions to aunts and uncles, in the middle of crowds."

EPILOGUE

"The task that I am leaving behind for you is very big: it is nobody's fault": this is the rough translation of the Esan *"Ironmhon ni me fiya nu uwe okpolor gbe e: e ye mhon oria".* Baba Okogun said this many times as his time approached to fall asleep. He was aware of the task and he also meant that he did not deliberately create the task. He would do everything, alive or dead to assist me in the task. I believe that writing this biography was part of the task. From very early in life and until his death, he revealed a lot of things to me about his life verbally including through dictation and audio recording. I have not written everything in this book. I could not remember everything, and I have deliberately left some out. The opportunity to write this historical biography came "e in a circumstance aptly reflected in the adage "Every disappointment is a blessing in disguise". Some health challenges made the children and family to recommend that I spend mor time in the USA than Nigeria, West Africa. As a retired man with little to engage me formally, I found more time from 2016 to devote to writing this book.

I thank God for giving me the grace and the means to face the task that Okogun left behind. My wife, children, brothers, sisters, cousins, nieces and nephews and several other persons have helped me in this task, and I thank them all. John Okogun Egualeona Omovuon's life, as has been pointed out by Reverend Dr. Father Charles Imokhai and Dr. Osahon Chris Eigbike respectively in the Prologue and Foreword was unique and filled with positive contributions to family and community in general; and provides models for us all.

He always "acted in the living present", burying the past, not trusting the future but always trusting God.

The last stanzas of Harry Wadsworth Longfellow's poem[90] A Psalm of Life say the rest

"Lives of great men all remind us
We can make our lives sublime,
And, departing, leave behind us
Footprints on the sands of time;

Footprints, that perhaps another,
Sailing o'er life's solemn main,
A forlorn and shipwrecked brother,
Seeing, shall take heart again.

Let us, then, be up and doing,
With a heart for any fate;
Still achieving, still pursuing,
Learn to labor and to wait.

REFERENCES

1. Omovuon, Okogun J. E. 1971. Dictated historical notes taken by Joseph I. Okogun at Ibadan. Appendix I.

2. Iriana, Monday kindly supplied the Shell Map of Nigeria. Mr. Monday Iriana was at a time Head of Shell BP Public Relations Office

3. Okojie, Christopher G., OFR. https://www/esanland.org/p/blog-page.html

4. Okojie, Christopher G. 1960. Ishan Native laws and customs, Unknown binding.

5. Butcher, H L M and White, H F M 1932 Intelligence Report Series Intelligence Reports on Ishan Division of Benin Province. National Archives of Nigeria pp 105, 109 - 110

6. Iyi–Eweka, Ademola, 2011. in Edo Nation website

7. National Archives, Ibadan document on the creation of Ewohimi Forest Reserve,1931 -1939

8. a. Ero, O O and Owie, S P. 2016. The Benin Monarchy and Ogiamen Connection The historical facts. Mindex Publishers pp. 1 -22

   b. Emafo, P 2019. An ethnographic account of Ohordua Kingdom Floreat Publisher

9. Butcher, H L M and White, H F M 1932. *Ibid.* p. 102

10. Ighedosa Omovuon, Joseph 2017. Private Communication. He is the most senior grandson of Pa Ighedosa Omovuon.

11. Eweka, E.B. 1992. Evolution of Benin Chieftaincy Titles, Uniben Press

12. His Royal Highness Usifo S. Enosegbe II, 1989. Welcome address to UkuAkpolo Oba Erediauwa I., Oba of Benin on his inaugural visit to Ewohimi.

13. Butcher, H L M and White, H F M 1932. *Ibid.* pp. 80 and 102

14. Odigie, Joseph O. A. Private Communication to the author

15. a. King-Ovonramwen Institute.: Inhabitants of ASABA-AGBOR ARE EDOS.

king-ovonramweninstitute.blogspot.com/.../inhabitants-of- asaba-agbor-are-edos.html 15b. Private Communication from Festus Odigie, one of Johnson O Odigie's sons.

16. https://www.esanland.org/p/esan-markets.html

17. Abhukhegbe, Asuerinmen, 2008. Pronouncement at a meeting chaired by Idinrio Odionwele Pa Isikhuemen Agbonselobhor of Idumobo at the residence of the author to resolve the controversy between Okogun Omovuon and Ikekhua Ogbeide families over the burial rites for late Mrs. Gladys Ikhumen who died September 28, 2008(records of Mr. Michael Omovuon) and was a granddaughter of Madam Arhetuemen Omovuon: "A man" *(arheobhuwa)* in Omovuon's family.

18. In Ewohimi tradition if someone maintains the same answer of "yes or no" when asked four times consecutively, the answer is accepted and acted upon. Hence the saying *Itamen enen ole anon ohe-ema* meaning the person refusing to eat offered pounded yam must be asked four times before the food is taken away from the person if the person maintains rejection of the food four times.

19. Oghunmun, Patrick of Izumen, Ewohimi. 2015 and 2019. Private information to the author

20. Okojie, Ogbidi – Wikipedia. https:// en.wikipedia.org/wiki/Ogbidi_Okojie.

21. Ukpe is the Esan common word for a feast. There were many feasts in Ewohimi. The other feasts like *ukpe-eze, ugi-odu, ukpe-Ezelomon*, *ukpe-arinmin*, etc. are qualified. When *ukpe* is not qualified, it refers to the celebration of ancestors.

22. Okoduwa, Anthony I. 2006. Tenancity of gerontocracy in Nigeria: an example of the Esan people in Edo State, Stud. Tribes Tribals, 4(1), 47-51

23. Oboite, Lawrence, 2013. Private Communication to the author on the description of the beauty of Enimaluole that he got from a man at Ikeken, Ewohimi while attending the burial ceremonies of late Mr. Festus Aiya. Mr. Festus Aiya died 30 August 2013, buried 28 September 2013 and was an Assistant Director at the National Agency for Food and Drug Administration, NAFDAC

24. Ilekhomon was the father of Madam Ebhulu who was married to an Idumu-agho family. Madam Ebhulu's junior brother, Akhigbe and his son respectively in turn inherited and took the Obasenyen of Omen-Eguae, Ewohimi chieftaincy title.

25. Ehibor, Robert Agoro, aka *Man Must Wak*, 2018. He kindly reminded the author of the name of this drum.

26. "Esan Acrobatic dance YouTube" video sites on Igbabonanlimin/Igbabonanrimin acrobatic dance: YouTube video sites on Egbabonanlimi/Igbabonelimin/ Egbabonelimwi acrobatic dance.

27. Benin-Idah War 16th Century: http://ihuanedo.ning.com/group/healtheducation/forum/topics/the-benin-idah-war; https://www.nairaland.com/4383454/famous-benin-idah-war

28. Esekhor's declarations clearly indicate that Esekhor, like people of her time, believed in Heaven for those who had lived good lives in the sight of God and that the people were not sure about the phenomenon of reincarnation as believed.

29. One yard is 36 inches while one meter is 39 inches; a meter is slightly less than a yard.

30. One British pound (Sterling) was twenty shillings. When Nigeria changed her currency on 1 January 1973, one British Pound exchanged for two Naira. One Naira (one hundred kobo) was thus ten shillings. Two shillings six pence in 1973 would be twelve and half kobo. Today, one British pound exchanges for about four hundred and eighty Naira (N480). Two shillings and six pence in about 1935 would today be sixty Naira(N60). Today a piece of abadan costs about three

thousand Naira (N3000) – over six times the equivalent in 1973 and much more times the cost in 1935 taking inflation between 1935 and 1973 into account

31. The marriage was consummated about 1954 shortly after Enimaluole's death. Akpolo and Mary settled in Port Harcourt, Rivers State after the marriage. Mary gave him two daughters. Mary and her daughters died at their respective early ages

32. Full text of "A Concise Dictionary of The Bini Language of Southern ... https://archive.org/.../Melzian+-+A+Concise+Dictionary+of+the+Bini+Language+of+S...gang of timber workers who square the logs; cf. gbe 1 [•], osiko [./]

33. Woman's wife: In those days, if a prosperous woman had no issues, she would perform all the customary rites as if she were a man for the marriage of a girl into her father's family if she is regarded as a son in her father's family or into the husband's family if she is married. Such a girl was known as *amen-okhuo* (woman's wife) and she was informally attached to a cousin in the affected family so that she would have offspring for the family.

34. Ora (Owan) Quarters was located opposite the present late Honourable Joseph O. Odigie's premises on the right-hand side of the road when going from Okaigben to Eguae just before Omen-Eguae quarters.

35. Yoruba Quarters was directly opposite Ogidigbo (present day Agbado) Market at Eguae, Ewohimi.

36. The Urhobo's exit from Ewohimi coincided with the emergence of the crude oil exploration in the Delta Region of Nigeria which brought jobs and some prosperity to the people of the area and to Nigerians in general.

37. I thank Engineer Osahon J. Okogun for reminding me of the momentum explanation for the throwing of tubers of yam into the River.

38. Adodo, Anselm 2017. Integral community enterprises in Africa: Communitalism as alternative to capitalism (Transformation and Innovation) 1st Edition, First published by Routledge, Abingdon, UK, and New York.

39. Joseph, Robert, and Felix were born during Okogun's stay at Umunede

40. Native gin was produced locally from palmwine tapped from Raphia Palm and from the Oil Palm tree through fermentation and distillation. Palm wine contains its own natural yeast and hence did not require exogenous yeast for fermentation. The relatively crude distillation equipment was fabricated from local materials. It was made illegal by the Colonial Government on health grounds to control crime from drunkenness and its competition with imported gins and other strong drinks. It was subsequently found to contain methanol in small quantities which caused blindness from excessive chronic consumption.

41. Ogbe and Ohen shrine was located and surrounded by forest on the spot in front of the present *Chief Osoh's Palace* in Idinrio. Ohen means Priest.

42. Documents on the creation of Ewohimi Forest Reserve are preserved in the Nigerian National Archives. Ewohimi forest was rich in old mahogany trees. DSP (rtd) Gabriel O. Ogiata before he died related his experience as a child when they were paid, for the fruits of mahogany trees that they collected from Ewohimi forests, by those who planted trees in Sapoba Forest Reserve, near Benin.

43. Mr. Okotie was an Itsekiri man from the Delta Province and he was the Contractor in charge and owner of the Timber logging business at Igueben.

44. Mr. Dick Odigie, one of Chief Paul Odigie's junior brothers was accused of talking to Aituagie, one of the Enogie's wives. A fine that included a cow was imposed and Chief Paul Odigie had not presented the cow. The subsequent settlement included paying the complete fine. The Enogie gave the cow's first female offspring to Okogun as its caretaker/owner. In those days Ewohimi reared local cows which were very different from the Llama reared by the Fulanis. Its meat is also somewhat tastier than that of the Llama. Such cows were still seen in 2017 at Ugbegun in Esanland.

45. Pa Okogun informed Joseph that Joseph wrote the letter to him. I have a faint memory about the letter

46. Except for Mr D.D. Smith, the names of the UAC Managers as written may not have been correctly written because Okogun called out the names as he thought he heard them being addressed.

47. The baby was born on March 25, 1950 at Idumagho, Ewohimi. The baby grew to become Reverend Pastor Mrs Felicia E E Ailende

48. This is one of the lists of heroic achievements for which a person is given special recognition and gift of a goat or a fruit tree by parents. The Enogie usually awards a chieftaincy title in recognition for such heroism. In 2017, Mr. Monday Ideh's son of Idumu-Oleghe, Okaigben shot and killed giant python near the Odu River and was decorated with a chieftaincy by His Royal Highness, the Enogie of Ewohimi Lord Peter Ogiefoh Usifoh II

49. The body of Enimaluole was wrapped in white cloth and then folded with a mat and buried at Omen-Eguae. It was not usual to use coffins in burying the dead in those days. Enimaluole was one of the earliest converts at Ewohimi (Okaigben) to the Christian faith as a member of the Assemblies of God Mission. She took her co-wives and children to the Church. Before she fell ill and died, Okogun's sisters decided that she and her colleagues be banned from going to Church. They feared that their brother Okogun could die prematurely because Enimaluole was always praying to Jesus Christ.

50. Pa Osagie Aki on his deathbed confessed that with the collusion of his wife, Ebhodaghe, he drugged the palm wine which Okogun drank and got into the violent mood that led to Enimaluole's injury, illness, and subsequent death.

51. Aiterebhe was born in August 1949. Madam Telefi Oshioaye Momoh was kept in Purdah in the Hausa Quarters at Ubiaja. Aiterebhe was brought up as a Hausa child. She learnt to speak Hausa and was not sent to school until late when Pa Okogun went to persuade Madam Oshioaye to release Aiterebhe to him so she could regularly be in school.

52. Lady Justina I Okogun, Joseph's wife received the old metal plates from Mrs. Christiana E. Ilegbodu before informing me about my mother's wedding gift so to say for her. The plates were metal and had become partially rusty.

53. Pa Johnson Iyamah Imhanrhedon, originally of Uzebu, Okaigben, Ewohimi explained to me why Ehi was not worshipped. He said the people believed that since Ehi represented the presence of God in their residence, there was nothing that God did not create to use in worshipping: everything belonged to God. He further explained that when going for battle or war dance when people tied

charms to their bodies, the charms were tied after kneeling and praying to God at the door and leaving the house. The charms were also removed from the body, kneeling in prayers of thanksgiving to God through Ehi for the safe return before entering the house.

54. Johnson Iyamah Imhanrhedon also explained that the young palm leaves, Igiomen use during festivals was to usher the good spirits of their ancestors into the premises during the celebrations. The Catholic Church and some other Christian denominations use palm leaves buds, igiomen in the Church and in processions on Palm Sundays to mark the triumphant entry of Jesus Christ into Jerusalem to complete His salvific mission on Earth.

55. He used *Cleome orientalis* or *Cleome ciliata* Schumach. &Thonn. (umomo otor) as the herbal component of a formulation for his treatment of swollen spleen. He taught Madam Julie, his youngest wife the art of managing swollen spleen with the formulation.

56. a. In very small amounts, skatole loses its vile scent for something a little more floral and it is added to certain kinds of ice cream to enhance their flavours. Skatole in foods: 10SurprisingIngredientsFoundInCommonFoods–Tested www.tested.com/food/460640-10-surprising-ingredients-found-common.../skatole/,

    b. Ojinnaka, C.M., OKOGUN, J.I.Okorie, D.A. [1984].MYRICATHIC ACID: *A Triterpene acid from Myrianthus arboreus (Urticaceae). Phytochemistry, 23, 1125-1127.*

57. It must be noted that Chief Paul E. Odigie before death boldly and courageously took the unusual step to renounce his membership of the Ogboni Confraternity. It was said that by joining earlier, he had violated their father's injunction that his children should not take up membership of any secret cults.

58. The property at Agbor was sold by Joseph in 2014 due to the difficulties in maintaining the structure and its surroundings, the deaths at Agbor of Messrs Josiah Ajieh, Gabriel Iyoriobhe, Gabriel Ehikhamen, caretakers Ekwunife senior and later his son Joseph, the continued waste of funds to maintain the property, little profitability and possible loss of property.

59. St. Camillus Hospital, Uromi: Card receipt number 1330 of 2/8/67 and the final receipt number 4527 of 28/12/67. There was a total of four payment receipts in Okogun's records.

60. I gave the tank to Felix. Felix used it to construct a water supply system for his house and it is still by the side of his house.

61. The duties included assessing males for the purpose of tax payment, collecting taxes, and paying the collected taxes into the Government Treasury.

62. The Eze family: The Eze family: The clearly identifiable families belonging to the Eze family are the Omovuon lineage of Ebikade, Uhomonye, Omolafe, Arhetuemen, Owobu, Akasi and Okogun; Aki lineage of Osagie and Iribhor; Okede lineage of Erinho, Okede, father of Iyamabhor and James, Osimen lineage of Abielekpen, Ebehigie and Amhandin; Abielekpen, Ugbotiti, Omovuon's sister and grandmother the Otoboh family of Idumuguokha; Omonakhin and children of the Igbeta group of Idumu-Agho. Appendix III

63. Okaigben Memorial School was later taken over by Government after Okaigben people lobbied Government through Hon, J. O. A. Odigie, Chief Jeremiah A Ighodalo and Mr. Peter O. Odigie during the era of Mr. Ayewoh of Uromi as Inspector of Education. At that time, Chief J. A. Ighodalo was a staff of Mandillas and Karraberis, M&K Benin City. The School's name was changed to Native Authority School and through several other name changes to the present name.

64. Mary as the first daughter of Okogun was to be the chief priestess of Esekhor's gods of *ake* and *oza* and *hence was like an apprentice under Uhomonye at Uzebu.* Obeto, Owobu's senior daughter also lived with Uhomonye at Uzebu.

65. Minutes of family meeting: Appendix II

66. There were five Customary Court appearances of Okogun and Ailegbesuan at Emu in a litigation instituted by Aiyobase claiming Amuda as her family's son.

67. According to Mr Johnson Okonobo Ikhuiriona, he was crying because he wished to go to School as he was being taken early in the morning to farm by his father. They were accosted by Hon Joseph Odigie who on being told the reason for his

tears, forcibly took him from his father back home to go to School. He started School from that day with his mother paying most of the fees.

68. The son involved was Robert Okogun. Robert was tagged as being a reincarnation of Ebikade, Okogun's senior brother. Archbishop Millingo of Zambia before his "Moon" slip had explained in his book titled "The World in Between" that Africans used the reincarnation claim to cast a jealous spirit on a someone claimed to be a reincarnation of a dead person. This may have been part of the problem.

69. The accuser at the oath-taking ceremony was Mr Asuerinmen Abhukhegbe

70. The young men came from Lagos where they said that they were told by some diviners that the witches and wizards at home were responsible for the failures they were experiencing in business ventures.

71. The use of the live cock parallels the scapegoat practice of the Jews though I did not ask Pa Okogun what eventually happened to the cock.

72. Eigbike, Osahon C 2018. Private information to the author Joseph Okogun

73. Ikhola shortened form of *Ikhon la* = I fought my way through an obstacle is a deep Esan name given if the circumstances of a child's birth involved a trial occurrence. As Ikhola was about to be born, her senior sister Izegbua took seriously ill as we arrived by ship in December 1970. Pa Okogun associated a night episode when his healthy big goat cried as if in agony and died with the threat to the lives of Izegbua and Ikhola who was born in February 1971

74. The old car was the then prestigious Toyota Crown bought ex works in 1972.

75. The document was the plan of Okogun's property at Agbor enclosed in an envelope addressed to me and stamped by the University of Ibadan. The envelope was earlier used to deliver a letter from the University to me. It was Okogun's way of concealing the document from being stolen

76. We found nothing fetish in Angelina Ailegbesuan's apartment. She disposed of such objects and returned to the Assemblies of God Mission Church Okaigben before she left for Benin

77. Silvester Eraze graduated and registered at the appropriate year as a Medical Doctor graduate of the University of Ibadan College of Medicine and left for Ghana to practise his profession

78. Several of the Professors were my contemporaries as students at the University of Ibadan while many of the House Officers and Registrars were taught organic chemistry by me. I thank them all.

79. Hon. Joseph O. A. Odigie died suddenly in 1986 on the day he took ill and his case was what the wife was referring to by name.

80. Coincidentally, Sir Amao was knighted by His Grace Archbishop Felix Alaba Job of Ibadan, on the same day as the author both as Papal Knights of Saint Sylvester Pope in 1985 at Oke Padre Catholic Cathedral Ibadan

81. The part of Okogun's ancestral land that the larger family, *egbe*, decided he gave to Asuerinmen; he said had a palm tree nicknamed *ukherie* meaning women's apartment which he was told gave very good palm wine. He was delivered as a baby when his parents had their abode around the palm tree.

82. The ceremony took place in 1987 and has already been described underage grade system. Samuel Osabhuohien Igue, BA, MA had only primary school formal education but through home study gained admission to University and was a lecturer at Niger Delta University,Bayelsa, State, Nigeria when he died.

83. Mrs Margaret Ehimika's husband Godfrey was my contemporary at Saint Patrick's College, Asaba. He was a Class one year behind mine, and we became family friends at the University

84. There was a report that Reverend Father Murumba had taken part in organizing a Christian Crusade at Ewohimi during which many fell involuntarily during his prayers. Many had to flee the arena saying that the Church had brought *Olumba Olumba* to them.

85. Saint Patrick's College was officially founded in 1944. The delegation was part of the 50 years Anniversary Celebration Committee.

86. Davidson Okunfolue grew up in Ekpoma, Esan as a son of one of Anglican Church Missionaries for Esan. He said that Ewohimi rejected Church Missionary

activities according to his father who said they could not penetrate Ewohimi. He expressed surprise that a University of Ibadan academic staff of my grade could hail from Ewohimi. He became friendly and spoke Esan very well.

87. Gregory Osabhuohien Onakhinor was a top Scout, a great rural development officer, public spirited, social, and selfless volunteer worker for community and the Catholic Church in Ewohimi

88. I was the Chairman, ITF Governing Council for two terms: 1984 – 1986 and 1987-1989 and was the first Chairman of ITF to serve two terms. It is noteworthy that over 4 years after ending my last term as Chairman, the Organisation mobilized to give me so much support at the burial of Okogun

89. Enomen sent his contribution by Email

90. Poetry Foundation https://www.poetryfoundation.org/poems/44644/a-psalm-of-life

APPENDIX I

DICTATED NOTES IN THE OLYMPIC EXERCISE BOOK

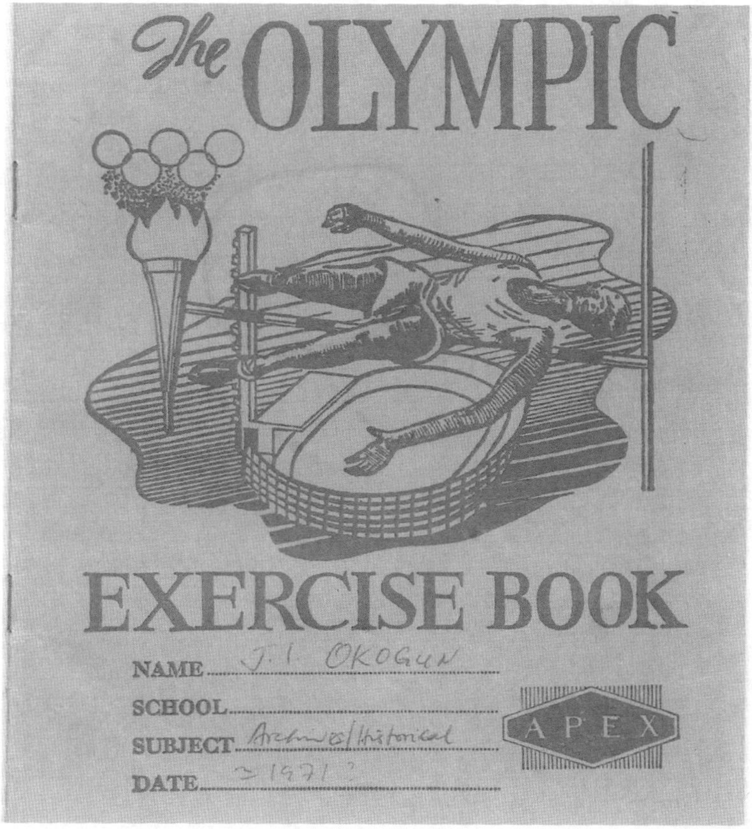

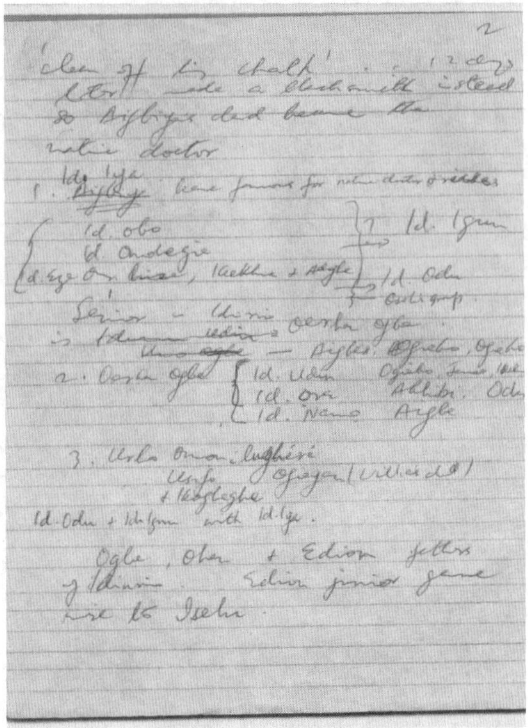

2

'clean off his chalk' ... 12 days
[illegible] a blacksmith instead
so [illegible] dad became the
native doctor

1. Id. Iyo [illegible] became famous for native doctor [illegible]

Id. Obo
Id. Ondegie
Id. Ege [illegible], [illegible] + [illegible] → Id. Igun
→ Id. Odu
→ [illegible] group.

Senior – [illegible] is [illegible] Oorta Ogbe
— [illegible], [illegible], [illegible]

2. Oorta Ogbe
Id. Udin [illegible]
Id. Ora [illegible]. Odu
Id. Nemo [illegible]

3. Urla Omon Iughere
Usifo Ofoyan (William [illegible])
+ [illegible]

Id. Odu + Id. Igun with Id. Iyo.

Ogbe, Oben + Edion fathers
of [illegible]. Edion junior gave
rise to Iseku.

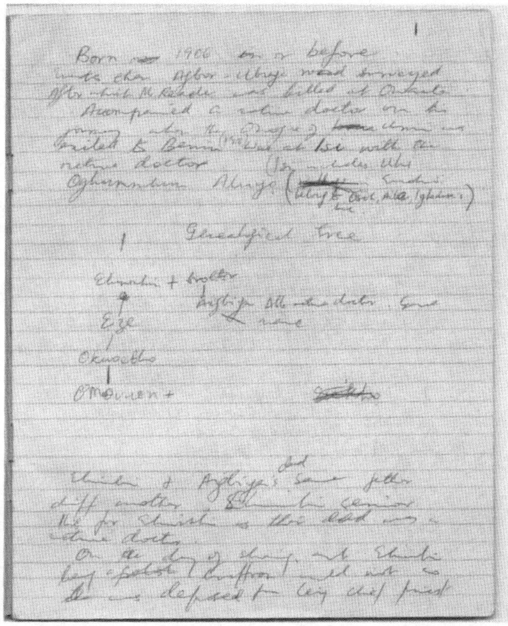
1
Born 1906 or before
Accompanied a native doctor on his
native doctor
Genealogical Tree
Eze

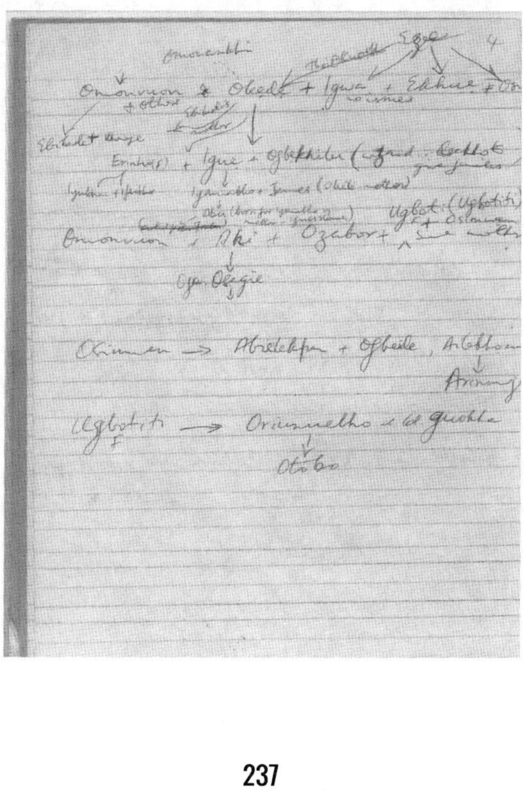
4
Eze
Otobo

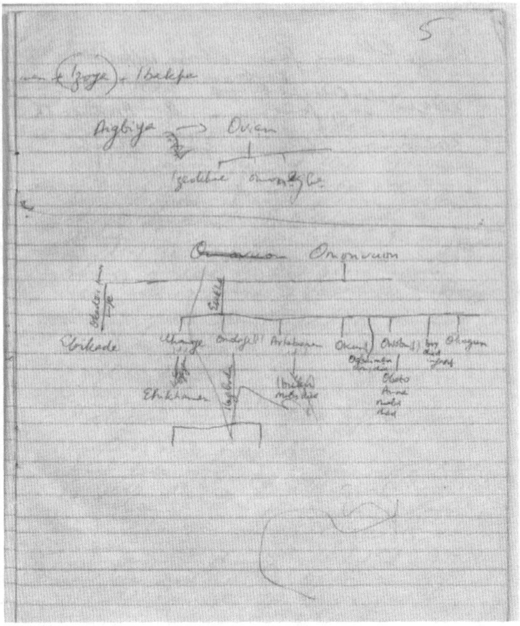

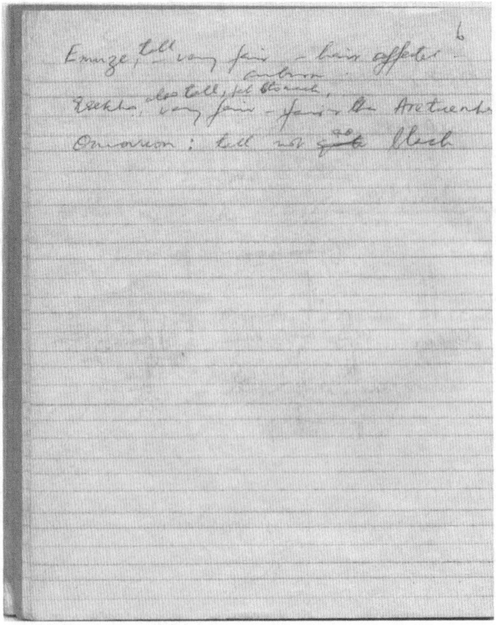

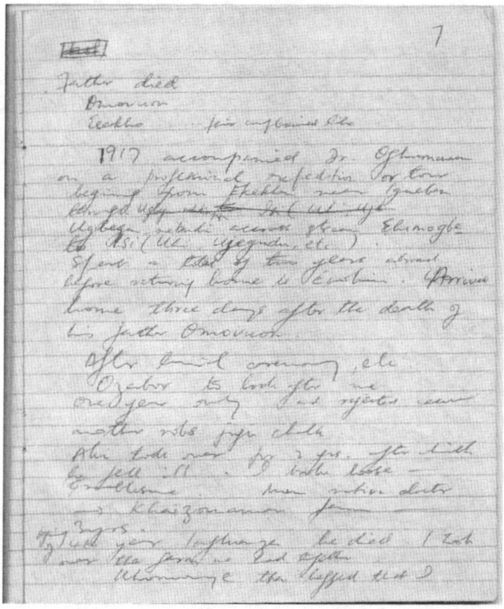

7

Father died
Omoruon
[illegible] ... [illegible]

1917 accompanied Dr. [illegible]
on a [illegible] expedition or tour
beginning from [illegible] near [illegible]
~~[illegible]~~
[illegible] across [illegible] Ehinogbe
to Asi ([illegible], etc.).
Spent a total of two years abroad
before returning home to [illegible]. Arrived
home three days after the death of
his father Omoruon.

After burial ceremony, etc.
Ozebor to look after me
one year only [illegible] rejected [illegible]
mother [illegible] child
[illegible] for 2 yrs. after [illegible]
he fell ill. [illegible]
[illegible] native doctor
[illegible] Khaizomamon [illegible]
3 yrs.
[illegible] year [illegible] he died. [illegible]
[illegible] the [illegible]
[illegible] that I

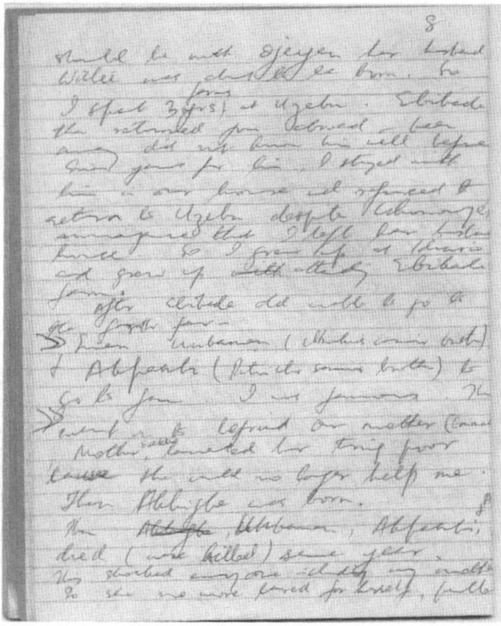

8

should be with Ojeyen [illegible]
[illegible] was [illegible] be born. So
I spent 3 yrs at Uzebu. [illegible]
the returned from abroad [illegible]
[illegible] did not [illegible] before
[illegible] for him. I stayed with
him in our house and refused to
return to Uzebu despite [illegible]
[illegible] that I left [illegible]
[illegible] So I grew up at [illegible]
and grew up [illegible] [illegible]
farm.
After [illegible] old [illegible]
[illegible]
[illegible] ([illegible] brother)
& [illegible] ([illegible] brother) to
[illegible]. I was [illegible]. The
[illegible] our mother [illegible]
Mother [illegible] being poor
because she could no longer help me.
Then [illegible] was born.
The ~~[illegible]~~, [illegible], [illegible],
died (were killed) same year.
[illegible] shocked everyone including my mother
So she no more [illegible] for herself, [illegible]

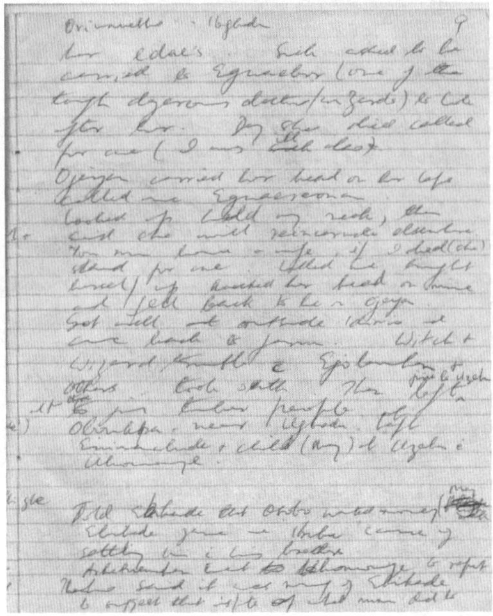

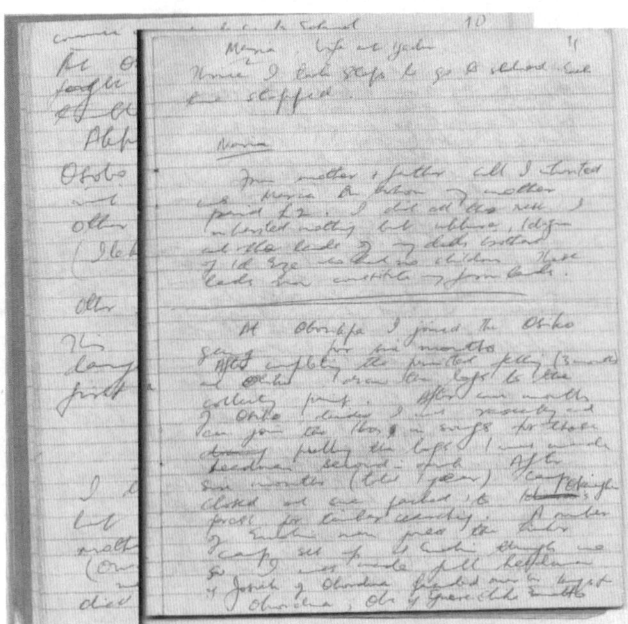

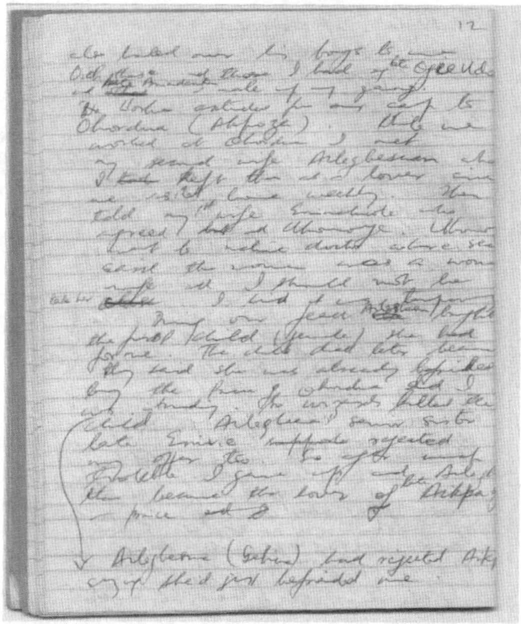
12

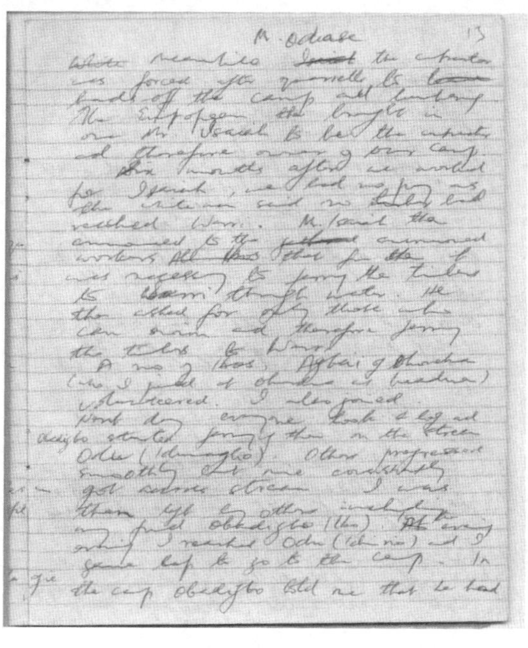
M. Odiase
13

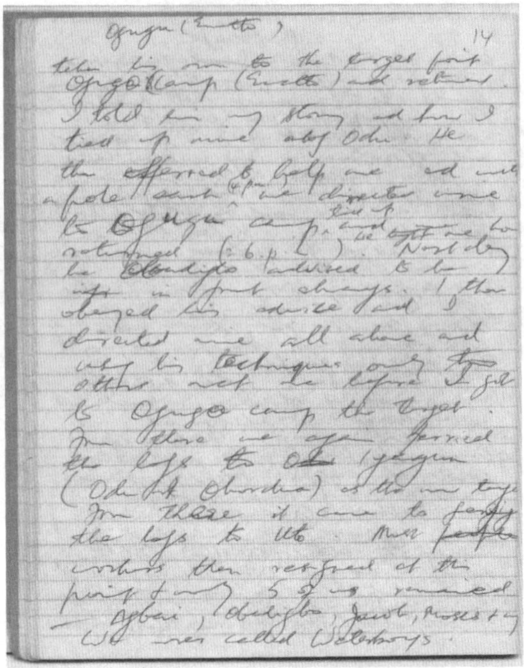

Ogugu ([illegible]) 14

taken [illegible] to the target point
Ogugo camp ([illegible]) and returned.
I told him my story and how I
tied up mine along Odu. He
then offered to help me and with
a pole [illegible] he directed me
to Ogugu camp and [illegible]
returned (i.e. 6 p.m.). Next day
he [illegible] advised to be
in front always. I then
obeyed his advice and I
directed me all alone and
using his techniques [illegible]
others met me before I got
to Ogugo camp the target.
From there we again ferried
the logs to [illegible]
(Odu [illegible] Oburdua) as the new target
From there it came to ferrying
the logs to Uto. Most people
workers then resigned at this
point and only 5 of us remained
Agbai, Obaligbo, Jacob, Moses and [illegible]
We were called Waterboys.

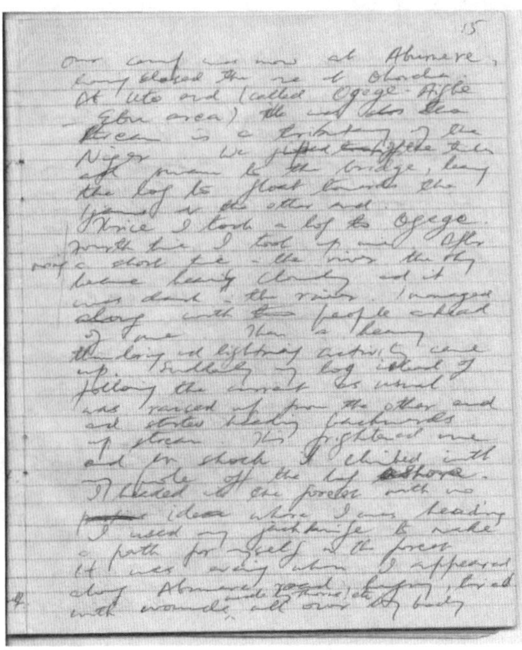

15

Our camp was now at Abunere,
having [illegible] the [illegible] Oburdua.
At Uto and (called Ogege-Afibe
Ebu area) the [illegible]
stream is a tributary of the
Niger. We [illegible]
[illegible] to the bridge, leaving
the log to float towards the
[illegible] on the other end.
Twice I took a log to Ogege.
[illegible] I took up mine. After
a short [illegible] the sky
became heavily cloudy and it
was dark in the rain. I managed
along with the people ahead
of me. Then a heavy
thundering and lightning activity came
up. Suddenly my log instead of
following the current as usual
was raised up from the other end
and started heading backwards
up stream. This frightened me
and in shock I climbed with
my [illegible] off the log ashore.
I headed into the forest with no
idea where I was heading
I used my jackknife to make
a path for myself in the forest
It was evening when I appeared
along Abunere road, hungry, tired
with wounds all over my body

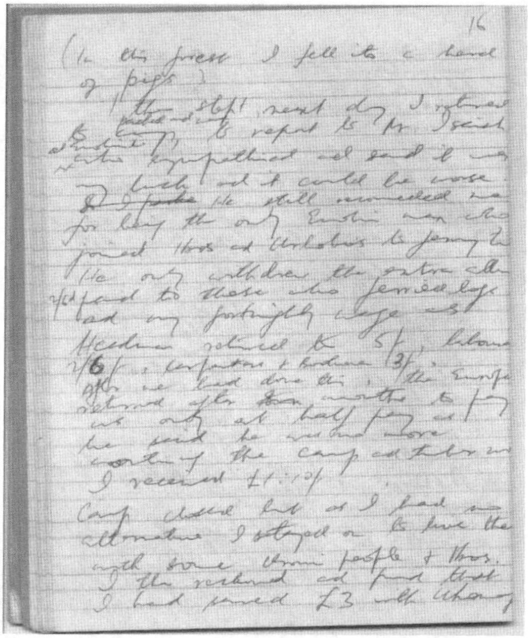

16

(In this process I fell into a band of pigs.)

[illegible] next day I returned [illegible] to report to [illegible]. I said [illegible] sympathetic and said it was [illegible] luck and it could be worse. He still [illegible] me for being the only [illegible] man who joined [illegible] and Urhobos to ferry [illegible]. He only withdrew the extra [illegible] paid to those who ferried logs and my fortnightly wage [illegible]. Headman received [illegible] 5/-, labourer [illegible] 3/-. After we had done this, the European returned after [illegible] months to pay us only at half pay and he said he [illegible] more [illegible] of the camp and [illegible]. I received £1:10/-

Camp closed but as I had no alternative I stayed on to live there with some Urhobo people + Ibos. I then reckoned and found that I had saved £3 with [illegible]

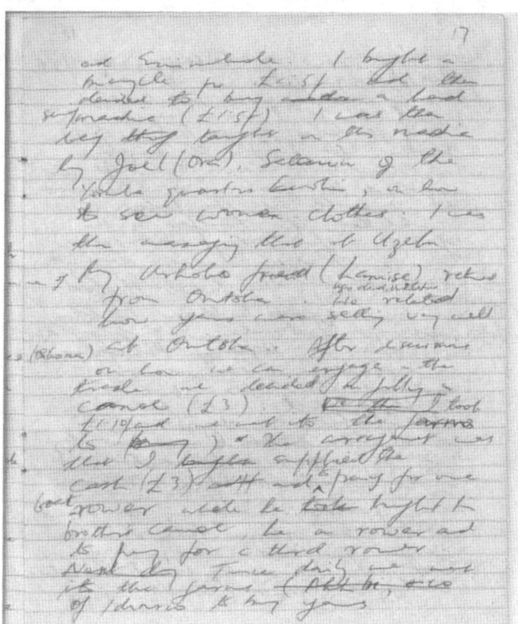

17

and [illegible]. I bought a bicycle for £1:5/- and then decided to buy [illegible] a hand sewing machine (£1:5/-). I was then being taught on this machine by Joel (Oru), [illegible] of the Yoruba quarters [illegible] to sew women clothes. [illegible] the [illegible] of Uzebu [illegible] my Urhobo friend (Lamise) returned from Ontola. He related how yams were selling very well at Ontola. After discussing on how we can engage [illegible] the trade we decided to [illegible] canoe (£3). I took £1:10/- and [illegible] to the farms to [illegible]. The arrangement was that I supplied the cash (£3) and [illegible] pay for one boat rower while he [illegible] brother's canoe, be a rower and to pay for a third rower. Next day [illegible] we went [illegible] the farms [illegible] of Idrisso to buy yams.

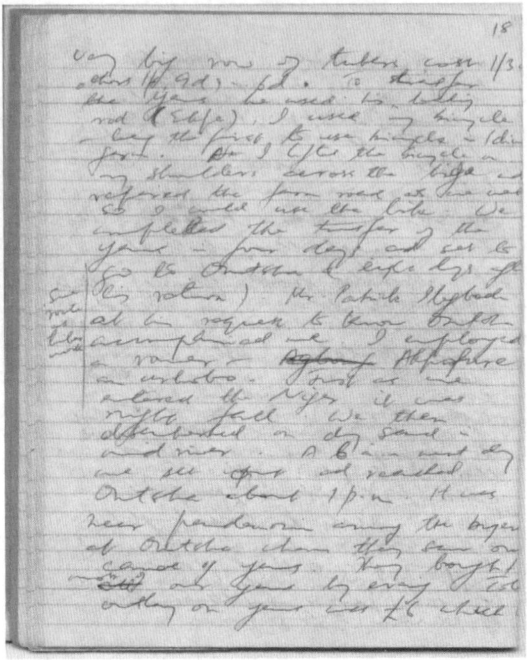
18

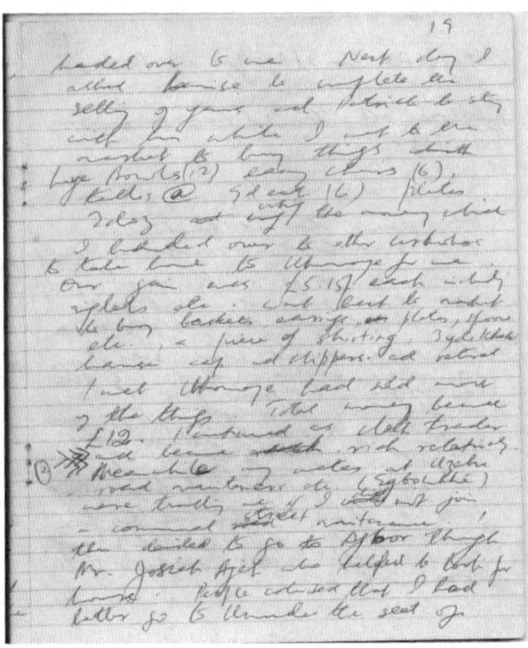
19

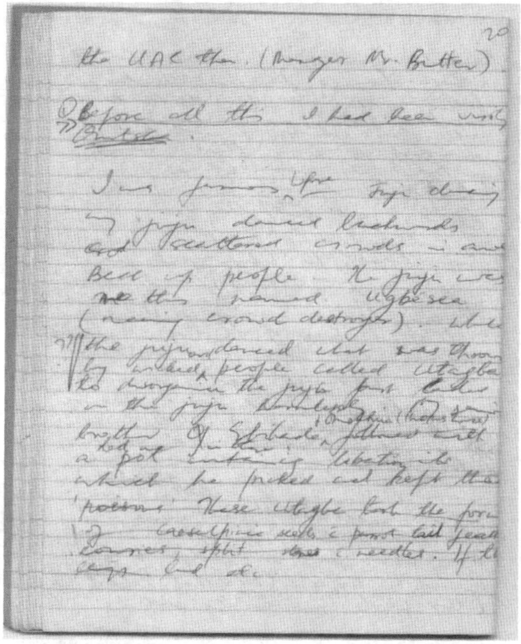

20

the UAC then. (Manager Mr. Butter)

① Before all this I had been visiting Onitsha.

I was famous upon [illegible] juju dancing by juju danced backwards and scattered crowds – and [illegible] of people. The juju was [illegible] named Ugbesea (meaning crowd destroyer). While the juju danced what was thrown by wicked people called Utagba to [illegible] the juju [illegible] in the juju [illegible] brother of Egbuche [illegible] [illegible] followed with a pot [illegible] [illegible] into which he picked and kept the 'poisons'. These utagbe took the form of [illegible] [illegible] [illegible] [illegible] cowries, split [illegible] & needles. If the [illegible] [illegible] [illegible]

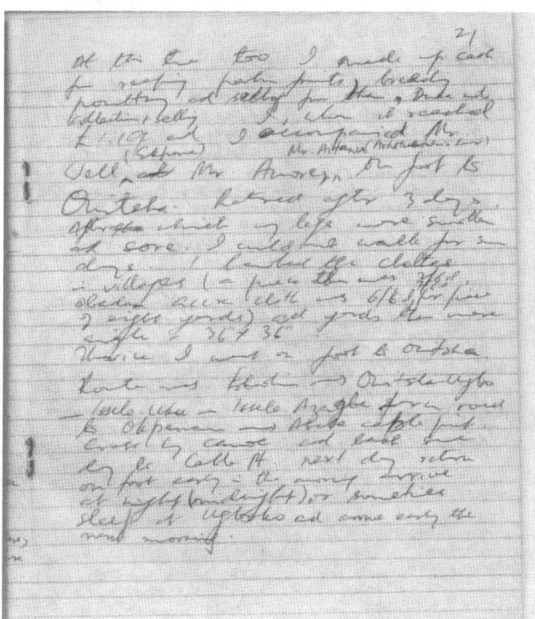

21

At this time too I made up cash for [illegible] palm fruits, breaking, pounding and selling for them & [illegible] [illegible] [illegible] [illegible] I [illegible] & recorded £1.10/- and I accompanied Mr. (Sakpona) Mr. Attanasi [illegible] Uell and Mr Amorey on foot to Onitsha. Returned after 3 days. After which my legs were swollen and sore. I could not walk for some days. I hawked the clothes in villages (a piece then was 2/6d, [illegible] [illegible] cloth was 6/6d for piece of eight yards) and yards then were [illegible] = 36" x 36".

Thrice I went on foot to Onitsha. Route was [illegible] → Onitsha [illegible] – [illegible] [illegible] – [illegible] Azagba [illegible] road to Okpanam → Asaba [illegible] [illegible]. Cross by canoe and back [illegible] [illegible] to Cable Pt. next day return on foot early in the morning arrive at night (midnight) or sometimes sleep at Ugbolu and come early the next morning.

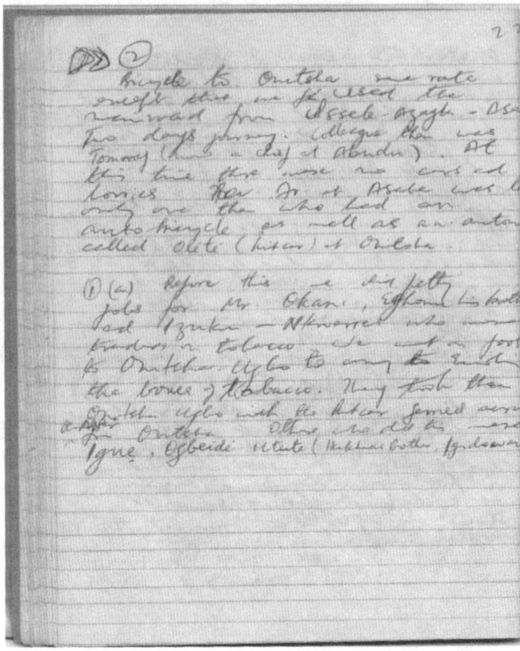

22

② bicycle to Onitsha same route except that we [illegible] used the main road from Issele-Azagba - Asaba. Two days journey. Colleague then was Tommy (now a chief at Abudu). At this time there were no cars and lorries. [illegible] at Asaba was the only one who had an auto bicycle as well as an auto[illegible] called Olete (hitcar) at Onitsha.

① (a) Before this we did petty jobs for Mr. Okani, [illegible] his brother and Izuka - Nkwocha who were traders in tobacco. We went on foot to Onitsha Ugbo to carry [illegible] the boxes of tobacco. They took them Onitsha Ugbo with the hitcar ferried across to Onitsha. Others who did this were Igue, Egbeide [illegible] ([illegible] brother, [illegible]

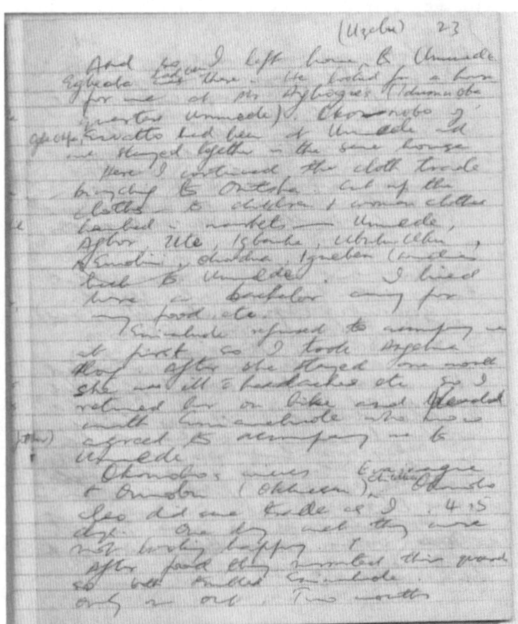

(Uzebu) 23

And so I left home to Umuede. Egbeola [illegible] there. He looked for a house for me at Mr [illegible] (Idumuoba quarter Umuede). Okonnobo of [illegible] had been at Umuede and we stayed together in the same house.

Here I continued the cloth trade bicycling to Onitsha. Cut up the cloths to children & women clothes [illegible] in markets — Umuede, Agbor, Ute, Igbanke, Ubulu-Uku, [illegible], [illegible], Igueben ([illegible]) back to Umuede. I lived there a bachelor cooking for my food etc.

[illegible] refused to accompany me at first so I took Agatha along. After she stayed one month she was ill with headaches etc so I returned her on bike and pleaded with [illegible] who now agreed to accompany me to Umuede.

Okonobo's wives Evangeline & Onnobu (Okhuesan), children [illegible] also did same trade as I. 4 & 5 days. One day we noticed they were not looking happy & after food they [illegible] this quarrel so we pulled [illegible] only 2 out. Two months

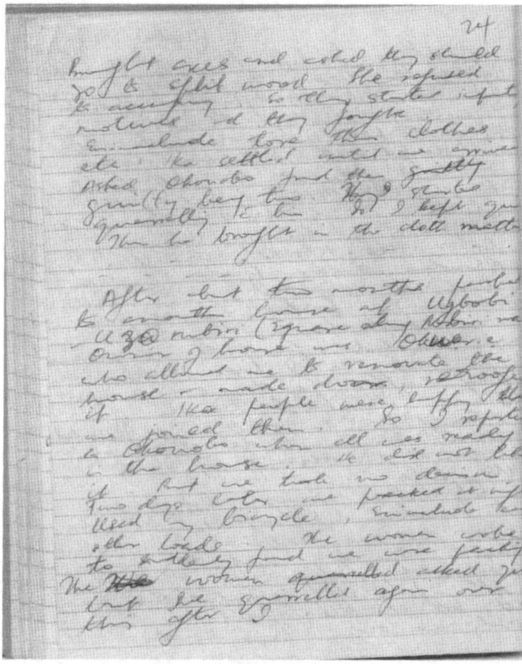

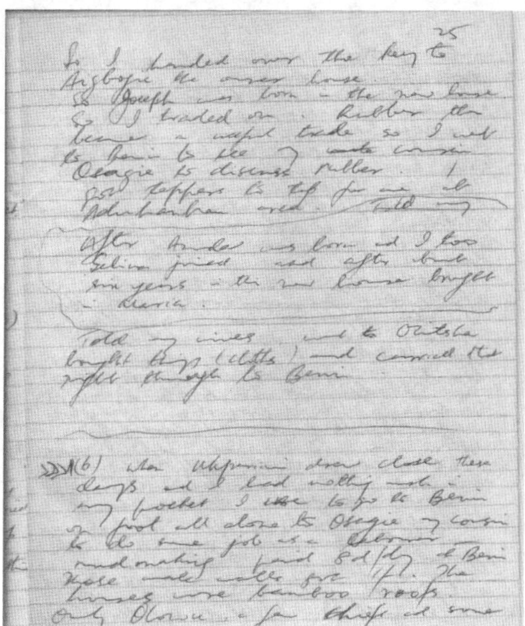

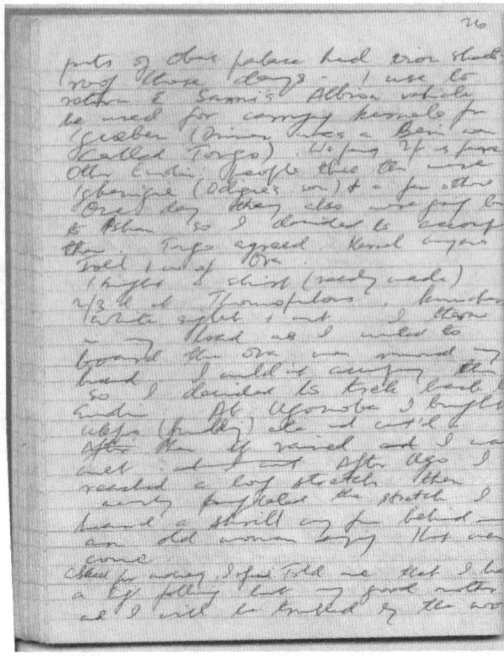

26

parts of Oba's palace had iron sheet roof [illegible] days. I use to [illegible] Sammi's Albion vehicle he used for carrying kernels for [illegible] (Driver was a Bini man called Tongo). [illegible] 2/- [illegible] Other [illegible] people [illegible] Igbanigue (Odigie's son) + a few others. One day [illegible] also [illegible] to Ashun so I decided to accompany them. Tongo agreed. Kernel [illegible] [illegible] of Ora.
I bought a shirt (ready made) 2/3 [illegible] Thomopulos, [illegible] white [illegible] I [illegible] [illegible] Road as I wanted to [illegible] the Ora [illegible] [illegible] I could not accompany the [illegible] so I decided to trek back to [illegible]. At Ugonoba I bought [illegible] [illegible] After the [illegible] rained and I was wet [illegible]. After Ogo I reached a long stretch. When [illegible] [illegible] the stretch I heard a shrill cry from behind — an old woman [illegible] [illegible] come. Asked for money, I refused. Told me that I [illegible] a [illegible] [illegible] my good mother and I will be troubled by the wo[illegible]

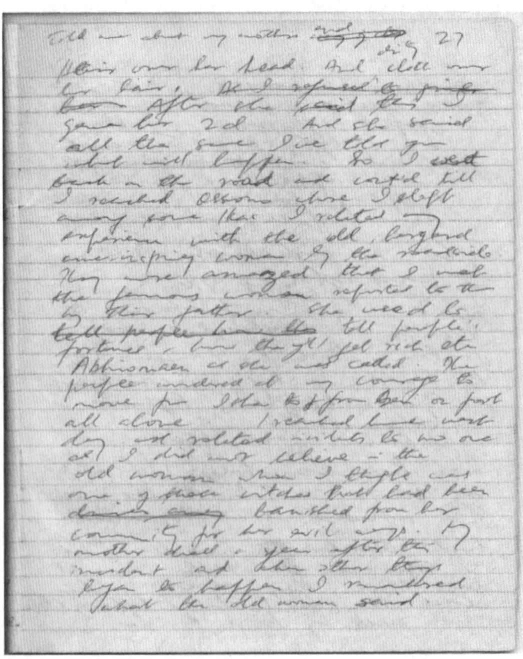

Told me that my mother [illegible] 27
[illegible] over her head. And [illegible] her hair, ~~[illegible] refused [illegible] ~~. After she said this I gave her 2d. And she said all the same I've told you what will happen. So I went back on the road and [illegible] till I reached [illegible] where I slept among some [illegible]. I related my experience with the old, [illegible] [illegible] woman by the roadside. They were amazed that I met the famous woman referred to them by their father. She used to ~~tell people [illegible]~~ tell people's fortunes [illegible] [illegible] Abhionaen as she was called. The people wondered at my courage to move [illegible] [illegible] from [illegible] or [illegible] all alone. I reached home next day and related incidents to no one as I did not believe in the old woman [illegible] I [illegible] was one of those witches that had been ~~[illegible]~~ banished from her community for her evil [illegible]. My mother died [illegible] years after this incident and when other things began to happen I [illegible] what the old woman said.

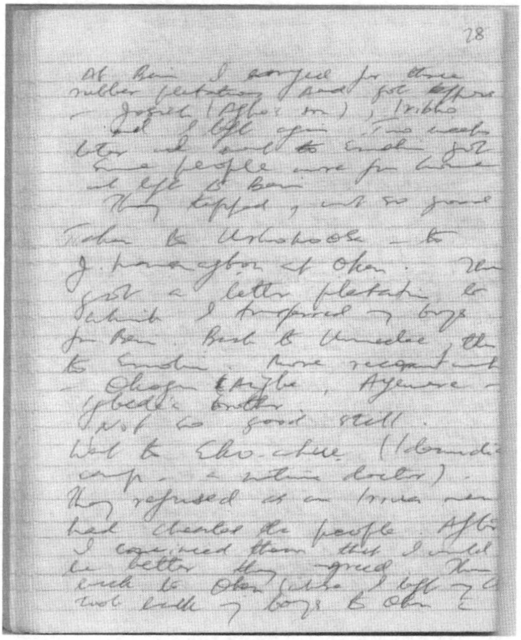

28

At Beni I arranged for three
rubber plantations and got tappers
– Joseph (Agbo's son), Iribho
and I left again. Two weeks
later when I went to [illegible] [illegible]
[illegible] people were [illegible] [illegible]
and left to Beni
They tapped, [illegible] so [illegible]
Taken to Ushokooke – to
J. [illegible] at Okon. Then
got a letter plantation to
[illegible] I transferred my boys
from Beni. Back to Umuedae, then
to [illegible]. More recruitment
– Okoga [illegible], Ayemere –
Igbede's brother
Not so good still.
Went to Eko-[illegible] ([illegible]
camp – a native doctor).
They refused as an Iroma man
had cheated the people. After
I convinced them that I would
be better they agreed. Then
back to Okon [illegible] I left my [illegible]
[illegible] with my boys to Okon [illegible]

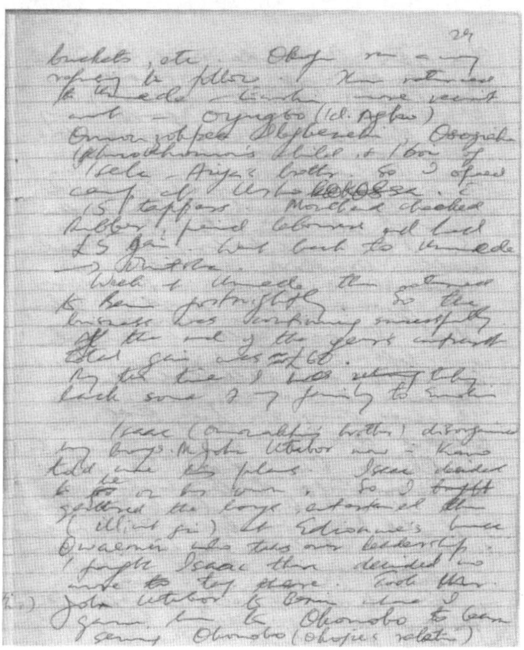

29

buckets, etc. Okoje [illegible] [illegible]
refusing to follow. Then returned
to Umuede – [illegible] more recruitment – Oyiugbo (Id. Agbo)
Omon [illegible] [illegible], Osagie
([illegible] child) + 1 boy of
Isele – Ariya's brother. So I opened
camp at Ushokooke.
15 tappers. Month end checked
rubber, paid labourers and had
£5 gain. Went back to Umuede
[illegible]
Went to Umuede then returned
to Beni fortnightly so the
business was continuing successfully.
At the end of the year's expected
total gain was £60.
By this time I was [illegible] taking
back some of my family to [illegible]

Isaac ([illegible] brother) disorganised
my boys. Mr John Utabor [illegible] [illegible]
told [illegible] [illegible] plans. Isaac decided
to be on his own. So I ~~fought~~
gathered the boys, abandoned the
(illicit gin) at Edosomwe's [illegible]
Owaemen who takes over leadership.
I fought Isaac then decided no
more to tap there. Took then
John Utabor to Benin where I
gave him to Obonobo to learn
sawing. Obonobo (Okoje's relation)

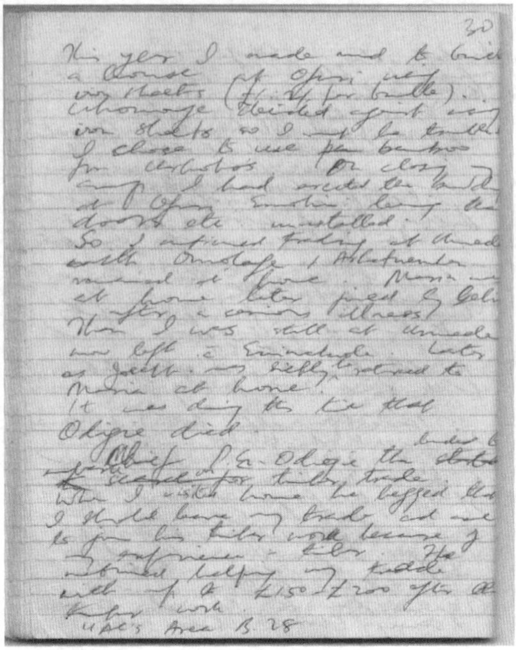

30

This year I made [illegible] to build
a house at Ofosi using
iron sheets ([illegible] for [illegible]).
[illegible] decided against using
iron sheets so I [illegible] [illegible]
I chose to use [illegible] bamboo
for [illegible]. On closing
camp I had erected the building
at Ofosi [illegible] leaving the
doors etc uninstalled.
So I continued trading at Umede
with Omolafe / [illegible]
[illegible] at home. Maria [illegible]
at home later joined by [illegible]
after a [illegible] illness)
Then I was still at Umede
[illegible] left [illegible] [illegible]. Later
as [illegible] my [illegible] returned to
Maria at home.
It was during this time that
Odigie died.
[illegible]
Chief P.E. Odigie the [illegible]
~~[illegible]~~ for timber trade
When I visited home he begged that
I should leave my trade and come
to join his timber work because of
my experience in timber. He
[illegible] helping my trade
with up to £150-£200 after the
timber work.
UAC's Area B.28

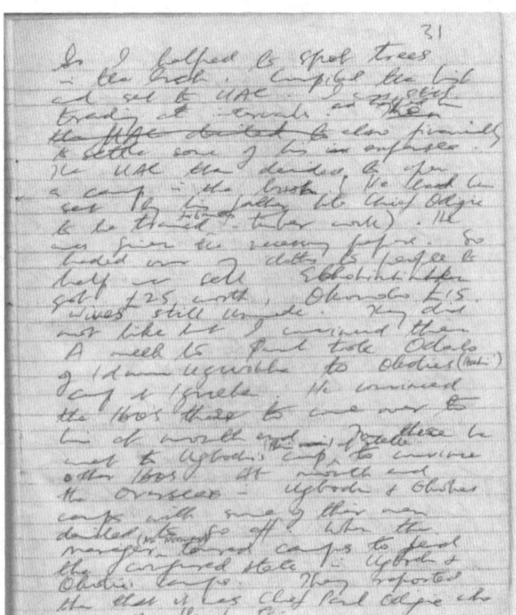

31

So I helped to spot trees
in the bush, compiled the list
and sent to UAC. I was still
trading at Umede. [illegible]
~~the UAC decided~~ to close financially
to settle some of his [illegible].
The UAC then decided to open
a camp in the bush (the land be
set [illegible] by his father late Chief Odigie
to be [illegible] timber work). He
was given the necessary papers. So
[illegible] over my debts to people to
help me collect. [illegible]
got £25 worth, Okomolo £15.
Wives still Umede. They did
not like but I convinced them.
A week to [illegible] took Odalo
of Idumu Ugwoke to Obodies ([illegible])
camp at Igueba. He convinced
the Ibo's there to come over to
him at [illegible] and [illegible] these he
went to Ugbodu's camp to convince
other Ibos at [illegible] and
the Overseas - Ugbodu & Obodies
camps with many of their men
[illegible] ([illegible]) go off. When the
managers toured camps to find
the confused state in Ugbodu &
Obodies camps. They reported
then that it was Chief Paul Odigie who
was responsible for this

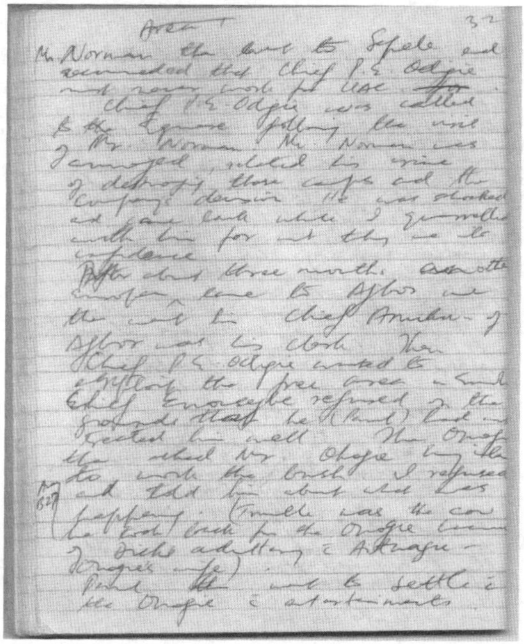

Arrest [illegible] 32
Mr Norman then went to Sapele and
recommended that Chief P.E. Odgie
must never work for UAC.
Chief P.E. Odgie was called
to the [illegible] following the visit
of Mr. Norman. Mr. Norman was
[illegible], related his crime
of destroying those camps and the
company's decision. He was shocked
and [illegible] while I quarrelled
with him for not [illegible]
confidence
After about three months, [illegible]
[illegible] came to Afloro [illegible]
[illegible] Chief [illegible] of
Afloro was his clerk. Then
Chief P.E. Odgie wanted to
[illegible] the free area [illegible]
Chief [illegible] refused on the
grounds that he [illegible] had [illegible]
[illegible] him well. The [illegible]
[illegible] by Odgie [illegible]
to work the bush. I refused
and told him about what was
happening. (Trouble was the [illegible]
he took back for the Onogie [illegible]
of [illegible] adultery [illegible]
[illegible] wife).
[illegible] went to settle [illegible]
the Onogie [illegible]

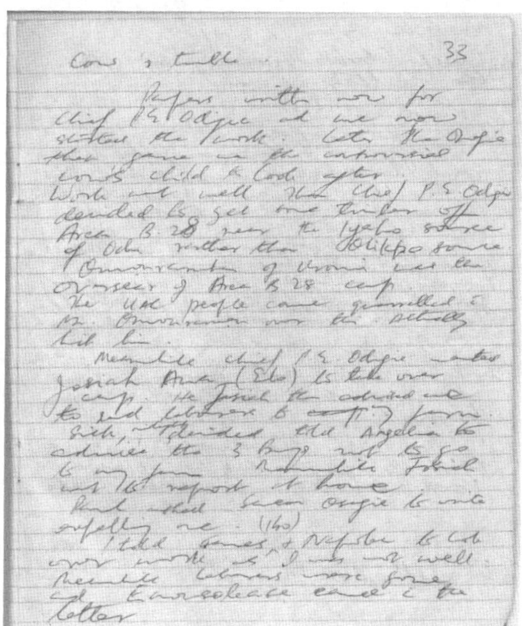

Cons [illegible] trouble. 33
[illegible] written now for
Chief P.E. Odgie and we now
started the work. Later the Onogie
[illegible] in the [illegible]
[illegible] child [illegible] after.
Work went well. Then Chief P.E. Odgie
decided to get some timber off
Area B.28 near the [illegible] source
of Odin rather than [illegible] source
[illegible] of [illegible] was the
Overseer of Area B 28 camp.
The UAC people came [illegible]
Mr. [illegible] over the [illegible]
[illegible].
Meanwhile Chief P.E. Odgie wanted
Josiah [illegible] (Edo) to take over
camp. He Josiah then advised me
to send labourers to [illegible] farm.
[illegible] told Angelina to
advise the 3 boys not to go
to my farm. Meanwhile Josiah
went to report at home.
[illegible] Osagie to write
[illegible] me. (140)
I told [illegible] to [illegible]
over work as I was not well.
Meanwhile labourers were going
and [illegible] came [illegible] the
letter

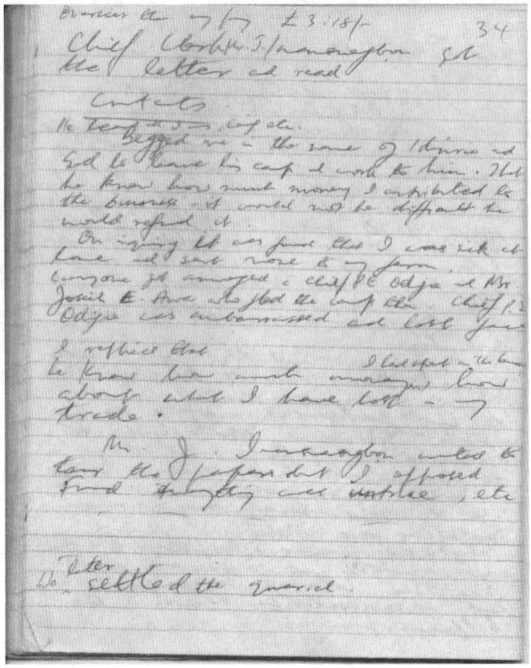

Overseer etc 7/- £3:18/- 34

Chief ... got the letter and read

Contents

... Begged me in the name of ... to leave his camp and work for him. That he knew how much money I contributed to the business – it would not be difficult he would refund it.

On inquiry it was found that I was sick at home and sent none to my farm. ... Chief P.E. Odjie and Mr. Josiah E. Area who ... the camp etc. Chief P.E. Odjie was embarrassed and lost face.

I replied that he knew how much money ... about what I have lost in my trade.

Mr. J. ... wanted to ... the papers but I opposed ... etc.

Later ... settled the quarrel

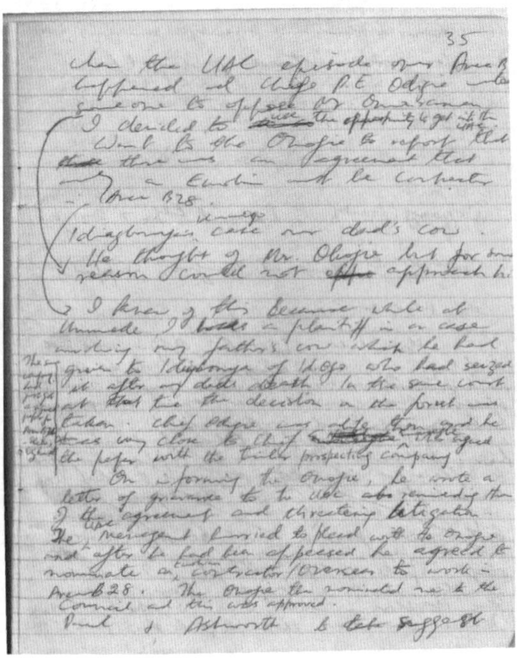

35

When the UAC episode over Area B ... happened and Chief P.E. Odjie wanted someone to oppose ...

I decided to use the opportunity to get ...

Went to the Onogie to report that there was an agreement that ... be contractor ... Area B28.

Idiagbonya's case over dad's cow.

He thought of Mr. ... but for some reason could not approach him.

I knew of this because while at ... I was a plaintiff in a case involving my father's cow which he had given to Idiagbonya ... who had seized it after my dad's death. In the same court at that time the decision on the forest was taken. Chief Odjie was ... and he was very close to Chief ... the agreed the paper with the timber prospecting company.

On informing the Onogie, he wrote a letter of grievance to the UAC ... reminding them of the agreement and threatening litigation. The UAC management hurried to plead with the Onogie and after he had been appeased he agreed to nominate a timber contractor/Overseer to work in Area B28. The Onogie then nominated me to the Council and this was approved.

... Ashworth ... suggest

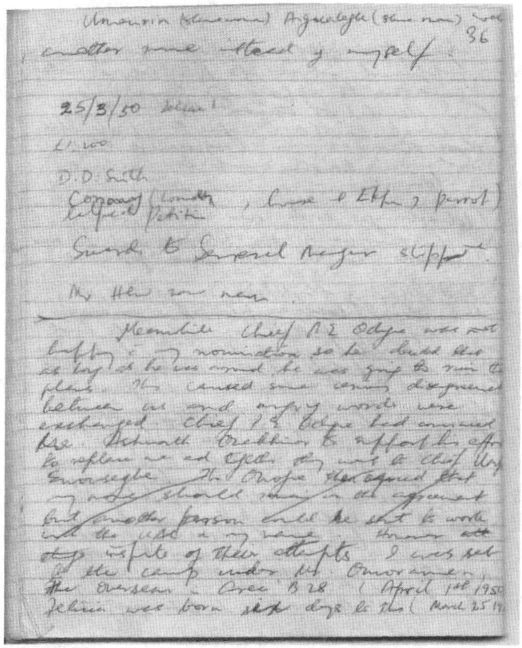

Umorurin (Kinsman) Agwulegbe (same name) was [illegible] 36
another name [illegible] of myself.

25/3/50 [illegible]

£1,200

D.D. Smith

Company (London [illegible], [illegible] Petition [illegible])

[illegible] to [illegible] [illegible] [illegible].

Mr [illegible] [illegible] [illegible].

Meanwhile Chief P.E. Odje was not happy [illegible] my nomination so he [illegible] that as long as he was around he was going to [illegible] the plans. This caused some [illegible] disagreement between us and angry words were exchanged. Chief P.E. Odje had [illegible] the [illegible] [illegible] to support his effort to replace me and [illegible] [illegible] [illegible] to Chief [illegible] [illegible]. The Okope [illegible] agreed that my name should remain in the agreement but another person could be sent to work with the UAC in my name. However all [illegible] in spite of their attempts I was sent to the camp under Mr. Omoraneme, the Overseer in Area B28 (April 1st 1950). Jelima was born [illegible] days to this (March 25 19[illegible]

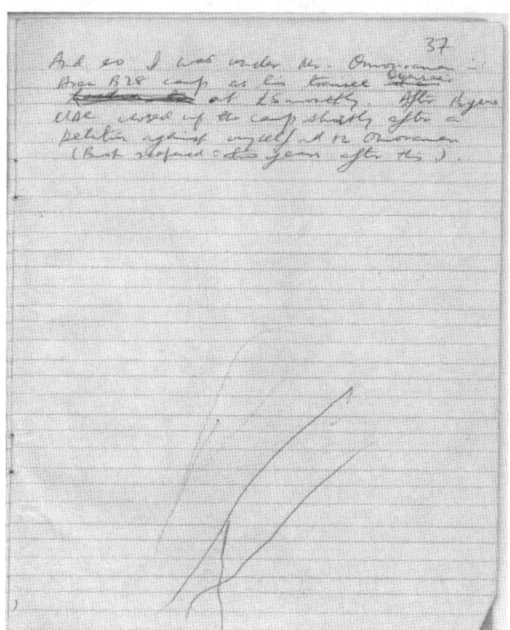

37
And so I was under Mr. Omoraneme in Area B28 camp as his trainee Overseer ~~[illegible]~~ at £5 monthly. After [illegible] UAC closed up the camp shortly after a petition against myself and Mr Omoraneme (But [illegible] [illegible] years after this).

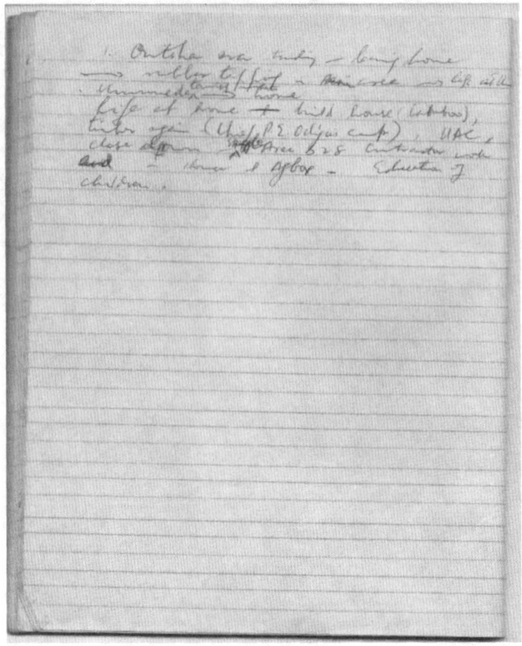

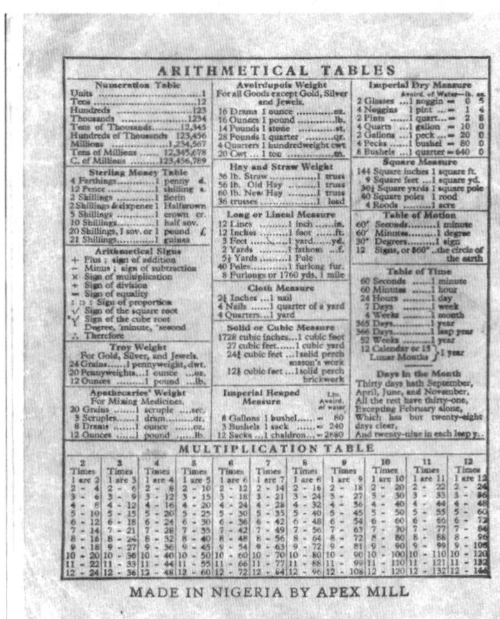

ARITHMETICAL TABLES

Numeration Table

Units 1
Tens 12
Hundreds 123
Thousands 1234
Tens of Thousands..........12,345
Hundreds of Thousands 123,456
Millions 1,234,567
Tens of Millions 12,345,678
C. of Millions 123,456,789

Sterling Money Table

4 Farthings............1 penny d.
12 Pence ....1 shilling s.
2 Shillings ....1 florin
2 Shillings & sixpence 1 Halfcrown
5 Shillings ....1 crown cr.
10 Shillings............1 half sov.
20 Shillings, 1 sov. or 1 pound £
21 Shillings............1 guinea

Arithmetical Signs

+ Plus ; sign of addition
− Minus ; sign of subtraction
× Sign of multiplication
÷ Sign of division
= Sign of equality
: :: : Sign of proportion
√ Sign of the square root
∛ Sign of the cube root
° Degree, ′ minute, ″ second
∴ Therefore

Troy Weight
For Gold, Silver, and Jewels.

24 Grains......1 pennyweight, dwt.
20 Pennyweights...1 ounce ...oz.
12 Ounces ....1 pound ...lb.

Apothecaries' Weight
For Mixing Medicines.

20 Grains ....1 scruple ....scr.
3 Scruples.......1 dram..........dr.
8 Drams ....1 ounce ....oz.
12 Ounces ....1 pound ....lb.

Avoirdupois Weight
For all Goods except Gold, Silver and Jewels.

16 Drams 1 ounce ....oz.
16 Ounces 1 pound ....lb.
14 Pounds 1 stone ....st.
28 Pounds 1 quarter ....qr.
4 Quarters 1 hundredweight cwt
20 Cwt ... 1 ton ....tn.

Hay and Straw Weight

36 lb. Straw ....1 truss
56 lb. Old Hay ....1 truss
60 lb. New Hay ....1 truss
36 trusses ....1 load

Long or Lineal Measure

12 Lines ....1 inch ....in.
12 Inches ....1 foot ....ft.
3 Feet ....1 yard.......yd.
2 Yards ....1 fathom ...f.
5½ Yards ....1 Pole
40 Poles.............1 furlong fur.
8 Furlongs or 1760 yds. 1 mile

Cloth Measure

2¼ Inches ...1 nail
4 Nails ....1 quarter of a yard
4 Quarters....1 yard

Solid or Cubic Measure

1728 cubic inches...1 cubic foot
27 cubic feet.......1 cubic yard
24¾ cubic feet ...1 solid perch mason's work
12¼ cubic feet ...1 solid perch brickwork

Imperial Heaped Measure (Lbs. Avoird. of water)

8 Gallons 1 bushel....... = 80
3 Bushels 1 sack .... = 240
12 Sacks ...1 chaldron... = 2880

Imperial Dry Measure

	Avoird. of Water—lb.	oz.
2 Glasses ...1 noggin =	0	5
4 Noggins 1 pint ... =	1	4
2 Pints ....1 quart... =	2	8
4 Quarts ...1 gallon =	10	0
2 Gallons ...1 peck ... =	20	0
4 Pecks ....1 bushel =	80	0
8 Bushels ...1 quarter =	640	0

Square Measure

144 Square inches 1 square ft.
9 Square feet ...1 square yd.
30¼ Square yards 1 square pole
40 Square poles 1 rood
4 Roods ....1 acre

Table of Motion

60″ Seconds..........1 minute
60′ Minutes..........1 degree
30° Degrees..........1 sign
12 Signs, or 360° ..the circle of the earth

Table of Time

60 Seconds ....1 minute
60 Minutes ....1 hour
24 Hours ....1 day
7 Days ....1 week
4 Weeks ....1 month
365 Days..............1 year
366 Days..............1 leap year
52 Weeks ....1 year
12 Calendar or 13 Lunar Months } 1 year

Days in the Month

Thirty days hath September,
April, June, and November,
All the rest have thirty-one,
Excepting February alone,
Which has but twenty-eight days clear,
And twenty-nine in each leap y..

MULTIPLICATION TABLE

2 Times	3 Times	4 Times	5 Times	6 Times	7 Times	8 Times	9 Times	10 Times	11 Times	12 Times
1 are 2	1 are 3	1 are 4	1 are 5	1 are 6	1 are 7	1 are 8	1 are 9	1 are 10	1 are 11	1 are 12
2 - 4	2 - 6	2 - 8	2 - 10	2 - 12	2 - 14	2 - 16	2 - 18	2 - 20	2 - 22	2 - 24
3 - 6	3 - 9	3 - 12	3 - 15	3 - 18	3 - 21	3 - 24	3 - 27	3 - 30	3 - 33	3 - 36
4 - 8	4 - 12	4 - 16	4 - 20	4 - 24	4 - 28	4 - 32	4 - 36	4 - 40	4 - 44	4 - 48
5 - 10	5 - 15	5 - 20	5 - 25	5 - 30	5 - 35	5 - 40	5 - 45	5 - 50	5 - 55	5 - 60
6 - 12	6 - 18	6 - 24	6 - 30	6 - 36	6 - 42	6 - 48	6 - 54	6 - 60	6 - 66	6 - 72
7 - 14	7 - 21	7 - 28	7 - 35	7 - 42	7 - 49	7 - 56	7 - 63	7 - 70	7 - 77	7 - 84
8 - 16	8 - 24	8 - 32	8 - 40	8 - 48	8 - 56	8 - 64	8 - 72	8 - 80	8 - 88	8 - 96
9 - 18	9 - 27	9 - 36	9 - 45	9 - 54	9 - 63	9 - 72	9 - 81	9 - 90	9 - 99	9 - 108
10 - 20	10 - 30	10 - 40	10 - 50	10 - 60	10 - 70	10 - 80	10 - 90	10 - 100	10 - 110	10 - 120
11 - 22	11 - 33	11 - 44	11 - 55	11 - 66	11 - 77	11 - 88	11 - 99	11 - 110	11 - 121	11 - 132
12 - 24	12 - 36	12 - 48	12 - 60	12 - 72	12 - 84	12 - 96	12 - 108	12 - 120	12 - 132	12 - 144

MADE IN NIGERIA BY APEX MILL

APPENDIX II

MINUTES OF TWO-FAMILY MEETINGS

1. Training of girls;
2. Death;
3. Co-existence of the Mothers - copied by children; and
4. The ladies have their part to play in the family.

The facts behind Robinson (Amudah's) case. Quarrels and court cases - Five court cases over Dad taking away Amudah's mother from Aiyobese who paid the dowry. After all the troubles - court cases and superstitious struggles - it was decided that Amudah should perform for Aiyobese to compensate her. He also uses her father's name Enato. This compensates her and according to advice to Dad this should ward off the causes, etc. of the woman. For this reason Joseph is the first son as already announced. Amudah then is the second in rank.

Amudah mentioned later the letter he received from someone about not leaving any brother or sister behind and people at Qhodua who talk about that not being his father etc. Dad assured him that he was his son fully but that events led to the decision and his use of the name Enato. It was in the interest of all. In my case he was to participate fully in the house. Events leading to the training of the older children were also discussed and reasons given for various events of Robert not goint to secondary school - 1957/58.

1	2	3	4	5	6
Lucy	Amudah '38	Uwamusi '49	Vick. '56	Mami '58	Egbeke
Joseph '38	Felix '42	Emmanuel '58	Thomas '63	Rose '60	
Robert '42	Felicia '50	Bartho. '63	Solo. '64-'65	Akhere	
Anthonia Aug. '49	Omisi 1952			Florence	
	Odion Obhokhan 23/12/55		Odion		

* Dates of Birth: Some are estimated & not correct

After all explanations for the decision above the girls - Anthonia, Felicia, Uwamusi and Omisi in that order were asked what they intended to do. Robert was also asked about his plans. Joseph told the house that Felix had definite plans for self improvement.

Appendix II

OKOGUN OMOVUON

FAMILY MEETING HELD ON THE 27TH DAY OF MARCH 1978 AT FAMILY HOUSE - OKAIGBEN-EWOHIMI

Present:

1. Pa J. O. Omovuon - Father
2. Mr. R. A. Enanto - Son
3. Prof. J. I. Okogun - "
4. Mr. R. E. Okogun - "
5. Mr. F. O. Okogun - "
6. Miss Celestina U. Okogun - Daughter
7. Miss Antonia A. Okogun - "
8. Miss Teresa O. Okogun - "
9. Miss Lydia O. Okogun - "
10. Master Emmanuel O. Okogun - Son
11. Miss Victoria Okogun - Daughter
12. Master Batholomew Okogun - Son
13. Miss Mammy Okogun - Daughter
14. Miss Rose Okogun - "
15. Master Thomas O. Okogun - Son
16. Master Solomon Okogun - "

OTHERS

1. Madam M. C. Ehikhamhen - Aunt
. J. I. Itama - Brother

Absent:

1. Miss Imome O. Okogun - Daughter
2. Felicia E. Okogun - "
3. Two married daughters who were not invited to attend and three others (two daughters and one son) who were too young to attend.

In attendance: Mr. F. O. Okogun

The meeting opened at about 5.30 a.m. with a short prayer by our Father Pa J. O. Omovuon.

Making the first speech, our father said that we knew what we wanted to say since we organised the meeting. Then prof. J. I. Okogun answered by saying that, though Mr. F. O. Okogun initiated the call of the meeting there were other things he would include in the agenda.

There was a hot debate over Mr. F. O. Okogun's failure to inform Amuda of the meeting, knowing fully well that he had written Prof. Joe about it. After everything being said and done, Felix defended himself and it was resolved amicably.

Another controversial matter was the issue of headship of the family between Joe and Amuda. Joe was not happy over the behaviour of Amuda in respect of some family issues. As a result, Joe wanted things to be clearly defined once and for all in respect of order of assuming headship in the family. This issue received very hot debate among the family.

Our Daddy, gave details to support the reason why Prof. Joe is given the headship of the family. This resulted from the controversial way his now senior wife was married. There were several court cases between Pa and the late Madam Eyobase Enato as well as diabolical battles. In the end Pa paid no dowry over Mama Angelina, an a compliance with a strong advice.

- 2 -

He summarized by saying that it was for the safety of the family in General and the children of Mama Angelina in particular that Amuda has to bear a separate surname. The idea of changing the name to R. A. Enanto Okogun was however suggested by Prof. Joe.

Opposing the idea Amuda said in order to keep to what father enumerated as the reasons behind his bearing that name, and the safety of everybody, he (Amuda) deemed it necessary to keep the name Enanto. This was later supported by Felix, though according to him (Felix) he was not trying to be sectional. At this stage the discussion about changing Enanto to become Enanto-Okogun was dropped.

Father also reminded Amuda and Felix to remember to erect a house at Ohordua (their mothers homeland) to the name of Eyobase's family when the fund is available.

Robert: The house was not happy over the uncompromising attitude of Robert with most members of the family. After very hot debate of accusation and criticism it was agreed that everybody should change his/her attitude towards Robert and feel free with him and pay him constant visits to make him feel happy.

On his marriage, he was vehemently opposed to it, as according to him he is financially not balanced to cater for any woman. The house did not agree that one has to be very rich financially before talking of marriage. However the most important thing is getting the house in good shape and well furnished. After long debate, it was agreed that his house should be furnished for him by the family. In doing so, everybody could do what he is capable of doing instead of being specific on the items to to be bought by every individual.

Mammy: It was announced to the house that Mammy has decided to marry .tead of going to school. After interviewing her by the family, it was hoped that she should be able to think of something to do when she gets to her husband. Joe however talked well of the boy's behaviour and felt that he is a nice boy.

Celestina: It was also announced that Celestina has been put in the family way by a class-mate to the surprise of the majority of the family. After full discussion, it was agreed that if they love themselves they could be allowed to marry themselves as the house does not support abortion. Now that she has paid for her final examination, everything should be done to see that she completes her school. Celestina was however advised to inform the boy to write Prof. Joe to explain and state his mind.

Antonia and Batholomew: Antonia gave reasons why she told Batholomew to go to boarding house. She enumerated the insubordinate attitude of Batholomew, Benjy and the worst of all them - Philip. She could no longer cope hence the action. Batholomew was however reprimanded and advised to change.

Children's Education: Joe commented that it could be seen that he and Felix have been doing most of this task. But since his problems became more, he has not been able to meet the demand of a great deal of family problems especially with the distance being another stony block. In this respect he said, Felix has been doing all in his power to keep the family going. He made reference to the cabinet bed made for Pa.

He was therefore very grateful to Felix and asked the family to thank and pray for him for all his good activities towards the family. After this the payment of the children's fees was distributed as follows:-

1. Thomas - Joe
2. Odion/Emmanuel - Felix
3. Obhokhan - Felicia
4. Victoria - Pa (Equipment mainly)

- 3 -

5. Batholomew - Antonia

6. Solomon - Irene (when admitted)

7. Rose - Celestina (tentatively when Rose is admitted)

It is hoped that by the time these children complete their education, they will in turn take over the junior ones coming up.

Father: It was decided that there should be monthly contribution for fathers maintenance of the wives with special reference to feeding. Individual contribution was agreed as follows:-

		₦ k	
Joe	-	13.00	Monthly
Amuda	-	10.00	"
Robert	-	5.00	"
Felix	-	11.00	"
Antonia	-	7.00	"
Felicia	-	7.00	"
Irene	-	7.00	"
Total	=	₦ 60.00	

It was also agreed that Celestina should start contributing after her education. It was also made clear that anybody could contribute more. The amount stated is minimum. Pa was happy over this and prayed for our happiness and long life.

Earlier on Pa said that he also gets monthly collection of about ₦80.00 (Or ₦40.00 I do not remember) from his house at Agbor. He was then told to use that for his up keep.

Emmanuel: Joe reminded the family of the prospect of Emmanuel. With his present performance at School, it is hoped that he should be in the University anytime.

In this regard therefore, he appealed, everybody should be ready to contribute to his University Education or any institute of higher learning. This was quite welcome by the house.

Jacob: He was asked to state his problems since the family felt that he looks amaciated. He then said that his job is not lucrative, as a result he goes for other private jobs on Saturdays and Sundays hence there is no time for him to rest. Otherwise, he had no other problem.

Pa then asked if he has any trade test or certificate for his profession. He said no. Felix was therefore directed to find out ways and means for his getting registered for trade test. With this he could be employed into the service or good company. Felix promised to do his best.

This was the last item on the agenda. Pa later brought in a bottle of hot drink for the occasion with which he prayed for us and the meeting closed at about 10.45 a.m.

3

APPENDIX III

EZE FAMILY TREE...........

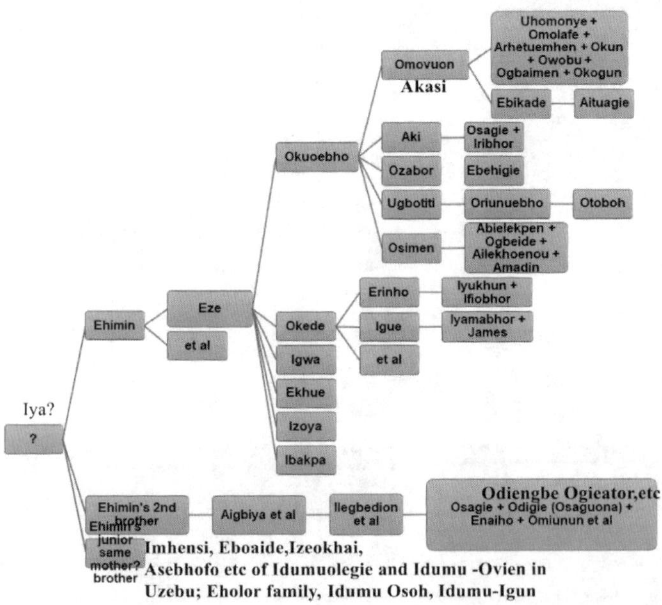

The senior rank Group in Idinrio is the Oeren Ogbe Group of Idumunamo, Idumu-udin Idumu-igele in Uzebu, the second is Idumu-Iya where the head house is Ehimin-Eze consisting of Uwi-Idinrio, Idumu-Obo with Ikogbe and Idumu-Omolegie with Idumu-Ovien in Uzebu while the third in rank Group is the Omonikhere Group of Ikogheghe, Omhen-Idinrio and Idumunegbon

APPENDIX IV

PA JOHN E. OKOGUN OMOVUON ACADEMIC PRIZE WINNERS AWARDS; FIRST YEAR AND 16TH YEAR 2017/18, OKAIGBEN PRIMARY SCHOOL

FIRST WINNERS 2002/03

	Primary 1	
1ST	**2ND**	**3RD**
Akhere Ekeomen* error	**Eucharia Eloebhose f**	**Magnus Okoro**
	Primary II	
1ST	**2ND**	**3RD**
Titus Eloebhose	**Godiom Nwachukwu**	**Juliet Enojiasun f**
	Primary III	
1ST	**2ND**	**3RD**
Chukwudi Godson	**Luke Eriaremhien**	**Omonon Adoghe f**
	Primary IV	
1ST	**2ND**	**3RD**
Saturday Ojo	**Joy Ehibor f**	**Osaigbevo Akowe**
	Primary V	
1ST	**2ND**	**3RD**

Theophilus Eloebhose	**Ezekiel Odile**	**Emmauel Agbonkpolor**
	Primary VI	
1ST	**2ND**	**3RD**
Akhere Omonjiade f	**Edujie Egedege f**	**Collins Owobu**

The first pupil winners of Pa J. Okogun Omovuon Academic Prizes, Teachers and some Okaigben Elders : 13th June, 2003. From left to right: sitting are Mrs Theresa Azenodion(teacher), Messrs. Thomas Omonfuegbe, Iyere Odiana, Imhontu, Chief Esongban of Okaigben (David), Sergent Major rtd Obiazi Odigie,

Aikamhenze Aitanu, Smallboy Oaikhena(Chairman PTA), Benson Imhontu and Mrs Felicia Odigie(teacher); standing are Mrs. G E Aguele (teacher), Mrs Joyce Iboi (teacher), Mrs Clestina Ukabose (teacher), Mrs Christiana Imhenrion (teacher), Mrs Juliana Ehikhamhenn (teacher), Mrs C Ukpebor(Headmistress), Mr Victor I Eloebhose (teacher) and Professor Joseph I Okogun

17TH YEAR WINNERS 2017/2018

	PRIMARY 1	
1ST.	**2ND**	**3RD**
GODWIN EDWIN(M)	JOHN IFADA(M)	PROMISE FELIX(M)
	PRIMARY 2	
1ST	**2ND**	**3RD**
GREAT OKODUGHA (M)	NOSA FRIDAY(M)	BENJAMIN PANAMA(M)
	PRIMARY 3	
1ST	**2ND**	**3RD**
MERCY AIKAMHENZE(F)	FAVOUR OTAIGBE(F)	WISDOM IMHONTU(M)
	PRIMARY 4	
1ST	**2ND**	**3RD**
NSEBON MEME-OBONG PETER(M)	ENEHIZENA E NEREMHANGBE(M)	CHUKWUEBUKA OGBUBIA(M)
	PRIMARY 5	
1ST	**2ND**	**3RD**
PRECIOUS UGUOKE(F)	EZEKIEL ISERIA(M)	PRAISE AKONOFUA(M)
	PRIMARY SIX	

1ST	2ND	3RD
SEFIAT ADIGUN (F)	ENDURANCE ERHOMHONSELE(M)	RUTH IMHANGUI(F)

M =MALE, F = FEMALE

10TH Award, 12th October 2012

Lady Justina I Okogun nee Odigie addressing the pupils before giving out the awards. Standing by her is the Headmaster Mr. P. Aisaboluokpea Omoigiahio. Standing with the pupils from the right are Mr. Frank Otaigbe, Mrs. Theresa Azenodion, Rosaline Okogun nee Odiana and Mrs. Bertha Izebhokhai.

Some Okaigben Elders in attendance on 12/10/12 to witness the 10th Prizegiving ceremony: from right are Obiazi Odigie Army Sergeant Major rtd., Gabriel Osadolo Ogiata DSP rtd., Robinson Aguele aka Charity Community leader and past National Secretary OKDA and Vicoria Iyoha.

Okogun alias Ogi e-ese, Ogun gbein gbein, Ogun N'Ose departed 4th December 1993 with a smile on his face Pictured in front of his house with Ofuri Market to his left and defunct John Holts premises and Idumodu-Ologhe Street in the background.
Photo by Dr. Victor A. Ilegbodu

Printed in Canada